LIVE & WORK IN

USA AND CANADA

LIVE & WORK IN

USA AND CANADA

Deborah Penrith
Susan Catto

Distributed in the USA by
The Globe Pequot Press, Guilford, Connecticut

Published by Vacation Work, 9 Park End Street, Oxford
www.vacationwork.co.uk

LIVE AND WORK IN THE USA AND CANADA
by Deborah Penrith & Susan Catto

First published 1995
Second Edition 1999
Third Edition 2002
Fourth Edition 2005

Copyright © Vacation Work 2005

ISBN 1-85458-336-0

Publicity: Charles Cutting

Title page illustration by Mick Siddens

Cover design by mccdesign

Text design and typesetting by Brendan Cole

Cover photograph: Native American costume

Printed and bound in Italy by Legoprint SpA, Trento.

Contents

UNITED STATES OF AMERICA

SECTION 1
LIVING IN THE UNITED STATES

DAILY LIFE

SECTION II
WORKING IN THE USA

STARTING A BUSINESS

CANADA

SECTION I
LIVING IN CANADA

GENERAL INTRODUCTION

RESIDENCE & ENTRY REGULATIONS

RETIREMENT

SECTION II –
WORKING IN CANADA

EMPLOYMENT

STARTING A BUSINESS

FOREWORD

Following the American dream – the United States was founded on the belief that individuals can take control of their destiny and create their own favourable environment. American history is full of examples of people making that journey, from the arrival of the Pilgrim Fathers escaping religious persecution to the start of the American Revolution, or the pioneers moving westward to shiploads of new immigrants arriving in New York Harbor. The US is a nation that still believes opportunities should be taken and hard work rewarded. If this mythology is too rose-tinted, at least we should acknowledge that it is a reputation which remains highly attractive, particularly to those people around the world who are willing to take a gamble to improve their quality of life. In this seductive scenario the successful (the alternative is not often considered), are showered with rewards.

In almost every suburb of the States newly arrived families from around the world are seeking the good life: a home with a yard, decent education and healthcare, a prosperous retirement, and maybe better opportunities for the kids. But today's immigrants are less likely to be escaping persecution and dire poverty. Many are educated professionals who are either transferred from one office of a multinational company to another or they are equipped with special skills that the American government wishes to attract in order to stoke the engine of the economy.

As George Bernard Shaw once said 'England and America are two countries separated by a common language'. If your first language is English, the language is the same, the wages generally higher than in Europe, the cost of living lower and the landscape infinitely varied, uncluttered and vast.

The devastating impact on the United States of terrorism on September 11, 2001 undoubtedly had an affect on the nation's psyche. The two biggest vote winners in George W Bush's re-election in 2004 turned out to be moral issues and the war on terror. Despite being the world's sole superpower, Americans see the world as a far more dangerous place after a decade of unprecedented prosperity following the collapse of Soviet Communism.

Not since the Japanese assault on Pearl Harbor have Americans felt so beleaguered. While many parts of the world, including Europe, have long coped with terrorism and violent conflict, American citizens have felt safe at home. The rest of the world has, until recently, seemed very far away. To protect themselves, Americans have introduced effective counter-terrorist measures, stricter visa controls, and intensive checks at entry ports. Travelling by plane now entails far greater patience and reserves of time.

However, the American economy's ability to sail through strong headwinds in 2004 is the best evidence yet that the economic recovery from the 2001 recession is now sustainable. This has been brought about by an increasingly balanced mix of growing consumer spending, business investment, federal government spending, and exports. Output of the national economy grew at almost its fastest rate in 20 years which bodes well for this greatest democracy in the world.

Despite periodic and inevitable economic downturns, the United States continues to exude an almost mystical appeal. American influence on world culture remains enormous and its economic power stretches to every area of global activity. Many people around the world either hope to emigrate to improve their prospects in life or wish, at least, spend a substantial amount of time living and working in this seemingly blessed country.

This revised edition of *Live & Work in the USA and Canada* continues to explain how to navigate the complex immigration requirements, find a job, home or school. You'll also learn how to adapt to American life, what to expect, and how to find help. Whether you are an employee or entrepreneur, a student or a retiree, the book should provide an introduction to fulfilling an aspiration.

The US and Canadian immigration systems are far more complicated than those which allow free movement of Europeans around the European Union. Furthermore, the immigration systems of both countries are unequivocally biased towards those whose qualifications, skills and experience are deemed to be of benefit to the USA or Canada. When it comes to eligibility the system is extremely selective for both the United States and Canada. *Live & Work in the USA and Canada* explains the points system and how best to go about maximising your chances of being accepted as an immigrant and where to get professional help with your application.

In Canada, the links with Britain are stronger – more than ten million Canadians are of British extraction. On balance therefore, Canada is probably less of a foreign country to Britons than the USA. This book helps to lessen the culture shock of daily life and gives guidance on socialising North American style.

If you do not wish to live permanently in the United States or Canada you can spend six months of the year there as a property investor/holiday home owner. Many retirees (as well as younger people) do this already; in both the USA and Canada there are hundreds of thousands of British retirees. This book will put you in touch with property agents and indicates the most likely places for retirement or holiday homes.

North America is not a continent easily left once you have established yourself; its respect for the individual, its big-heartedness, its pace and extraordinary diversity are all part of the attraction. We hope that *Live & Work in the USA and Canada* will help you make the move successfully.

Deborah Penrith
Susan Catto
May 2005

ACKNOWLEDGEMENTS

The authors and the publishers of this book would like to thank all those people who have contributed to the content over the years. In this revised edition special thanks go to:

USA: James R LaVigne of LaVigne, Coton & Associates, Orlando, and Richard Robinson of Robinson O' Connell for their help on new immigration procedures; Paul Bishop of the National Association of Realtors; Anne Favreau, Internship Coordinator at the United Nations; Simon Ruben at the Fulbright Commission; and staff at BritishAmerican Business Inc. In the fourth edition Dr John Philip Jones and his son Philip Jones shared their experiences of moving to the USA.

CANADA: Kitty Pierce, Martin Catto and the kind people who shared their experiences and served as case studies provided valuable insight on the process and problems of immigrating to Canada. Andrew, Ella and Spencer Clark, Sally Catto and Helen Thomas are also warmly thanked.

TELEPHONE NUMBERS

Please note that the telephone numbers in this book are written as needed to call that number from inside the same country. To call these numbers from outside the country you will need to know the relevant international access code; these are currently 00 from the UK.

To call the USA or Canada: dial the international access code + 1 + the complete number as given in this book.

To call the UK: international access code +44 + the complete number as given in this book – *but omitting the first 0 in the British number.*

Section 1

LIVING IN THE UNITED STATES

GENERAL INTRODUCTION

RESIDENCE AND ENTRY REGULATIONS

SETTING UP HOME

DAILY LIFE

RETIREMENT

General Introduction

CHAPTER SUMMARY

○ The size and range of the US is hard to grasp: every state is like a country in itself and the country is large enough to have something for everyone.

○ America is a country built by immigrants seeking the liberty to improve themselves, and freedom is enshrined in the constitution.

○ Although historically the land of opportunity, the US has some of the world's strictest immigration rules; but those who plan to start a business are welcomed with open arms.

○ The Economy. America has the world's largest economy; with only 4% of the world's population it uses a quarter of its energy resources.

○ Government. The US is a federal republic with a government composed of three separate branches: the Executive, headed by the president; the Legislature (Congress) and the Judiciary.

○ The federal government is mainly in charge of defence, foreign affairs, justice, security, currency and the mail: much of the remaining government is handled at state level.

○ Politics. The Democrats and Republicans, the two main parties, are broad coalitions containing different factions.

○ Americans base their vote on issues and personalities rather than through party loyalty.

○ Geography. The 50 US states contain a population of some 294 million of whom around 75% are white, 12.3% black, 12.5% Hispanic and 3.6% Asian.

○ There is enormous climatic variation, from the Arctic conditions of Alaska to the deserts of the south-west.

DESTINATION USA

Europeans are fascinated by the United States. While Americans may see Europe as a wonderful land of history, castles, and misbehaving aristocrats, we look at America as the embodiment of everything modern, glamorous and sophisticated. This is changing as the speed of communication means that things previously unattainable (and American) are now in our shops as soon as we hear of them, but there is still something exciting about America. No other country is as visible and as talked about. We grow up on a diet of films and television from the States. We know so much about the country: what they eat, how they dress, how they talk. Many children in Europe have seen the Rocky Mountains or Monument Valley a hundred times before they have heard of the Matterhorn. But what always takes the visitor by surprise is the sheer foreignness of it all. They speak English, but that is often the only point of contact. Attitudes and ways of life are so different to what we are used to that some Europeans are lost. Nothing could seem more foreign than New York late at night, with your head running with scare-stories (as Norman Mailer said, visitors to New York 'just want to be reassured that they are not going to be mugged within the next few hours'); or a redneck nightclub in Phoenix where the customers wear stetsons and the temperature outside is in the high nineties.

America is a different country. To know it you would have to travel for twenty years. Every state is a country in itself: Utah is as different to Louisiana as London is to Prague. Every city and every state is as American as anywhere else, but there is no such thing as a place that is typical of the USA. New Orleans is no more nor less American than Chicago.

For hundreds of years people have been flocking to America, millions of them escaping hardship and repression in their home countries. No matter that it is closing its doors to immigrants and making it more and more difficult to plead economic hardship as a reason to get into the country, and despite the fact that hopes turn sour for so many who arrive and sink into poverty, still they come over the desert from Mexico and across the sea from Cuba. For those who are successful, of course, the dream comes true, and this is how the myth lives on: it is the millionaires who shout loudest about the American Dream. When the novelist G K Chesterton said, 'There is nothing the matter with Americans except their ideals' he wanted them to keep a firmer grip on reality. America does sometimes seem full of contradictions. The land of opportunity has some of the strictest immigration laws in the world; in the country that considers itself a flag-bearer for human rights, by December 2003, 880 people had been executed since 1977; in California, the Golden State, the byword for non-aggression and non-judgment, the population has approved legislation stripping illegal immigrants of their rights to public services.

But it is a stunningly beautiful country. Americans often talk with wonder

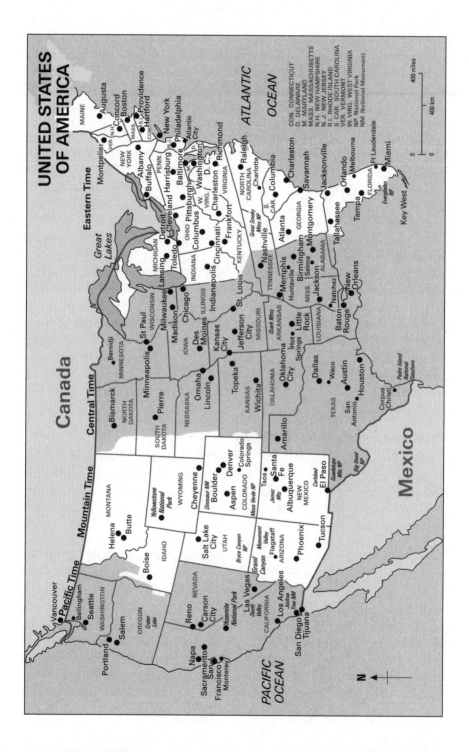

and respect of the beauty of the land, and you know that they feel privileged to live there. The Grand Canyon or the autumn colours of New England are famous sights, but the real beauty of America is the size of it, and the emptiness. In Europe there are few open spaces on the scale of some of the great national parks. In Yosemite it is possible to wander for days without seeing another soul. There are roads that never seem to end, vanishing in the heat-haze on the horizon. It is a country in which you can disappear with ease, which is one of the reasons why hitch-hiking is forbidden in most states. Too many people have not treated the country with the respect it deserves: it is not France, with a farmhouse round the corner and a colony of English advertising executives down the road. Wyoming, for example, has a population the size of a small city, and a land mass as big as the British Isles.

The American people are famously friendly. It is true that to the reserved British they might seem overly so, but if you are newly arrived in a town you will be delighted by the attention and the interest you receive. If you are naturally outgoing you will fall easily into any community, and if you have a reclusive nature you will be able to find an isolated spot, somewhere in the Rockies perhaps, or Arizona, or upstate New York, where you will be bothered by nobody. This is the greatest attraction of America: it has something for everyone. You cannot say it is too cold, or too hot, or too mountainous, or overpopulated, or the people are too inquisitive, or not interested. America is the land of opportunity, and you simply have to decide where to go to find your ideal environment.

Pros and Cons of moving to the USA

Those who decide to move to the USA will be assured of a standard of living as high as anywhere in Europe. At the same time they will find that the cost of living is a good deal lower than many other countries. America is an exceedingly attractive country to live in, which is one of the reasons that it is so difficult to get permission to do so.

For much of the 1990s the United States enjoyed a period of enormous economic growth and prosperity. A combination of deficit reduction by the Clinton administration in 1993 and significant innovation in computing and technology drove the economy to new levels of prosperity. But this success also fuelled a speculative frenzy, especially in Internet stocks, which have since lost much of their value. The market gradually realised that valuations were absurdly inflated and that these internet and technology stocks needed to be earning real revenues like any business. Following a period of recession in 2002, the US economy is now in good shape with an annual growth rate of between 3.5% and 4%. The United States economy is historically dynamic and resilient and is currently powering ahead creating about 10,000 jobs a day.

While UK entrepreneurs and would-be exporters have the advantage of a shared language, the US government is anxious to attract as much inward investment as possible. States are given federal grants with which to start up business advisory centres, and to offer investment initiatives. There is no control over the nationality of those benefiting from these grants, and many states actively encourage foreign investment. The UK government has fostered links between UK businesses and the USA. US chambers of commerce have opened in the UK in order to encourage business enterprise between the two countries.

Setting up a business is not difficult, and can be accomplished in some states in a matter of days. If you run a business that employs people and invests in the USA, you are eligible for a visa that will allow you stay as long as the business is going. Taxation of businesses in most states is lenient, payroll regulations are straightforward; the bureaucratic burden is generally lighter than in most of Europe. The downside of this is, of course, the competition that you will be up against. It may be easy to register your business, but it is another matter entirely to make it work. Experts advise that unless you identify a niche that has not been exploited, you will quickly be overcome by aggressive home-grown competition. The federal and state governments will help you set up, but will not hold your hand while you are encircled by sharks.

Pros
- High standard of living
- Healthy economy with good prospects
- The Special Relationship: UK\US business relationships are friendly
- Incentives for new businesses and investment
- Few bureaucratic burdens on business
- Low taxation
- Common language
- Locals are very friendly and open
- High wages
- Beautiful and diverse country
- Housing and rental sector cheap

Cons
- Visa and immigration controls
- Distance from Europe
- Bureaucracy on domestic level can be a problem
- Executive job prospects are not as good as they have been
- Punishing work ethic – few holidays
- Weak regulation of guns
- Unfamiliar customs

Britons who are employed by a US company should find a few differences in the way things are done. The US work ethic is famous: 'Rise early, work late, strike oil' was John Paul Getty's formula for success. If you cannot do the third, you will be expected to do the first and second. In America, more than any other country, success is measured in concrete terms: money and position. The drive to do well is enormous: the nation was built by people who for one reason or another were driven out of their homelands. Many arrived in the USA with no money and no belongings; the boss who 'built himself up from nothing' is a stock figure, but one who has left his mark on the American company. You will be expected to work harder and longer than you are used to. Too many breaks will be noted, as will an unwillingness to work the odd weekend. Two weeks holiday is the norm. The rewards are substantial: wages in the US, especially at senior management levels, are high. The housing and rental sector is cheaper than in Europe: a typical middle manager lives in a three bedroomed semi-detached house on its own plot of land. Out of the office, great demands will be made on your free time, in the form of recreational activities. Americans work hard, and they set out to enjoy the little leisure that they have. You will be invited to sports clubs, to dramatic evenings, to debating clubs, to fishing week-ends and mountain walks. You will never be lonely.

There are many advantages to living in America, and a few disadvantages. The very popularity of the country is the reason for one major drawback: the immigration laws. It is very difficult to get permission to stay more than six months at any one time, and even more difficult to work legally unless you can prove that no American can do your job. California's notorious Proposition 187, a raft of draconian immigration controls, deprives illegal immigrants of their rights to state and local non-emergency health care, welfare services and education. The chances of getting a green card (and permanent resident's status) are somewhat easier for victims of repressive regimes and for certain nationalities. Each year there is a green card lottery but only certain nationals are eligible each time because the process is designed to increase the diversity of the population and encourage nationals from countries with low rates of emigration to the US. Western Europeans (except the Irish) are given no special dispensations for residency applications.

Once you do get permission to work (or if you decide to work illegally, as thousands do, at the risk of deportation), you may find that many prejudices about the US are confirmed. Inner city areas sometimes suffer high rates of crime, particularly involving guns. This can be a shocking to people more used to living in Europe where gunfire on the streets merits headline news. In every city there are no-go areas that only the most foolhardy would penetrate. Racial tension also remains a distinct problem in American society, but there has been improvement since the 1960s and the creation of many Federal programmes to limit discrimination and improved economic assistance for minorities. Despite the high standard of living enjoyed by the majority there is desperate poverty in both cities and rural areas: in some states 18.5% of the population lives below the poverty line.

America is a foreign country, with many customs and attitudes that Europeans find difficult to understand. What is seen as a joke in the office in London may land you in trouble in New York. Americans' greater sensitivity toward the constituent parts of its society involves some adjustment but simply reflects its truly diverse character. The national ideal of a melting pot is taken seriously.

Americans have strange habits and play an incomprehensible version of rugby, called football, that is nothing like football. They invented the Big Mac. They eat strawberry jelly and peanut butter. They have strange names, their beer is weak, their dress sense poor, they are too friendly, they are too loud. But all criticism says more about the critic than the criticised. Trying to compile a comprehensive list of the pros and cons of living in America is an exercise doomed to failure but the summary of the main reasons either to move to the States, or not to, is reasonable from a British point of view.

The US offers a distinctly better standard of living than most of Europe and obviously even more so than the developing world. In many parts of the country, especially on the coast, the climate is temperate and appealing. Life as a rule is generally easier than the congested cities of Europe and commercial choices are endless, shopping malls offer abundance at good value and services are delivered with a smile around the clock. America continues to have an enduring appeal largely because self-improvement is so central to the culture. That hackneyed phrase, 'the American Dream' has staying power because it reflects the nation's cultural support of individual self-improvement. Unfortunately, the flip-side is that an individual can also fall very far, but that is not often advertised in the brochure for America, Inc.

POLITICAL AND ECONOMIC STRUCTURE

The United States has one of the best-known written constitutions in the world. It was drawn up in 1787, ratified by the 13 original states by June 1788, and has been continuously in operation ever since. In a country which is made up of representatives of just about every nation on earth, the constitution is the glue which holds people together. All nations and populations have something which they consider gives them 'nationhood'. This might be language, race, history or a past struggle for independence; for Americans, the most powerful thing that they have in common is the belief in individual freedom, enshrined in the constitution. Its aims were to create a 'more perfect union' through justice, domestic tranquillity, common defence, general welfare and liberty. Today, anybody wishing to become a citizen of the United States must swear to uphold the constitution, and must also be able to answer a series of questions about its meaning and purpose.

The structure of American government and politics has always been rooted in individual freedom. The Bill of Rights is designed to protect the average citizen from governmental abuse of power: the rights of women, ethnic minorities and all other groups are taken for granted by all Americans. This has led to a highly litigious society (Americans are quick to use the law to assert their rights), and there are more lawyers per head in the States than in any other country. One of the most notorious of these rights, the right to bear arms, is jealously guarded by many Americans.

There is a historic distrust of regulation by the Federal government which goes back to the roots of the Revolution, and this suspicion of authority is reflected in well-organised resistance to the regulation of firearms and any new taxation. Competition for power between the Federal government and the states has a long history and reflects the constitution's concern for the balance of powers between local communities and the centre. These disputes are often resolved by the Supreme Court. Contempt for Washington was most horrifyingly demonstrated by the blowing up of a federal government building in Oklahoma in 1995 with a 4,000lb bomb. One hundred and sixty-six people lost their lives in an outrage that was at first pinned on radical Islamic terrorists, but the culprits were later linked to a home-grown right-wing militia group. Speaking after this disaster, President Clinton felt compelled to remind the nation that government officials and institutions are both honourable and respectable.

The key to understanding American politics lies in the pioneering history of the country. Among the first settlers were English puritans escaping religious persecution. They landed at Plymouth Rock in 1620, and over the next decades were joined by successive waves of their countrymen, as well as Dutch (who bought Manhattan from the native Indians in 1624), Scots, Irish and Germans. Gradually the frontiers of the new colonies were pushed westwards over the Appalachians and beyond, until by 1763 the whole of the continent east of the Mississippi had been colonised. Over the next century, millions of new settlers from Europe fought and traded with the Native Americans for land, and as they became more powerful, herded them into reservations. This was the frontier spirit that opened up the west.

Americans by and large order their lives in the belief that they have built the greatest and most powerful country on earth. The cowboy with pistols and rugged sense of justice might be a Hollywood invention, but myths are rooted in reality: there are more handguns than TV sets in the USA – 212 million at the last count – almost one for every man, woman and child in the country.

Independence was fought for. The Native Americans displaced from their territories, a precarious living was wrested from the soil, the British colonial government was defeated. In the popular imagination, hostile inhabitants and unfamiliar lands were subdued and civilised by a pioneering spirit. In 1789 America was a tiny nation of thirteen states hugging the Atlantic seaboard; today it is a federation of fifty states and 294 million people. The early Americans knew as much about California as they did about the moon: today it has a population of 35.9 million.

All this was built from nothing. When we say glibly that America has no history we are speaking in terms of time. The quality of its history is a distillation of the dreams of millions. To Americans it is a vast history, packed into 200 years, the history of the greatest nation on earth. Each individual, arriving with a handful of precious belongings, carved out a detail of it. This is echoed again and again in the lives of Americans: they love their country powerfully and emotionally because they believe they created it, and are responsible for its welfare. Never was an anthem sung with such feeling as 'God Bless America'. Perhaps more than any other nation in the world, Americans believe their country has a unique destiny which is often attributed to the religious nature of the Plymouth colony, founded by the Pilgrim Fathers, religious refugees looking for a safe harbour and a pure expression of their faith.

The revolution later built on this notion of freedom, in resistance to 'taxation without representation.' Americans believe that they have intrinsic human rights, which is articulated in the Constitution as the inalienable right to 'life, liberty, and the pursuit of happiness.' When this phrase was written, these were radical ideas, but these beliefs continue to inspire people around the world. Historically then, Americans have valued individual effort and merit but the country can be introspective despite its enormous power, wealth and influence in the world. In the early years of the 21st century it stands as the indisputable superpower. However, the population, particularly beyond the two coasts, leans towards isolationism, a feeling that the US should not be active in international affairs unless there is a distinct threat to American security. Often in the past 60 years, American presidents have cajoled their countrymen to sanction a greater role for the country overseas in order to maintain the international order.

The architects of the constitution believed that they were creating the formula for the perfect balance of power between the people and the government. Democracy in America is as good and as bad as democracy everywhere, but with all its problems, at its best it can still be a beacon for liberal democratic values. But as the infamous events of September 11, 2001 illustrated, the United States is often seen by some groups around the world as an enemy to be confronted and even aggressively attacked. The long-term significance in historic terms of the destruction of the World Trade Center remains uncertain but what is clear is that following the end of the cold war the US continues to be an inspirational force for its economic and cultural vigour; unfortunately this also attracts a degree of fanatical hostility and anger. Not since the outbreak of World War Two have Americans been so pressed to examine their place in the world

Economy

The United States is the world's largest economy and continues to be highly productive and successful. Despite having only having 4% of the world's population, it produces 25% of the world's economic output. This fact alone explains the nation's enormous importance to the world economy and its influence. It is self-sufficient in every major product except for petroleum, chemicals and some manufactured items with a strong, resilient, and diversified economy. Balancing the budget remains an annual battle between the executive led by the President and the legislature on Capitol Hill. Taxation remains highly contentious and politically perilous.

In the early 1990s the deficit was ballooning out of control and the country's debt was becoming a major problem. George Bush's famous promise, 'Read my lips – no new taxes' might have helped him into the White House but it came back to haunt him when he bit the bullet and agreed to some higher taxation. When Bill Clinton assumed office in 1993 his economic advisers pressed for a deficit reduction package which also included new taxation. After a mighty struggle the proposed budget was passed by the narrowest of margins in both houses of congress, but many observers attribute the booming economy in the 1990s to this measure. George W Bush cut taxes which added about a one percentage point growth since mid-2001. In his second term, President Bush has promised not to raise taxes which may pave the way for an overhaul of the 'archaic' tax system.

Nevertheless economic pressures remain on the 'middle class', the vast majority of working Americans. Whereas in the 1950s only one breadwinner was necessary to keep the average middle-class family in comfort, now normally both parents have to work. At the same time there is still a substantial underclass, especially in the inner cities, which remains trapped in poverty. Caught in vicious circles of poverty, inner city decay and a reluctance by the middle class to finance remedies, 35.9 million Americans, a disproportionate number of them black, live below the poverty line. In some states, such as Mississippi, Louisiana and New Mexico, 18.5% of the population is extremely poor.

> But the United States is a phenomenal economic power. Current GDP is $10.9 trillion. The country consumes a massive percentage of what it produces – exports only account of 11.3% of GDP, as compared to a European average of 25%. The USA uses a quarter of the world's energy resources even though it has only 4% of the world's population. It imports 33% of its oil, and 18.8% of the country's energy is produced by nuclear power.

The economy is now overwhelmingly based on service industries. Agriculture accounts for 1.3% of the GDP, industry 16% and services 74.7%. The principal components of the manufacturing industry are machinery and transport, which also make up the major percentage of US exports.

The strongest sectors overall are steel, motor vehicles, aerospace industries, telecommunications, chemicals, electronics and computers, and a broad range of consumer goods. Other leading sectors are pharmaceuticals, entertainment and the media, and financial services.

After 1992 the US economy expanded at a gallop for eight years. The takeover mania that took hold as the recession came to an end in the early 1990s continued well into 1998. During the Clinton presidency enormous corporate mergers took place in an economic climate of growth. The government also encouraged the process of globalisation, whereby trade tariffs were lowered and multi-national companies supported. Clinton saw the creation of NAFTA, the North American trading area of the US, Canada, and Mexico as one of his greatest achievements. It faced substantial opposition from the unions and American nationalists who predicted that American companies would be free to move production lines to Mexico where they could employ labour at a fraction of the usual cost.

Following the end of the Cold War, politicians in both parties supported the notion of a 'peace dividend' which would arise from reduced military spending. Funds could now be channeled towards national infrastructure, social programmes or returned to the citizens through tax cuts. This had a profound impact on military manufacturers and many areas of the country, like Southern

California, suffered high unemployment. Twelve billion dollars was spent on programmes to retrain workers and help companies to adapt and develop lines for civilian use. Fortunately too, the economy continued to expand enabling the government to keep unemployment low.

After a decade of lower military spending, President Bush proposed a massive increase in the military budget for 2003 of $45 billion, an increase of 15%, to equip the country for the 'war on terrorism'. The military budget for 2005 is $417 billion.

Farmland makes up 46% of the US land surface. In 1900, half the US workforce were farmers. Continuing the twentieth century trend, numbers employed in farming have fallen further in the 1990s. Now 2.1% of the population work on farms. The traditional family farm is under severe pressure because economic pressures favour agribusiness, agriculture on an industrial scale. Increased mechanisation and biotechnological advances have made agriculture an exact and efficient science. At the same time the farming world is coming under serious public pressure to reduce the use of chemical pesticides and factory farming methods. The chief crops are cereals, cotton and tobacco; cattle ranching for beef is another important sector.

Outlook

The US economy grew by 4.4% over the whole of 2004, the fastest pace since 1999, creating 2.23 million jobs. When the economy began to lose its momentum at the end of 2000, the picture was complicated by the terrorist assaults on the country in September 2001 and the ensuing 'war against terrorism,' which certainly affected consumer confidence, particularly in the travel and tourism sectors. Certainly the simultaneous hijacking of four planes has had a devastating impact on the airline industry – 100,000 Americans in the aviation industry and 80,000 travel agents lost their jobs. At the time of writing, the national rate of unemployment was down to 5.4% and average hourly earnings rose 2.4% in 2004. Although inflation was picking up, wages and salaries had risen 1.2% more than inflation therefore increasing disposable incomes. The Federal Reserve (the US's central bank) made ten cuts in the interest rate during 2001 in an attempt to prevent recession but at the end of 2004, eleven of the twelve Federal Reserve districts were experiencing expanding economic activity.

Although the dollar has fallen 26% against the pound and 35% against the euro since February 2002, the weaker currency could stimulate US exports. This could help reduce the current trade deficit of $600 billion (6% of GDP) caused through importing more than exporting. While GDP has slowed to 3%, America is strong enough to power its way to continued economic growth and is inherently dynamic and adaptive and tends to rebound quickly from cyclical downturns.

Regional Trends

Since the 1970s there has been a migration of industry from the north of the country to the sunbelt regions of the west and south, which have a heavy concentration of light and high-tech industries. The fastest-growing municipal economy anywhere in the USA in the 1990s has been the area around Raleigh-Durham in North Carolina.

The economies of the individual states vary widely. California is known for the San Francisco high-tech industries and the Los Angeles entertainment industries, but manufacturing and farming are found throughout the state. It is the largest and most prosperous state and tops the league in terms of Gross State Product, although it is now declining as businesses move east to Arizona and north to Oregon, where the tax burden is less. The economy of the state was hurt in 1994 and 1995 by the shutdown of various military bases, but by 1996 there had been a turnaround when total personal income grew by 5.4%. In the fourth quarter of 2004, this income grew by 2.6%, the fastest pace since the beginning of 2000.

Other states with a high GSP are New York, Texas, Florida, Illinois, and Pennsylvania. The least productive states are Vermont, North Dakota, Wyoming, Montana, and South Dakota. Measuring the prosperity of states by the rate at which they are developing gives a different picture. Recent figures for job creation show that the fastest growing states are Nevada, Arizona, Florida, Idaho, Georgia, Texas, Utah, and Delaware. California used to be the Golden State, the favoured destination for entrepreneurs and businesses, but years of recession have caused many organisations to think again and to locate in cheaper areas with faster growth.

The decline in the heavy industrial base of the north east, (the Rustbelt, ranging from Pennsylvania to Iowa) has been offset in New England by an expansion in the service industries, and now Boston, for example, is a centre for computer services. But these states have generally shared much less in the economic boom of the last few years: New York and New England have barely increased employment since 1994. The exception is New York City, which has enjoyed a boom because of abnormally high profits on Wall Street and rapidly-declining crime rates. New Jersey has the highest median household income with $54,932 compared with a national average of $43,318.

Another state which is regarded as up-and-coming is Texas, which has diversified away from oil into high-tech and computers. It will also benefit from its proximity to Mexico, as the North American Free Trade Agreement increases cross-border activity. Florida is also benefiting from increased Latin-American trade.

Government

The United States of America is a federal republic with a government composed of three separate branches: the Executive, headed by the president; the Legislature (Congress, which includes the House of Representatives and the Senate); and the Judiciary, headed by the US Supreme Court.

Each of the 50 member states has a measure of self-government. The federal government is responsible for defence, foreign affairs, justice at the higher levels, internal security, the coinage and the mail. In many ways the USA is a collection of independent states: it is sometimes easy to see how after the War of Independence the architects of the Union were not at all sure that it would work. When Pennsylvania was created, for example, it was considered imperative that it had a corridor leading up to the Great Lakes, to avoid having to go through New York State. To this day, many Texans will not accept that their state is part of the Union.

The president is both head of the Executive and Head of State (in contrast to the British system, for example, where the two are separated). The president must be at least 35 years old, a US citizen by birth, and have been resident in the USA for at least 14 years. Presidential elections are held every leap year on the day after the first Monday in November. Each president is limited to two terms of four years each. He (there has not yet been a woman president) is elected along with a vice president who takes over if a president dies, is removed from office, or is unable to continue. The last time that this happened was when Gerald Ford took over from Richard Nixon when the latter resigned.

The Legislature is made up of the House of Representatives (the House) and the Senate. The House of Representatives consists of 435 representatives, or congressmen and congresswomen, elected every two years by universal suffrage. The number from each state is determined by the population of the state: Texas sends 27 representatives to the House, Montana only two. The Senate has 100 senators, two from each state, who are elected every six years.

The Judiciary, which is made up of the US Supreme Court and various lower federal courts, interprets, reviews, and applies federal laws. Federal courts can also apply state laws in certain cases. Supreme Court judges are nominated by the president and approved by the Senate. Although it is not the final authority on state law (that function is fulfilled by a supreme (state) court in each state) the Supreme Court can declare void any state law that conflicts with federal law. It also has the final ruling in test cases which cannot be settled by the state courts and may have a profound impact. During the 1950s it was the Supreme Court that ruled segregated education as a violation of the US Constitution. In 2000, the presidential election was locked in conflict over disputed ballots in Florida. Eventually, the decision about how to proceed fell to the US Supreme Court which ruled that the relevant Florida election officials could declare a final result in George Bush's favour. It remains a highly controversial decision but illustrates the power of the court to influence American life as the final arbiter of the Federal Constitution.

Each state has its own constitution and a government modelled on the federal one, with a state legislature, a governor, and a court system. Within each state, power is devolved even further, to city and county authorities. In the 1980s, the Reagan administration tried to reduce the role of the federal government, and transfer as much power as possible to the states, with the result that now states play an important part in the making of domestic policy.

In the United States television has long played a vital part in the voting process, with election campaigns focusing heavily on the visual and instantly recognisable qualities of the leader and of the party's policies. Because the population identifies a national president when it is voting (although in a presidential election an entire administration is voted in), a presidential campaign usually articulates simple and powerful themes of patriotism, defence, crime, the family. One of the reasons for Ronald Reagan's popularity was his ability to articulate the most traditional of American ideals, such as individual success and freedom. He preached the message that American power should be revived after the humiliations caused by the Iranian revolution and subsequent hostage taking of more than 400 US citizens, and wrapped the whole thing in layers of easily-digested policy: fight crime, fight drugs, and defend the country against Communism. Bill Clinton too – despite the Monica Lewinsky scandal – was immensely popular, in part because of his telegenic charisma and talent for connecting with ordinary Americans.

Unlike European parliamentary democracies, the US cabinet members are not members of the legislature, but political appointees of the president. There are 14 executive departments which they head, of which the most important are the State Department, responsible for foreign policy, the Treasury and the Defense department. Other departments deal with agriculture, transportation and so on.

The two houses of Congress sit at either end of the Capitol Building. Both houses are extremely powerful, possessing the legislative power both for proposing bills and passing them into law. A powerful president is normally able to persuade Congress, but this is by no means certain, particularly if his party does not control either of the chambers. The party system is less rigid than the British model in which executive authority depends upon strict party discipline in Parliament. Both congressmen and senators are by nature more independent figures who tend to build coalitions of interest across the two parties according to different factors like regional influences and personal idealogy. As a result the president can be frequently thwarted in his wishes.

In the 1994 mid-term elections, the Republicans took control of the House for the first time since Eisenhower and retained a precarious hold on the Senate. It is possible for a president to win the White House without a majority in either of the houses as George Bush Snr experienced in 1988, but an administration's legislative agenda will be weakened without ample support 'on the hill', as Congress is colloquially referred to. Clinton was hamstrung by Republican control of the House for six of his eight-year administration. But he managed to put this setback to his advantage by effectively portraying the gung-ho Republican opposition as obstructive and irresponsible, most notably when the federal government effectively shut down in 1995 owing to the lack of a budget agreement between the President and Congress.

When George Bush Jnr became President in January 2001, he enjoyed narrow Republican majorities in both the Senate and House of Representatives, but in an illustration of the power of American legislators, particularly in the senate, Senator Jim Jeffords of Vermont 'crossed the aisle', leaving the Republicans to become an independent. The Democrats controlled the Senate by one vote, but this gave them the power to derail the president's legislative agenda. The tables turned and a Republican president compromised with congress as his Democratic predecessor learnt before him. Clinton lost, for example, his radical proposal to reform the American healthcare system. Each scenario illustrates well the system of divided powers, which the Founding Fathers conceived in the effort to prevent any re-emergence of 'tyrannical' government they experienced under British rule.

Written into the constitution, therefore, are checks and controls to prevent the state from becoming too strong. All laws have to be ratified by Congress: they have to run the gauntlet of both Houses, and are often heavily revised in the process.

President George W Bush won a second term in the general elections of November 2004. He enjoyed a 3.5 million margin in the popular vote – the biggest by any US president – over his opponent Senator John Kerry.

Political Parties

At both federal and state level, the American political system is a two-party one. The Democrats and the Republicans are among the oldest political parties in the world: the Democrats were formed at the beginning of the 19th century, the Republicans (known as the GOP, the Grand Old Party) in 1854 by opponents of slavery, with Abraham Lincoln as their first President. Both parties are not really parties in a strictly whipped sense but broad coalitions encompassing wide ideological spectrums and regional interests. During the first stages of any presidential campaign (the primaries), candidates from the same party will run against each other, often with devastating results. In 1980, George Bush, a moderate Republican, lost in the primaries to Ronald Reagan, on the right of the party. There are many different factions within the parties. One of the best known is Jesse Jackson's Rainbow Coalition, another is the Christian Coalition, a powerful lobby made up of various groupings of the evangelical right. There are fewer differences between the parties than we expect. A right-wing democrat could be mistaken for a left-wing Republican and it is not uncommon for politicians to change parties. Democratic socialism as commonly found in Europe barely registers any electoral support. Occasionally an independent candidate will make an impression on the voting public, especially in times of great disaffection with the government In 1992, the Texan Ross Perot won 19% of the vote as an independent. In 1912, Theodore Roosevelt got 27% of the vote: this is the nearest an independent has ever come to the White House.

This may be changing, however. In the USA party allegiance is less important than it is in the UK. The public prefers to see things in terms of individual personalities and single issues: a politician's stance on abortion or homosexuality is more important than which party he or she belongs to. Congressmen rely far more on the ability of the media to put their personalities across, than on standing on a particular party platform. In the past voters were loyal Republicans or Democrats, but many more are now registering as independent, and voting for the individual rather than the party.

GEOGRAPHICAL INFORMATION

Area

The United States of America is the fourth largest country in the world. The North American continent, consisting of Canada and the Arctic archipelago as well as the United States, covers 8.3 million square miles (21.5 million square kilometres), of which the United States takes up 3.6 million square miles (9.3 million square kilometers). It is bounded in the north by Canada, in the south by Mexico and the Gulf of Mexico, in the east by the Atlantic Ocean and in the west by the Pacific Ocean. From east to west, New York to San Francisco, is 3,000 miles (4,800 km). From the town of Brownsville, the southernmost point of Texas, to the 49th parallel (the boundary between the USA and Canada), is 1,600 miles (2,560 km). This vast landmass covers a huge spectrum of different landscapes, environments and climates. The eastern coast (New England, where the first white settlers landed) is rocky and richly wooded. South and west of New England are the Appalachian Mountains, which rise up out of the Atlantic coastal plain. Further west are the Great Lakes and the central lowlands, undulating plains cut through by the mighty Mississippi, which begins its journey near the Canadian border and finally flows into the Gulf of Mexico, 2,348 miles (3,779 km) later, by then a huge and sluggish river, broad and deceptively slow. Going west from the Mississippi the landscape changes to the Great Plains, called the breadbasket of America, and then rises to the Rocky Mountains, a massive range that runs north to south. The highest point of the Rockies is Mount Whitney in California, 14,495 ft (4,418 m). Further west still is the great Californian valley, half of it desert, half fertile – and the Pacific Ocean. Mt McKinley in Alaska is the highest point at 20,321 ft (6,194 m) while Death Valley in California is the lowest at −282 ft (-86 m).

To a European the size of the United States is difficult to imagine. We tend to think of it as one country (as indeed it is) but forget to take the size of the continent into account. New York is almost as far from San Francisco as it is from London; Texas is bigger than France; Alaska is twice the size of Texas. You can drive west from Houston all day, and still not have left Texas; to drive from New York to California is the equivalent of driving from London to Cairo.

Regional Divisions and Main Towns

The USA is a federal republic of 50 states. The capital is Washington, the District of Columbia. The first states of the Union were: Maine, New Hampshire, Vermont, Massachusetts, Connecticut, Rhode Island, New York, New Jersey, Pennsylvania, Delaware and Maryland. As the 19th century progressed, further states were added to the union: Louisiana in 1812, Alabama in 1819, Arkansas in 1836. California became a state in 1850, Alaska and Hawaii, the newest additions to the union, in 1959. The states vary greatly in size (Rhode Island is tiny, 1,200 square miles/3,107 square kilometres; Alaska covers 600,000 square miles/1,553,994 square kilometres), geography and population. Each state organises its affairs independently, with a government that is designed to mirror the federal government. States set their own taxes and pass their own laws, and have their own police forces and jurisdictions.

Each state has its own capital, which may not to be the largest or best-known city. The capital of New York state, for example, is Albany; the capital of California is Sacramento. The largest cities (by population) in the United States are New York (8 million), Los Angeles (3.4 million) and Chicago (2.7 million). Detroit, Dallas, Houston, Philadelphia and San Diego; all have populations of more than a million.

American cities tend to sprawl and merge, and huge metropolitan areas are forming. New York City spills over into suburbs in New York, New Jersey and Connecticut, forming an almost continuous conurbation with a population of 18.3 million. The same has happened on the west coast, with Los Angeles, Anaheim, and Riverside in California forming a metropolitan area of 14 million people.

The fastest growing cities, in terms of population change in the last decade, are Moreno Valley CA (319% growth), Mesa AZ (89% growth), Rancho Cucamonga CA (83.5% growth) and Plano TX (77.9% growth). Other towns that are growing fast are Irvine, Escondido and Oceanside in California, Arlington in Texas, and Las Vegas. All have increased their populations by over 50% in the last decade.

The states with the highest standard of living are Connecticut, New Jersey,

Massachusetts, New York, Maryland and New Hampshire, all with an average income per head of $37,000. Mississippi, Arkansas, West Virginia, New Mexico, and Utah have the lowest standard of living in the country ($25,000 and less). California, New York, Texas and Florida have the highest Gross State Product; Vermont, North Dakota, and Wyoming have the lowest.

The most rural states are Vermont and West Virginia, where less than 40% of the population live in urban areas. In California, New Jersey, and Hawaii more than 89% live in an urban area.

The *Useful Business Information State by State* in the *Employment* chapter, lists all the states and their important statistics. A list of state abbreviations is given in *Daily Life*.

TABLE 1 AVERAGE MAXIMUM TEMPERATURES (FAHRENHEIT)

	January	July
Atlanta GA	50	88
Chicago IL	29	84
Denver CO	43	88
Honolulu HI	80	87.5
Los Angeles CA	66	75
Miami FL	75	89
New Orleans LA	61	91
New York NY	38	85
Phoenix AZ	66	106
St Louis MO	38	89
San Francisco CA	56	72
Seattle WA	45	75
Washington DC	42	88.5

Population

The population of the United States is 294 million and grew 1% between July 2003 and July 2004. The latest national survey found a birth rate of 14.5 per thousand and the death rate 8.8 per thousand. Twenty one per cent of the population is under 15, 12.6% over 65. There are 79.6 people per square mile. 75% of the total population identified themselves as white, 12.3% as black, 12.5% as Hispanic and 3.6% as Asian. Continuing an historically high rate of immigration, 9.5% of the US population was born in another country.

Religion

Total freedom of religion is written into the American Constitution. Church and State are separate. More than 90% of Americans claim to be members of one of the hundreds of Christian denominations; of these 40% to 50% are regular churchgoers. The main Protestant denominations are Baptists (36.6

million), Methodists (13.5 million), Lutherans (8.4 million) and Episcopalians (2.5 million). There are some 60 million Roman Catholics and 5.9 million Jews. Since the 1980s there has been a steady increase in the power of the Evangelical movement and 42% of all Americans describe themselves as 'born-again' Christians. 'Televangelism' is an established part of the American scene. There is no animosity between Protestants and Catholics (the latter tacitly accept divorce and contraception) and shared services are commonplace. The ethnic minorities practise their own religions and there are many other sects, such as the Church of the Latter Day Saints (Mormons) of Salt Lake City in Utah and a host of small sects or new age spiritual groups with members from different ethnic groups. There are estimated to be around four million Muslims.

Climate

Climatic variation within the United States is enormous, ranging from the Arctic conditions in Alaska to the deserts of the south west. Winter temperatures in Alaska plummet to -19°F (-28°C), whereas in Florida they are a steady 66°F (19°C) for most of the year. In California the weather hardly varies: it is constantly mild with a range of only 16°F (9°C). On the east coast the climate is similar to much of Europe, with severe winters and hot summers. New York city has particularly cold and wet winters, and hot and muggy summers. The centre of the continent is dry, but both the north-west Pacific (Oregon and Washington) and the New England Atlantic coast are humid, with a heavy rainfall.

Much of the United States is prone to the most powerful of nature's forces: the northeastern coast is vulnerable to blizzards, the southern lowlands are susceptible to thaw flooding in the spring (the Mississippi recently flooded vast tracts of land), and in the desert areas of the south tornadoes are a hazard.

Global Warming & US Pollution

The US is one of the world's worst polluters when it comes to greenhouse gas emissions. President Clinton agreed to back the 1997 Kyoto conference treaty to reduce emissions from cars, factories, homes and other energy users, but his successor President Bush decided in 2001 to revoke that support, provoking a storm of criticism around the world. His administration argued that the treaty unfairly penalised the United States for its dynamic rate of growth and productivity. Bush has instead proposed that the US offer incentives to its domestic consumers for reducing greenhouse gas emissions. He also argues that the burden for reducing them should be more evenly distributed across the globe. Much though could be achieved by improving conservation within the US and supporting renewable sources of energy. Following the terrorist attacks on the US, it remained to be seen if the Bush administration would adopt a more conciliatory approach to international co-operation as a reward for the coalition of countries which backed military intervention in Afghanistan and as recognition of international inter-dependence. The Kyoto Protocol has now come into effect (February 2005) committing the 34 countries that signed the agreement to cut emissions by 2012. President Bush has expressed a desire 'to work together' on environmental issues and will introduce his own 10-year programme to reduce carbon intensity of the US economy by 18% .

GETTING THERE

It is often cheaper to fly to the USA from Europe than it is to fly within Europe. There are over a dozen scheduled airlines and countless charter carriers who fly to destinations all over the States. In many cases flying from the UK means you have a choice of UK airports for your departure. Finding the best priced ticket takes some searching around in the advert pages of newspaper travel supplements and backpackers magazines like *TNT* or *Southern Cross*. The London *Evening Standard*, London listings magazine *Time Out* and the colour supplements of the Saturday and Sunday newspapers are also useful sources, as of course is the Internet and Teletext. Cheap, direct fares normally have an advance booking requirement of 14 or 21 days and with charters you cannot change the date or time of the booking once it has been made. Most operators can cater for those who wish to fly to one US city and return from another; these are known as 'open jaw returns'. For details of travel insurance and health insurance within the US see *Daily Life*.

The peak (most expensive) period is usually June to September and Christmas/ New Year. At other times it is generally easy to get cheap tickets for the date you want. In the low season, flights from London to Miami are priced around £250 return and London to New York about $196.

A reliable, independent booking service for low cost flights on scheduled and charter services to the USA is available from Flightclub (Guildbourne Centre, Chapel Road, Worthing, West Sussex BN11 1LZ; ☎0845-880 1808; or book online at www.flightclub.co.uk), who are members of ABTA.

Other agents specialising in the USA include: First American Travel (☎020-8673 8888), Unijet (☎0870-600 8009), and Trailfinders (☎020-7938 3939; www.trailfinders.com). Airline numbers for US flights include:

Air Canada	0870-524 7226
American Airlines	0845-778 9789
Continental	0845-607 6760
United Airlines	0845-844 4777
US Airways	0845-600 3300
British Airways	0870-850 9850
Delta	0800-414767
Virgin Atlantic	01293-747747
Northwest/KLM	0870-507 4074

Insurance. Working travellers and those on speculative job finding trips to the USA are strongly advised to take out comprehensive travel insurance. Insurers offering reasonable and flexible premiums include *Expatriate Insurance Services Ltd* (from the UK ☎0870-330 0016, International ☎+44-1273-703469, from within the USA ☎1-800-436 6267; e-mail info@expatriate-insurance. com; www.expatriate-insurance.com) who specialise in arranging international travel, health, and life insurance.

RESIDENCE AND ENTRY REGULATIONS

CHAPTER SUMMARY

○ The US has some of the most complex immigration rules in the world with more than 70 types of visas and derivatives.

○ Citizens of some countries, including the UK, are allowed to enter the US for up to 90 days for business or pleasure under the Visa Waiver Program: otherwise a visa is necessary.

○ Those found entering America illegally are barred from the country for five years for a first offence – or twenty for a second.

○ For a non-American to live and work in the US they either need the appropriate visa or a green card, which is a permit to live in the US with most of the rights of a citizen.

○ The Green Card. This is only given to people who intend to live permanently in the US: in effect it grants most of the privileges of US Citizenship apart from the right to vote.

○ **US Citizenship.** Those without special family connections to the US can only apply to become a US citizen after holding a green card for five years.

Useful Terms

Affidavit of Support: A form of contract required to be signed by the petitioner in family petition cases and some employment cases. The petitioner must live in the USA.

Dictionary of Occupational Titles: A book published by the US Department of Labour describing almost every job, its duties and the amount of training or education needed.

Diversity Lottery, or *Diversity Immigrant Visa Program*: The Green Card Lottery, also known as DV-2004, DV-2005, and so on.

Intending Immigrant: A person coming to the USA intending or hoping to make it a primary place of residence. If an inspector believes you are an intending immigrant you will only by allowed in with the correct immigrant visa or green card. If you are married to a US citizen, or plan to marry, you won't be allowed in with a non-immigrant visa or under the visa waiver program.

Labor Certificate: This is issued if no US worker can be found for a certain job. It shows that giving the job to a non-US worker will not harm the US job market.

Sponsor: A person or organisation – your employer – who files a visa petition on your behalf. Also called a petitioner.

Visa Waiver: A type of admission which allows citizens of the specific countries (includes all European Union members) to stay 90 days without a visa. Cannot be extended.

THE CURRENT POSITION

Although a million people a year emigrate to the United States, it still has some of the strictest and most daunting immigration laws in the world. There are more than 70 types of visas and derivatives, and a series of different categories of green card. Consular bureaucracy, which often requires the production of personal documents from birth certificates to property details, can make visa application an ordeal. Despite the complexity of the process, however, over 90% of British people are successful in their application for a visa.

British emigration to the US is currently running at between 8,000 to 10,000 per year. This means that these British citizens have been granted resident status. Such a high figure explains why the British are not eligible for the green card lottery, officially known as the 'diversity program' (see below) because they fill the quota set aside for each nationality. The lottery is designed to give greater access to nationals who might not have such a high degree of skills and to ensure that emigration to the US is culturally and ethnically balanced.

The UK leads the world in the numbers of citizens living in the US after being granted working visas (temporary workers, intracompany transfereers and exchange visitors). There are approximately 110,000 British citizens working or studying in the US as temporary workers, intracompany transferees or exchange visitors, which illustrates that with sufficient help, resources and determination it is highly feasible to consider the option of living and working in the US. Despite the bureaucratic hurdles, thousands of individuals pull off the ambition of spending part of their lives across the Atlantic.

For those set on going one step further and permanently emigrating, you will require even more persistence and dedication, but the figure quoted above of the people being awarded residency (green cards) again demonstrates that the option is viable, but one that requires tremendous commitment.

At present there are two ways of living and working legally in the USA. The first is to have the appropriate non-immigrant visa, and the second is to have an immigrant visa. An immigrant visa holder is processed for a Permanent Resident Card (PRC), known as the Green Card. Both are covered in detail later in this chapter: the essential differences between them are that the green card is a permit to live and work permanently in America with most of the rights of a citizen, while a non-immigrant visa is always temporary. It is quite possible to spend many years living and working legally with the right kind of non-immigrant visa, without ever applying for a green card.

Up to 1990, one of the prime qualifications for successful immigration was to be a relative of a US citizen. Green card quotas were designed to favour those with family connections above most others. Getting a green card through employment has also been a successful route for many people.

The 1990 Immigration Act brought about substantial changes in immigration policy. Although it is still extremely helpful to be related to a US citizen or permanent resident when petitioning for a green card, the Act created several new categories which are based on the personal qualifications of the applicant. There is now more priority given to the employment categories: if you are a person of 'extraordinary ability' in the arts or sciences, or an outstanding academic, it is slightly easier to get a green card than before. The Act created the H-1B category of working visa to allow qualified people to fill shortages in hospitals, universities, computer programming and other occupations. There are 65,000 H-1B visas available annually. Congress recently passed a law allowing an additional 20,000 H-1B visas a year. Therefore, the US Citizenship and Immigration Service (USCIS), formerly the Immigration and Naturalization Service (INS), now states there may be an exemption from the cap of 65,000 a year for those people who have a Master's degree or above in the USA. At the time of writing, the final regulations still had to be ratified.

In addition to working visas, the EB-5 investment visa was introduced. This is particularly desirable as, like family-based visas, it provides an immediate green card but requires a minimum 'at risk' investment of $500,000. Most non-family based visas are linked to a specific job or investment, which can prove restrictive. With EB-5 the investor does not need to have active day-to-day involvement in the investment enabling the holder, and his immediate family, to take any job, own any business, and even retire.

Further changes to the law came in with the Illegal Immigration Reform and Immigrant Responsibility Act of 1996. Most of these changes relate to enforcement of the law, and include such things as an automated entry-exit control system matching your next entry with your last exit, the setting up of inspection stations at foreign airports, and the provision of ten full-time immigration enforcement agents in each state. Penalties for illegal immigration have become more draconian – an illegal alien forced to leave is barred for five years, and any subsequent removal will result in a 20-year bar.

Anyone working for a multi-national company with offices in the United States is uniquely privileged and intra-company transfers (L category visa) cover this category. Many foreign nationals seem to slip into New York's financial world with ease. However for the majority of foreign nationals it is difficult, but certainly not impossible to get permission to work in the United States. Experts advise that if you do not fit into any of the visa categories, you should change your circumstances until you do. The visa system has many quirks: for example, a category may require 'degree or degree equivalent'. This might seem that those without degrees have little chance of getting through, but there are a number of qualifications that will satisfy the USCIS, including, in some cases, the right sort of experience. If you have done City and Guilds exams in the UK, or if you have twenty years experience as a senior engineer, this could count as 'degree equivalent'.

However, for an individual hoping to find work in the US the process of obtaining permission to work is uncertain and requires a degree of determination and commitment. Naturally, it's hard to apply non-vocational qualifications to the common working visa, the H1-B, particularly an arts degrees like History or English. But these degrees often offer an advantage in that they can be elastic in their applicability to many jobs. Describing yourself as a 'researcher' with a specialist knowledge in an area corresponding with your degree is one solution. With the assistance of an experienced immigration lawyer, it is possible to obtain one of the working visas, but you will need to have the support of an employer in the States first, patience and sufficient funds to support the often lengthy legal process.

It is important to remember that working illegally is regarded as a serious offence for the employer as well as the employee. The penalty for the former is a hefty fine, and for the latter deportation. If you are caught working illegally it will also prejudice any future visa applications that you make. The US is now charging a $500 anti-fraud fee for H-1B and L-1 visas.

The system is complicated and the USCIS is strict in its interpretation. To many people it may seem unfair, but it is worthwhile to keep in mind that although the system cannot be deceived, it can be worked to your advantage. The essential thing is to know the categories and to take the greatest care in ensuring that you fit into one of them.

Immigration is a contentious issue within the United States because it remains such a popular destination. Anyone other than native Americans is by definition descended from immigrants. Historically, it is a nation that has welcomed immigration and the huge ethnic and cultural diversity of urban neighborhoods remains extraordinary as new waves of immigrants continue to arrive. If you look through a New York city phone directory you'll see almost every ethnic group in the world represented there. But occasionally, especially during times of growing unemployment, certain pressure groups will campaign to restrict the numbers of new immigrants. Critics argue that Americans are being squeezed out of employment opportunities and that the country is facing problems of population density and all of the accompanying demand for services and land.

In one of his last acts as President, Bill Clinton signed into law the American Competitiveness in the Twenty First Century Act which raised the number of H1-B visas issued each year but in return sponsoring employers would pay a tax of a $1,000 per visa application to fund training of adult Americans for high-tech jobs and to teach children IT skills. Filing fees for H-1 visas have now increased substantially and you should be cautioned that the fees can change drastically in a short period of time. In January 2004, the US authorities introduced the US-VISIT Programme which means that all those aged between 14 and 79 travelling to the US with visas will be finger-scanned and photographed on arrival. This does not apply to those travelling under the Visa Waiver Program.

NON-IMMIGRANT VISA CATEGORIES

Overview

Virtually anybody wishing to enter the USA as an alien (anyone who is not a US citizen or holder of a green card) must hold a valid passport and an appropriate non-immigrant visa. In 2000, President Clinton signed into law the Visa Waiver Permanent Program Act. The Visa Waiver Program (VWP) allows visitors from 27 countries (including the UK) to stay as a temporary visitor for business or pleasure, for up to 90 days without a visa. You must travel with an airline which has agreed to take part in the scheme: this includes the main transatlantic carriers. During the flight they will hand out visa waiver forms which need to be completed and given to Immigration control on arrival. Check with the airline before you fly if you are not sure if they subscribe to the programme. As from October 2004, all VWP travellers must be in possession of individual machine-readable (biometric) passports. When you arrive at your port of entry you may be subjected to rigorous questioning as to the reason for your journey. You may need to prove that you have sufficient funds to finance your stay, that you have somewhere to stay and you may need to make a convincing case that you are intending to return to your country of residence within the 90 day time limit. Sometimes this may involve producing proof of continuing employment at home or enrolment in higher education. American immigration can be tough even to the point of putting you on a return flight home, so bring enough material to persuade the officials that you are truly just visiting for business or pleasure.

If you need to stay longer than 90 days, you should apply for a visa in the US consulate of your home country; only in the rarest cases are they issued in the USA itself. If you are temporarily abroad you can apply in the US consulate of the country that you are staying in.

If you are applying for a straightforward B visa, for tourists (B-2) and temporary business visitors (B-1), the process is simple and should not require assistance from a lawyer. It becomes more complicated when you want to stay for more than six months at a time, or when you want to work. It is essential to be quite sure which visa category you are applying for. If you are in any doubt about your status or what kind of visa you want, seek professional advice. There is a list of US immigration lawyers operating in the UK below.

US consular officials base their decisions on the applicant's documentation and, in some cases, a short interview. The US Embassy is currently processing more than 525 visa interviews on a daily basis. In the eyes of the consular officer every visa applicant is deemed to be an 'intending immigrant', and the burden of proof rests on you to convince the officer that you have a 'compelling commitment' to return to your own country. In most cases this is straightforward: for example if you are applying for a B visa and have a job or a college place to return to. There are two common reasons for refusal to grant a B-1 or B-2 visa. The first is when you want to extend your trip over the six month limit, and have no definite commitment to a job or a place at university when you return. Secondly, you may have left your job in the UK in order to look into the possibilities of starting or investing in a business in the USA, so that you can qualify for an E-2 (treaty investor) visa. In both cases it is up to you to convince the consulate that you are not an intending immigrant.

After you have been issued a visa there is a further hurdle in the form of the Immigration and Customs Enforcement (ICE) officer at the port of entry. These officers are unpredictable. They might search your luggage and demand to know why you have brought an ironing board and a full set of cutlery if you only intend to stay three months. They will certainly want to know how much money you have on you, and what access you have to more funds. They will ask questions that might seem difficult to answer if your reason for visiting the country differs even slightly from your visa category.

Once you are in the United States it is no longer possible to get your visa changed to another non-immigrant visa status without leaving the USA. As of 16 July 2004, all revalidation of visas must take place in the persons home country or place of usual residence or abode. Another caveat: while changing your mind is one thing, 'wilful misrepresentation of a material fact' is another. If you apply for one visa with the intention of changing your status when you arrive, you may get into serious trouble and find yourself ineligible for future visas. For example, if you have changed from B-1 to E-2 status once, and then return to the USA on another B-1, hoping to change status again, your application would almost certainly be turned down, and the USCIS would regard with extreme suspicion any future application.

The most important thing is to apply for the right visa in the first place. If you are thinking of staying for a long time, or looking for work, or if you are going out as a student and will want to stay, you will eventually have to apply for a green card (see below). This is a long and difficult process, especially for a Western European. The US Embassy can supply a full list of all the visas available: the following is a summary of the main categories.

Visa Categories

A Visa – Diplomatic Visa. To qualify you must be travelling to the US on behalf of your national government to engage solely in official activities for that government. Issued through diplomatic channels.

B Visa – Temporary Visitors for Business or Pleasure. If you are visiting the United States solely for business or pleasure, and are not eligible for the visa waiver programme, then you should apply for a B-1 (business) or B-2 (pleasure) visa. Business in this case means coming for the purpose of conferences, conventions or seminars, negotiation of contracts, consultation with business associates, and litigation while employed by a non-US company. You are allowed to incorporate but not to be employed by a US company, or to manage a US business, while visiting on this visa. However, you may also acquire property and sign contracts. A B-2 visa means that you may not take part in any business related activities at all. B-1 visas normally provide an admission for up to one year, B-2 visas for a maximum of six months. It is possible to use the B-2 as often as you like. If you have a holiday home in the USA and can prove that you have another, permanent, residence in your own country it is perfectly possible to spend six months of the year in the USA, using your visa each time you come back in. B visas are now valid for a maximum of ten years.

C Visa – Transit Visa. Most European visitors can simply transfer flights under the visa waiver program. Check with the local US embassy or consulate for information.

D Visa – Crew Member. Issued to crew members of international airlines and to aliens required for the normal operation and service of a vessel.

E Visa – Treaty Traders and Investors. E visas are valid for up to five years at a time and are not subject to quota restrictions. E-1 visas are for citizens of countries which have the appropriate treaties with the USA (which includes the UK). The US company that you work for can be owned by you or by another person, and must share a nationality with you. At least 50% of its business activities must consist of trade between the USA and your own country. As well as this the employees of the company must have the same nationality as their employer. You are restricted to working only for the employer or self-owned business which acted as your visa sponsor. E-2 visas are available to those who have made a qualifying 50% investment in a US company (of any size), or who are working for a UK company which has made an investment of at least 50% in a US company. E-2 visa holders can apply for a green card through the EB-5 program once they show they have made the minimum investment in the company ($500,000 to $1 million) and have hired 10 new workers.

E VISA

Privileges.
- You can work legally in the United States for a US business in which a substantial *cash* investment (at least $100,000) has been made by you or other citizens of your home country.
- You may travel in and out of the United States or remain there continuously until your E-2 visa expires.
- There is no legal limitation on the number of extensions that may be granted.
- E-2 Visas can allow you to live in the US on a prolonged basis, provided you continue to maintain E-2 qualification.
- Visas are available for your spouse and all unmarried children under 21.

Limitations
- Visas are available only to nationals of countries having trade treaties with the USA.
- You are restricted to working only for a specific employer or a self-owned business which acted as your E-2 visa sponsor.
- Accompanying relatives may stay in the USA with you, but they may not work.
- When children reach the age of 21 and wish to continue living in the USA they must apply for their own visa.
- You must renew your I-94 every year.

F and M Visa – Students. F visas are issued to full time academic or language students; M visas are for vocational, technical or other non-academic students. The privileges and restrictions that apply to both are more or less the same, except that with an M visa you can work legally on or off the campus if the work is considered practical training for your field of study. Restrictions that apply are that you must first be accepted by a school or college in the USA before you can apply, and you can only attend the school for which you were issued that visa. A spouse and minor children may qualify for a non-immigrant visa.

G Visa – International Organisations. For UN and similar organisations.

H Visa – Temporary Workers. Most non-resident foreigners given permission to work are admitted on an H visa but in there are in all four different types of this visa. Remember that you will need to have obtained a firm offer of employment first before making an application to the US Citizenship and Immigration Service (USCIS).

H1-B visas are issued to temporary workers in 'specialty occupations' – those that require a degree or certificate of higher education. Architecture, engineering, mathematics, physical sciences, social sciences, medicine and health, education, business specialities, accounting, law, theology, and the arts are all considered speciality occupations. H1-B visas are limited by a quota. The current law limit is to 65,000 the number of aliens who may be issued and H1-B visa. This makes the chances of getting one slimmer at the end of the financial year. The application process has been speeded up with a 'fast stream' system allowing employers to obtain visas for prospective employees within seven days. The employer is required to submit a petition (a form of sponsorship) to the USCIS; and a 'labor condition application' must also be submitted to the Department of Labor. When these have been approved then the employee applies to the consul in his or her own country.

H1-C visas are for registered nurses working temporarily in the USA.

H-2B visas are for those skilled and unskilled workers going to the US to perform a job which is temporary or seasonal in nature and for which there is a shortage of US workers. Technicians and skilled tradespeople can apply in this category.

H-3 visas are for trainees. The training cannot be available in your home country and must be for future employment outside the USA.

An H visa is valid only while you work for the employer who sponsored your application. If you change jobs you must apply for another visa, with a new employer's petition. You can only possess an H visa, whether with the original employer or a number of employers, for a maximum of six years. On expiration you must reside abroad for a total of one year before applying for another visa.

I Visa – Representatives of Foreign Media. These are available to people working in press, radio, film, television or other media, in their own country. They are issued for multiple admissions and are valid for an extended period. Holders are obliged to work only in the occupation for which the visa was issued. Freelancers must prove that they have a contract for work produced in the US.

J Visa – Exchange Visitors. J-1 visas allow you to come to the USA to participate in a specific exchange visitor programme approved by the United States Information Agency (USIA). These include summer employment programmes, intern programmes for university students, and au-pair programmes. For further information visit http://usinfo.state.gov/. Dependents receive J-2 visas. The USIA sponsors organisations such as BUNAC (see *Employment*), which provides those qualifying for its programme with the J-1. They are valid for 12 to 18 months, and allow multiple entry. You can work in a wide variety of occupations but you are restricted to those which are specified in the organisation's programme.

K Visa – Fiancé(e). For the fiancé(e) of a US citizen only who will travel to America to marry and take up indefinite residence after marriage. The K visa can only be issued when the fiancé(e) is outside the USA. A K-3 (spouse) and K-4 (child) visa has been created to reunite families that have been separated for a long period of time while their visa immigrant applications are being processed.

L Visa – Intra-company Transfers. L visas are available for certain executives, managers or employees with specialised knowledge who are transferred to the USA to work for their employer, its parent, branch subsidiary or affiliates. The visa category is valid for up to a total of seven years for executives or managers and for five years for workers with specialised knowledge, and allow multiple entry. Any legal form of doing business is acceptable, including but not restricted to, corporations, limited companies, partnerships, joint ventures and sole proprietorships. The USCIS is becoming increasingly more restrictive in allowing L-1 visa holders to convert to the green card through the I-140 Permanent Employment process. The USCIS reserves the right to re-evaluate all L-1 visas when you apply for the green card through the I-140 route.

L VISA

Privileges.
- You can be transferred to the USA and work legally for a US company that is a branch, subsidiary, affiliate or joint venture partner of a company which already employs you outside the USA.
- Visa can be issued quickly.
- You may travel in and out of the USA or remain there continuously until your L-1 status expires.
- Visas are available for your spouse and all unmarried children under 21.

> O If you have an L-1 visa for an executive or managerial level position in the US company and want to apply for a green card through employment you can do so but the USCIS is becoming more restrictive in allowing this form of conversion.
>
> O When you enter the USA your I-94 will be issued for the length of your L-1 approval.
>
> **Limitations**
>
> O You are restricted to working only for the US employer who acted as your L-1 visa sponsor and the US company must be a branch, subsidiary, affiliate or joint venture partner of the company that currently employs you outside the USA.
>
> O Visas can initially be approved for one year (new US company) or three years if your US company has been trading for more than one year. Extensions of two years at a time may be allowed until you have been in the USA for a total of seven years if you are a manager or an executive.
>
> O When children reach the age of 21 and wish to continue living in the USA they must apply for their own visa.

O, P, and R Visa – Temporary work visas for selected occupations. The Immigration Act 1990 created a number of highly specialised working visa categories. O and P visas are available for people with outstanding ability or achievement in business, the sciences, arts, education, entertainment, and athletics. R visas are for religious workers who have been a member of a religious denomination which has a bona fide non-profit religious organisation in the US. The application requires written evidence from an appropriate individual or organisation to back it up. These visas are often issued for a particular event or occasion (such as a festival) and are valid for the duration of that event, up to a maximum of three years.

Q Visa – Exchange visitors coming to the USA to participate in international cultural exchange programmes. Nicknamed the 'Disney Visa' because it was as a result of lobbying by that organisation that helped create it, the Q visa is granted to those who will be working in a job where they will be sharing a practical training with Americans, or the history, traditions or culture of their country. Nannies and au pairs (although they normally qualify for a J-1), or teachers of unusual arts would qualify. The visa is valid for up to 15 months, and has to be applied for by the prospective employer. It differs from the J visa in that it does not relate to specific exchange programmes.

S Visa – Suppliers of information in criminal or espionage cases. Self explanatory.

THE GREEN CARD

The green card, or the Alien Registration Receipt Card – the I-551 which includes a photograph, biometric indicators, and a fingerprint in the chip – is the best-known and most coveted of immigration documents. It entitles the holder to work and live permanently in the United States.

Significantly, the green card not only entitles you to live in the country – permanent residence is a necessity. If the USCIS suspects you of having another home abroad, and if you spend more than a certain amount of time out of the country (usually a year), you may lose your green card. You have to satisfy the authorities that you are, and mean to remain, a permanent resident.

This can cause problems if you want to apply for a visa and then for a green card, because a requirement of most visas is the absolute intention not to remain permanently. A certain amount of ingenuity is often needed to explain a sudden change in circumstances.

A green card holder is a tax resident of the United States, and has the right to apply for US citizenship after a certain time. One of the only differences between citizenship and green card status is that the latter does not give you the right to vote.

Everyone has an equal chance of getting a green card. Although some people consider that it is more difficult for a Western European to make a successful application, everybody applying through one of the normal channels (for example through employment, as a family member of a US citizen, or through a minimum investment of $500,000) has the same status whatever their nationality. The fact is that many Western Europeans in the United States do not have green cards because they do not see themselves as permanent residents. It is more common for them to stay for the duration of a non-immigrant visa and to return periodically to their own country, whereas many people from the developing world and from Eastern Europe tend to come to America to stay for good.

Another reason for the lack of Britons with green cards is that for several years they have not been eligible for the Green Card Lottery (see below), which is only open to nationals of countries which have not sent more than 50,000 emigrants to the US in the past five years. (An exception is made for individuals born in Northern Ireland.) There are a number of websites dedicated to facilitating entry to the lottery.

Many Europeans in the USA complain about the system, its expenses and difficulties.

One past applicant says
British people and Europeans have a very hard time staying here, and have to move through the immigration system from one visa to another and finally to

> *a green card. This is a very difficult process which I can testify to first hand. Many circumvent the system by marrying, although even then the immigration department checks up on them to see if the marriage is valid.*

The only case in which certain nationalities are favoured above others is in the Diversity Immigrant Visa program – popularly known as the green card Lottery (see below), by which 55,000 green cards are reserved each year for countries which traditionally have not sent many emigrants to the USA. The Immigration Act of 1990 introduced this category as a way of encouraging ethnic diversity in the US population. The odds of being selected are about one in twenty, according to the USCIS.

Certain categories are favoured above others: the vital distinction is whether you come from a country with a repressive regime. Political refugees are given priority above many other categories. Other ways of getting a green card include investment in the USA, although as a minimum of $500,000 must be invested it is not an option open to many.

Applying for a Green Card. Applying for a green card is usually a two-step process consisting of the filing of a petition (by your relative, spouse or employer) with the USCIS, and the application, which can be made at the US embassy or consulate in your home country. You can file with the INS if you are in the USA on a non-immigrant visa at the time. As applications differ depending on the category, you should ask the advice of the consulate.

The following are the categories of those who are eligible for green cards:

Immediate Relatives: Including spouses of US citizens; unmarried people under the age of 21 who have at least one US citizen parent; parents of US citizens if the son or daughter is over 21.

Preference categories: These are people with family members who are US citizens (under these categories certain family members will be given precedence over others: children of US citizens have priority over brothers and sisters, for example). The second preference category is those with job skills that are wanted by US employers and are in short supply in the USA.

Diversity Immigration Lottery. Also known as the Green Card Lottery: 55,000 green cards are given to those countries who in the past have sent the fewest immigrants to the USA. You must register by a certain date each year, and if the registration is accepted you file an application, with documents such as birth and marriage certificates, at a consulate. You must provide proof of a high school education or its equivalent, or two years' work experience within the last five years in a job which requires at least two years' training or experience. One hundred thousand people from six geographic regions are given the right to enter the Lottery, of which half will win a green card. Some seven million apply every year. There have been instances of fraudulent websites posing as official US government sites and 'scam' e-mails soliciting funds. Notification of success will come from the Kentucky Consular Center in the form of written notification and will never solicit payment.

Investors: As a result of the Immigration Act 1990, 10,000 green cards are now available to those who invest $1 million in new US businesses that will hire at least ten full-time workers or an existing business and hire an additional ten full-time workers. The minimum is reduced to $500,000 if the investment is made in a Targeted Employment Area, which is either rural or where unemployment is 150% of the national average. However, the requirement to employ ten citizens is waived if the investment is made in specific areas designated as Regional Centers and a competent professional, such as an economist, quantifies that it will stimulate employment. Many Regional Centers have immigrant investor programs which offer investments designed to meet the immigration requirements.

Special Immigrants. Over the years various laws have been passed covering certain 'special categories' of immigrant. These include religious workers, foreign medical graduates, former employees in the Panama Canal Zone, foreign workers who were formerly long-time employees of the US government, and several others. Check with the US consulate for details.

Refugees and those seeking political asylum: To qualify you must be fleeing political or religious persecution in your own country. Economic refugees (those escaping poverty) do not qualify.

Temporary Protected Status. This is not a green card category: Temporary Protected Status is given to those fleeing persecution who need a temporary safe haven. It will not lead to a green card.

Amnesty. The Immigration Control and Reform Act (ICRA) 1986 gave amnesty to aliens who had been living illegally in the USA since 1 January 1982, by giving them green cards. Special Agricultural Workers (SAWs) and Replenishment Agricultural Workers (RAWs). Under ICRA 1986 those who had worked in agriculture for 90 days between 1 May 1985 and 1 May 1986 were given green cards. The second category (RAWs) are those who worked for 20 days within a calendar year and registered before 31 December 1989, who were entered into a lottery. The system will be revived whenever there is a shortage of agricultural workers.

US CITIZENSHIP

United States citizenship can be acquired in one of four ways: if you are born in the USA, if your parents are US citizens, if you have been naturalised, or if your parents have been naturalised. For full details see the book *How to become a US Citizen* published in the US by Peterson's (www.petersons.com).

To be a US citizen you have to renounce citizenship of all other countries, although your country may not accept the renunciation, and may enable you to keep dual citizenship. US immigration laws are complicated, and there are many ways in which people qualify for citizenship without realising it. The rules governing whether or not a child born out of the country is a citizen or not have changed several times over the last 50 years. The basic law is that in order to qualify one or both of your parents must be US citizens, and have to have spent a certain amount of time in the USA. If you think that you may qualify as a US citizen, contact the consulate for details of the law as it stood when you were born.

If you were born between 1952 and 1986, and only one parent was a US citizen, he or she would have had to have spent at least ten years (at least five of them after the age of 14) in the USA.

From 15 November 1986 to the present the ten year residence rule changed to five years, with two years of compulsory residence after the age of 14.

When parents become naturalised US citizens, their children automatically have the same right, provided that they hold green cards and are under the age of 18 at the time of their parents' naturalisation.

Proof of US citizenship can be provided with a birth certificate from a state government, a US passport, certificates of citizenship or certificates of consular registration of birth.

A child born on US soil is automatically a citizen of the USA no matter what the laws of the parents' country. Children born in the USA to foreign diplomats are an exception to this rule: they are deemed to have been born on foreign soil.

Naturalisation. To become a naturalised citizen of the US you must be at least 18, and you must have held a green card for at least five years. You should also be a person of good moral character ('bad' moral character can cover anything from committing a crime to non-payment of taxes), have knowledge of the English language, and be familiar with American government and history.

At least half of the five-year waiting limit must have been spent in the USA. If you leave the country for a year or more this wipes out any time added up to the five years, and you must start the waiting period again.

If you are married to a US citizen the waiting period is reduced to three years; if your spouse works for the US government abroad there is no waiting period.

The process for naturalisation is surprisingly simple. The application is made with the USCIS on form N-400. After this has been processed (which may take anything from a few months to over a year) you will be called to an interview in which you will have to demonstrate the required knowledge of history and government, and spoken English. You may be asked the date of US independence, the meaning of the stars and stripes, what happens if both the president and the vice president die in office, who is the governor of your state, or what is the name of the national anthem and who wrote it? These questions are designed to imbue in anyone who wants to become a citizen a sense of the importance of what they are doing. It is not an exercise in nationalism, more a matter of taking your new country seriously by taking the trouble to know something about it.

The final part of the process is the swearing-in ceremony, when you will swear allegiance to the United States, and renounce citizenship of all other countries.

ILLEGAL PAPERS

All you used to need to fake a green card was a typewriter, a pot of glue, a cheap laminating machine and a polaroid camera. Many of the estimated five million illegal immigrants in the USA hold counterfeit green cards – but that is all set to change. In 1998, the then INS spent $38 million developing a green card they believe is impossible to counterfeit. Embedded with microscopic portraits of all 42 presidents, a hologram of the Statue of Liberty and other hi-tech wizardry, it should try the skills of the cleverest forger. You can still buy a fake for anything from $5,000 to $15,000 – but be warned that the government is notoriously touchy about illegal immigration, and if you are discovered with fake papers you will certainly be deported, and may never be allowed back into the country. Beware also of phoney 'immigration consultants' claiming to increase your chances of success in the green card lottery. They will tell you they have never had an application rejected, or they will claim to be affiliated to the government. The process for entering the lottery is free and simple, and there is nothing anyone can do to increase your chances of success.

SUMMARY

Once you have succeeded in getting the visa that you want, make sure that you work and live within its limits. It would be pointless to blacken your name by trying to cheat the system. Once you are on the files of the USCIS you will be amazed by how familiar they are with your circumstances and how soon they get in touch if you outstay your welcome.

Bear in mind that many people spend years in the States without getting permanent residence status, or applying for the 'ultimate goal', citizenship. The latter is probably not an option for most Europeans, who are unlikely to want to renounce their nationality for the sake of it.

If you have had an application turned down it would be best to get a lawyer. There are two schools of thought on this subject. Some say that it will do you no good, that the system is quite easy to work without resorting to expensive advice; on the other hand, for between $1,000 and $3,000 you can get enough help to open doors that you were not aware of, and it could save months of frustration. Treat lawyers with caution, and make sure that they are fully qualified to deal with your situation: the US Embassy will supply a list on request.

Useful Websites

The most useful websites come from law firms and other organisations specialising in visa applications; a small selection of the best are listed here. There are also hundreds of personal homepages of people who feel the need to share their visa application sagas – some of them make interesting reading.

www.uscis.gov. The official site of the US Citizenship and Immigration Service providing information about fees, applications, regulations and offices.

www.visanow.com. Provides online immigration law services, guidance and online applications.

www.lawcom.com/immigration. The immigration homepage from the law office of Richard Madison. An excellent and informative site.

www.us-immigration.com/imm.htm. Straightforward immigration information from the American Immigration Center.

www.imwong.com. From the law office of Margaret W. Wong and Associates.

Useful Addresses

US Embassies:

US Embassy, 24 Grosvenor Square, London W1A 1AE. Main switchboard ☎020-7499 9000, Visa Information Line ☎090-6820 0290, 24 hours (60p per minute).

Operator Assisted Visa Information Line ☎090-5544 4546 (£1.30 per minute); www.usembassy.org.uk.

US Consulate General Scotland, 3 Regent Terrace, Edinburgh EH7 5BW; ☎0131-556 8315; fax 0131-557 6023.

US Consulate General Northern Ireland, Danesfort House, 223 Stranmillis Road, Belfast BT9 5GR; ☎028-9038 6100; fax 028-9068 1301.

US Citizenship and Immigration Services, US Embassy, 5 Upper Grosvenor Street, London W1A 2JB; ☎020-7495 0551; fax 020-7495 4330; www.uscis.gov.

Foreign Embassies in the USA:

British Embassy, 3100 Massachusetts Avenue NW, Washington, DC 20008; ☎202-588 6500; fax 202-588 7866; www.britainusa.com/embassy.

British Consulates in: Los Angeles, San Francisco, Miami, Atlanta, Chicago, Boston, New York, Dallas, Houston, Seattle, and Denver.

Irish Embassy, 2234 Massachusetts Avenue NW, Washington, DC 20008; ☎202-4623939.

Visa Services and Immigration Lawyers:

Brownstein, Brownstein & Associates, Immigration Department, 1310 Greene Avenue, Suite 750, Montréal,

Quebec, Canada H3Z 2B2; ☎514-939 9559; fax 514-939 2289; e-mail immigrate@brownsteinlaw.com; www.brownsteinlaw.com. Canadian immigration lawyers with associates worldwide including the United States.

Ferman Law, 27 Bruton Street, London W1J 6QN; ☎020-7499 5702; fax 020-7236 2533; e-mail info@fermanlaw.com; www.fermanlaw.com An American attorney specialising in US and Canadian immigration, setting up businesses and taxation.

Four Corners Emigration, Strathblane House, Ashfield Road, Cheadle, Cheshire SK8 1BB; ☎0161-608 1608; fax 0161-608 1616; e-mail info@fourcorners.net; www.fourcorners.net. Specialists in assisting with immigration and visas to the USA. Full support with relocation and resettlement also given.

Global Visas, 20 St Mary at Hill, London EC3R 8EE; ☎020-7190 6592; e-mail info@globalvisas.com; www.globalvisas.com.

Jaffe & Co, 38 Queen Anne Street, London W1M 9LB; ☎020-7436 9409. US Visa and Immigration Attorneys.

Laura Devine Solicitors, 11 Old Jewry, London EC2R 8DU; ☎020-7710 0700; fax 020-7710 0719; e-mail enquiries@lauradevine.com; www.lauradevine.com.

LaVigne, Coton & Associates, 7087 Grand National Drive, Suite 100, Orlando, FL 32819; ☎407-316 9988; fax 407-316 8820; e-mail attylavign@aol.com; www.lavignelaw.us International attorneys dealing with immigration to the US, property, business, foreign investments, tax and contracts law.

Lesley Sillitto, 1 Powell Close, Edgware, Middlesex HA8 7QU; ☎020-8951 1082; e-mail visausa@btinternet.com; www.investorvisaUSA.com. US visa consultant specialising in business investment visas.

New Horizons Group, Gateway Professional Park, 301 N Cattlemen Road, Suite 205, Sarasota, FL 34232; ☎941-387 3829; and Liberty House, 222 Regent Street, London W1B 5TR; ☎020-7297 3000; e-mail info@newhorizonsgroup.com; www.newhorizonsgroup.com. One-stop relocation service to the USA.

Richard S. Goldstein, 96A Mount Street, 1stFloor, Mayfair, London W1K 2TB; ☎020-7499 8200; fax 020-7499 8300; e-mail lawoffices@goldsteinvisa.com; www.goldsteinvisa.com; and 145 West 57th Street, 16th Floor, New York, NY 10019; ☎212-957 0500; fax 212-957 2020; e-mail lawoffices@lorsg.com.

Travel Document Systems, 925 15th Street NW, Suite 300, Washington, DC 20005; ☎202-638 3800; fax 202-638 4674; e-mail support@traveldocs.com; www.traveldocs.com.

USA Immigration Law Center, 1717 K Street NW, Suite 600, Washington DC 20036; ☎202-973 0168; e-mail info@usailc.com; www.usailc.com.

Visaplus Relocation, 100 Pall Mall,

London SW1Y 5HP; ☎020-7724 5556; fax 0220-7724 5535; e-mail ea@visaplus.co.uk; www.emigratingabroad.co.uk.

Walker and Walker Emigration, 24 Church Street, Kirkby in Ashfield, Nottingham NG17 8LE; ☎01623-753240.

Walter F Rudeloff, 4 King's Bench Walk, Temple, London EC4Y 7DL; ☎020-7267 1297; fax 020-7209 9710. American attorney at law providing professional immigration services to obtain any type of US visa or green card.

Workpermit.com, 11 Bolt Court, Fleet Street, London EC4A 3DQ; ☎020-7842 0800; fax 020-7353 0100; e-mail london@workpermit.com; www.workpermit.com. Global corporate immigration service affiliated with the UK's Computing and Software Services Association.

Employment and Investment Specialists

AmblerCollins Visa Specialists, Eden House, 59 Fulham High Street, London SW6 3JJ; ☎020-7371 0213; fax 020-7736 8841; email info@amblercollins.com; www.amblercollins.com. A firm specialising in advising on all categories of US visas and assists in applying to appropriate government offices.

RWH International Inc, 3223 3rd Avenue South, Suite 200, Seattle, WA 98134; ☎416-636 3933; fax 416-636 8113; email info@usjoboffer.com; www.usjoboffer.com. A firm which assists the job hunting process in the US.

Robinson O'Connell, 10 Greycoat Place, London SW1P 1SB; ☎020-7960 6057; e-mail visas@robinsonoconnell.com. Specialists in the EB-5 investment visa, particularly those linked to Regional Centers for retirees.

Transatlantic Jobs; New York ☎212-7341541; e-mail peter@transatlanticjobs.com; www.transatlanticjobs.com.

Setting up Home

CHAPTER SUMMARY

o The US property market is efficient and fair, and so many foreigners buy houses there that specialised estate agents and relocation agents exist to help the process.

o Florida remains the most popular choice for the foreign househunter.

o House prices vary greatly across the country; generally the south is cheaper than the north or Midwest.

o The standard of living is high in the US, with an average household income of $43,318, and 68% of Americans own their own home.

o There are relocation companies who can help with every stage of moving to the US, but their services are not cheap; they are mainly used by employers sending staff overseas.

o **Buying property.** Americans tend to obtain mortgages through their estate agents or mortgage brokers rather than direct from a bank.

   o Most US estate agents are members of Multiple Listing Services which have information on all properties available in a region, not a selected few.

   o Contracts are signed earlier in the buying process than they would be in the UK, and legal advice is essential.

o **Renting property.** Most apartments are rented unfurnished – apart from a refrigerator.

   o Rental regulations vary from state to state but the law is generally weighted in favour of the landlord.

America continues to be a favourite choice of emigrants. According to the UK Office of Population Censuses and Surveys, over 30,000 people a year leave the UK in order to spend a year or more in the USA. Wherever you go, you will meet Europeans, and if you spend time in areas with the greatest concentration of foreigners, such as California, New York, Florida, Illinois, Colorado and Arizona, you will find ready-made communities to welcome you. Buying a house in the United States can be as traumatic as it is in your own country, but generally the US property industry is well-regulated, efficient and fair. There are so many foreigners buying property (especially in certain states), that extensive networks exist to smooth the buying process. There are large numbers of UK property companies that deal with the US; relocation agents will steer you through the entire process, from identifying properties to organising visits. The more a company is doing for you, the more important it is to brief them thoroughly: you do not want to make a series of abortive visits across the Atlantic to look at unsuitable houses. Names and addresses of agents and professional advisors are in the relevant sections below.

Another way of getting in touch with US property professionals is to go to one of the major international exhibitions aimed at domestic homebuyers. The main event for information about buying property in the US is the Homebuyer Show held annually in March at the ExCel centre in London's Docklands. There is an extensive section dedicated to buying property abroad and exhibitors include developers, agents, attorneys, removal companies, overseas lenders and property magazines displaying their services. The show is an excellent opportunity to familiarise yourself with prices, locations, and so on, and to collect addresses of companies which might be useful in the future. For more information about the show contact the organiser, Homebuyer Events Ltd (Mantle House, Broomkill Road, London SW18 4JQ; ☎020-7069 5000; fax 020-8877 1557; e-mail enquiries@homebuyer.co.uk; www.homebuyer.co.uk).

> The US housing market is buoyant and at its highest level in 20 years. According to the Office of Federal Housing Enterprise and Oversight, the average house price increased by 11% over 2004. The fastest pace of property increases was in Nevada where demand in Las Vegas pushed prices 32% higher over the year. Properties in Hawaii, California, and the District of Columbia all rose more than 20% in the same period. Palm Springs (California), popular in the 1940s and 50s, is facing a renaissance where huge demand for property has increased prices by 30% over each of the past three years. Florida continues to be the state where most foreigners choose to live, with Colorado, Arizona, Nevada and Montana increasing in popularity.

House prices vary enormously from state to state. It is more expensive to buy in a city than in the country, and generally cheaper inland than on the coast. You will also find the south cheaper than the north and midwest. Of the ten most expensive places to buy a house, seven are in California (Beverley Hills, Brentwood, San Francisco, La Jolla, San Mateo, Newport Beach and Palos Verdes). The others are Greenwich and Darien in Connecticut and Wellesley, Massachusetts. Other expensive states are Hawaii, Virginia, Montana, New Jersey and New York. The cheapest housing is in Wyoming, Nebraska, Idaho, Wisconsin and Alabama. The most affordable urban areas are Tampa Bay in Florida, Houston (Texas), St Louis (Missouri), and Minneapolis.

In some cases the decision whether to buy or not will not arise: if you are on a short-term job placement, or if you are intending to live in a major city, where prices are high even for the seriously wealthy. Otherwise this is a excellent time to buy.

Much long-distance planning can be eased by using the Internet where you search property listings, check prices, and make contact with attorneys, real estate agents, schools, local authorities. One useful starting point is *Life In the USA* (www.lifeintheusa.com) which provides a guide to immigrants about American society and culture.

HOW DO THE AMERICANS LIVE?

It is possible to answer this question either with a string of statistics, or with a brief sketch of the average American household.

The standard of living in the United States is considerably higher than in many European countries. In a country of 294 million inhabitants this can only be an average: there is also terrible poverty and deprivation, and not only in the inner cities. Some rural areas, such as the Appalachians and the Mississippi Delta suffer crushing poverty. But the national standard of living is high: the median household income is $43,318 and 89% of households own a motor vehicle, while more than 99% have a refrigerator, 76% a clothes washer, and 43.5% central air conditioning. Over 98% own a television, 34.5% a freezer, 28.5% an outdoor grill, and 12.3% a waterbed heater.

By 2003, 68% of Americans owned their homes, which means nearly seven out of 10 households own the home they live in. The US Department of Housing and Urban Development has specified a national homeownership goal of 70% by 2006. This is likely to be an apartment or condominium in a town, or a house (or bungalow) in the suburbs, with its own garden – called a yard. Land is not the scarce commodity it is in most of Europe, and although 80% of Americans live in urban areas, high-density housing is rare. The vast majority of the population live in big city suburbs which spread for miles with few limits on growth, in houses set in decent plots of land. Surburban living is encouraged by car ownership, and by the opening of out-of-town shopping complexes, which in turn cause city centre businesses to close down. And as shops and communities collapse in the inner cities, those who can afford to move out do so, leaving less and less reason for anyone to remain there – except those who are trapped by poverty.

There are more than 50 metropolitan areas with populations of over three-quarters of a million. Some of these are huge – in terms of area, rather than density of population. On the west coast, Los Angeles is a vast urban sprawl stretching 99 miles (160 km) along the Pacific coast and 49 miles (80 km) inland; and on the east coast there is a chain of large cities, from Boston to Washington

DC. A new and quintessentially American phenomenon is the Edge City. This is a suburb that has become a town, with shopping malls, cinemas, offices and streets of houses, but it has no name, and belongs to no particular place. There are more than 200 of these in the USA.

A third of all Americans live within 20 miles (32 km) of the old Route 1, the first federal highway which starts on the Canadian border and runs all the way along the East Coast until the tip of the country at the Florida Keys. The majority of people who emigrate to the States live on either the east or west coast: Florida is a favourite of retirees, both European and American.

With such a vast and diverse country, any generalisation will be misleading, but it is possible to make some observations about how the average American family lives. Every country has its stereotypes, and Americans seem to be lampooned by Europeans with more than average frequency. Just as Americans are delighted when they meet someone who conforms to their picture of the stuffy, polite, tweed-suited, red-faced Englishman, many Europeans expect Americans to be as brash and loud as the popular conception has it.

> In America, things often are on a larger scale than any European is used to. Even portions of food can seem immense. The average family lives in a bigger house, on a bigger plot of land. It is important to be aware of the great differences between states. A family in Los Angeles will lead a very different life to one in New England. On much of the west coast, three time zones away from the east, life is as 'American', and sometimes as foreign, as it comes.

In Illinois, between Chicago and Springfield, there is a town called Normal. The population of Normal is around 40,000. It is not quite in the geographical centre of the United States, but in terms of history, racial mix, lifestyle and attitudes it is probably as near to a 'normal' American town as you could find. It has a high school, a city hall, a police department headquarters, a flagstaff, a cinema and a shopping mall. It has average problems. The police are worried about the number of guns there are in the town, it has a minor drug problem, and a more serious problem with racism: Illinois has one of the largest Hispanic populations in America. To describe how an American family lives you could do worse than imagine the average family in the average town, and in Normal, Illinois, that is as near as you are going to get.

A middle-class family in Normal will live in a three-bedroomed house on the outskirts of town. It may be a bungalow, and will be no more than 20 years old. It would not appear very sturdy to a European, but the family will not expect to stay there for ever, and they certainly will not think that their children will remain when they are grown up. The house will have a garage and a garden. Everybody in the area will have one or two cars: public transport is highly unlikely to come near to the house, even if it exists in the town. There will be a well-cared-for front lawn. The inside of the house will be clean and roomy, and all the furniture will look new. There will be few old-fashioned decorations or knick-knacks. There will be four telephones. The kitchen will be packed with electric gadgets, as will the rest of the house. In a power cut, the refrigerator, the freezer, the microwave, the toaster, the electric coffeepot, the popcorn-popper, the can opener, the electric carving knife, the television, the VCR, the computer, the stereo, the answerphone, the garage door opener, the clothes washer, the dishwasher, the magimix, and the electric toothbrush would all be rendered inoperable. Europeans travelling in the States 10 or 20 years ago were always amazed by the gadgets, the sheer variety of *things* that Americans had in their homes. This has changed now, and our jaws no longer drop at the electric boot-wipers and heated pet blankets. What still has the capacity to astonish is the size of the refrigerator in an American home. It will invariably be of industrial size: at least six feet tall. This is to contain enough food for a family of four. The family shopping will be done once a month, or at the most once a fortnight, and fridge and freezer will be stocked full.

The higher standard of living is reflected in more than the size of the refrigerator. The children will have bedrooms groaning with toys, all more expensive, more automated, and generally able to *do* more than other kids' toys. A European ten-year-old visiting his American counterpart is usually delighted and envious at the magical kingdom in the bedroom.

It does not need pointing out that millions of Americans live in vastly different circumstances. The cities hide families that sleep three to a bed, and do not have hot water, let alone electric toothbrushes: the USA has some of the worst inner-city poverty in the developed world. For every affluent household in Normal, Illinois, there is a family living in a trailer park in a jobless community in a former industrial heartland, victims of recessions and the relentless closure of factories. Often travelling by train will take you through burnt out and decaying urban neighborhoods which have been left behind after failing industries have closed down. America has more millionaires than any other country, but its cities and rural areas can be poverty-stricken and squalid. Neither the country's wealth nor its poverty represent a true picture, rather they are aspects of the same reality.

FINANCE

TABLE 2	USEFUL TERMS

Adjustable Rate Mortgage (ARM): variable rate mortgage.
Annual Percentage Rate (APR): the finance rate on a loan.
Assumption of mortgage: buyer assumes responsibility for an existing mortgage note held by the seller. Subject to approval by the lender.

> *Balloon payment*: large accelerated payments due at the end, or during the life, of some loans.
> *Caps*: national limits on interest rates within an ARM.
> *Federal National Mortgage Association (FNMA, Fannie Mae)*: private corporation created by Congress that buys mortgage notes from local lenders. It can also set guidelines used by lenders to assess borrowers.
> *Origination fee*: application fees for processing a mortgage.
> *PITI* principal, interest, tax, and insurance: the basis of monthly mortgage repayments.
> *RESPA statement*: the Real Estate Settlement Procedures Act sets out a good faith statement (RESPA statement) which gives a breakdown of closing costs.

Mortgages Overview

American lenders will demand an astonishing amount of information before they will consider lending to you. As well as the standard information, you will be required to supply at least three years' pay slips, rental cheques, tax returns, credit reports, credit card accounts and any liabilities. Interestingly, they like to see evidence of money owed, and are suspicious of a regularly-cleared credit account, which may indicate you're not to be trusted with long-term credit.

Mortgage lenders come in many forms. As a first move you should go to a large real estate agent who will have a mortgage broking section. They will arrange the loan for you, either themselves or through a broker, and then farm it out to a local bank or larger institution. You can also go to a mortgage broker (listed in the Yellow Pages). They will charge around 1% of your mortgage.

Local lenders (banks and other financial institutions) will take on loans from brokers and real estate agents, tie around 100 together, and sell them onto large loan institutions, like the Federal National Mortgage Association.

Although it is possible to cut out the broker by arranging your own loan directly with a bank, unless you are conversant with US financial services practice you may find it too complicated, and as expensive as going to a broker in the first place.

The company *Conti Financial Services* (204 Church Road, Hove, Sussex BN3 2DJ; ☎01273-772811; fax 01273-321269; e-mail enquiries@mortgageoverse as.com; www.mortgageoverseas.com) can offer specialist advice on obtaining a mortgage from both American and UK lenders.

Mortgages on the Web

Until recently, the prospect of getting a mortgage online was too daunting for most people to contemplate. Issues such as security were uppermost in borrowers' minds, and the amount of variables involved – such as matching the best type of loan to the borrower – seemed to need human input. But computers are the ideal tool for matching infinite numbers of variables. There are now Web-based mortgage packages from companies such as Microsoft, Intuit, E-Loan, Amex, Priceline.com and the intriguingly-named HomeShark which allow you to compare and contrast current loan rates, and give a complete picture of loan costs, terms and how mortgages will affect individual borrowers. Some packages will ask how long you intend to stay in your home and will guide you to a shorter- or longer-term mortgage accordingly. California-based E-Loan has a facility called E-Track which tracks the progress of your loan and posts regular updates on your application.

Useful Websites

One of the most useful government sites is the US Department of Housing and Urban Development's (HUD) at www.hud.gov, which offers straightforward information. HUD is a federal agency responsible for national policy and programmes that address America's housing needs. Its website has information on all aspects of homebuying, from finding an agent to arranging a mortgage. The National Association of Realtors (estate agents) also runs a helpful site at www.realtor.com, which acts as a central reference source for finding information about realtors, properties for sale, moving services, and offers advice on finance and insurance.

Online borrowing has a long way to go before the majority of borrowers are getting their mortgages straight off the screen – the reams of paperwork still make a human facilitator essential – but some of these sites are worth a look, if only to give yourself an idea of what to expect from a visit to the mortgage-lender.

Many of the websites listed below offer enormous quantities of relevant information ranging from the latest borrowing rates to special tools which help you calculate the costs of buying a property.

www.bankrate.com – a comprehensive site for financial reference giving current mortgage rates and banking products.

www.realtor.com – the official site of American realtors (estate agents) with advice on financing and moving services.

www.eloan.com – well set-out information on all aspects of borrowing.

www.homeshark.com – information for buyers, sellers and renters. Another excellent site for the financially-uninitiated.

www.quickenloans.com – comprehensive online home loans, refinancing and financial services site.

www.mortgageexpo.com – offers financing options.

www.priceline.com – offers competitive rates and low costs. The site has an info centre explaining all the different types of mortgage and a glossary of terms.

Types of Mortgage

The expanding US economy will steadily apply borrowing and inflationary pressures and long-term interest rates are expected to rise accordingly. In March 2005, 30-year fixed-rate mortgages stood at around 6.01%, while one-year adjustables were 4.24%. Mortgage rates are predicted to rise to 7% by the end of 2006.

The US mortgage system is basically similar to that in the UK, although there are differences in procedure that need to be noted. The Federal National Mortgage Association (a.k.a. 'Fannie Mae') is a privately-owned corporation set up by Congress that is responsible for mortgage guidelines used by the majority of lenders. The main types of mortgage are:

Fixed Rate: the most popular type of mortgage, usually carried over 30 years.

Adjustable Rate Mortgage (ARM): initial payments can be 2% to 3% lower than the current rate, although rates can 'balloon' with changes in the interest rate. ARMs take account of national interest rates, and repayment is controlled by a cap on the mortgage. Lifetime Caps set the limits over the lifetime of the mortgage, Annual Caps regulate your interest rate over the year, and Payment Caps allow for one adjustment a year.

Convertible Mortgage: can be converted from fixed to adjusted rate at certain times during the course of the loan.

Graduated Payment Mortgage: has a low initial rate that increases over a period of time. The lender assumes that the borrower's income will increase in order to be able to service the higher rates.

Two-step Loans: fixed or adjustable rate mortgages with a built-in rate increase after five or seven years. Initial rates are usually low, but in the latter stages of the mortgage you will pay more than the going rate.

Fifteen-year Mortgage: paid off within 15 years.

Registration and Mortgage Costs

Some states require documentary stamps on mortgage and transfer deeds, although often at a low rate. In Florida, for instance, if you are buying a property then you will be charged 35 cents per $100 of mortgage amount. If you are selling a property, you are obligated to pay 70 cents per $100 of the full selling price. In states where you are required to record title documents there will be further charges for this. Some states also levy 'intangible taxes' on the loan amount ($2 per $1,000 of loan in Florida). Other states impose various transfer taxes and other duties. New York, for example, has a transfer tax of $2 per $500 of price, and a mortgage recording tax of 1% of the loan. There are many permutations.

Added to these are the closing costs which, depending on the state, will include mortgage recording fees, state and local closing taxes, as above, legal fees, inspection fees and other general costs. These can total between 2% and 6% of the purchase price. Mortgage lenders also usually charge one or two 'points' (a point is 1% of the total loan). The other main monthly costs associated with a mortgage are what is called 'PITI': the Principal mortgage payment, Interest, Taxes and Insurance. Annual property taxes can be between 1% and 3% of purchase price.

The lowest down-payment that can be offered is usually 5% (though it is possible to negotiate less). Normally, the buyer will put down 20% of the purchase price. Financial planners advise against paying more than 28% of your gross monthly income in mortgage repayments, although the lending environment makes it easy to shop around: look under *Real Estate Loans* in the Yellow Pages. Overall, the typical monthly house payment, including insurance and taxes, is around $1,000 per month.

Title insurance is usually a requirement of the mortgage, and the lender will not close the deal without proof that a policy has been arranged. Make sure that you get an Owner's Policy (which will cover your equity, in the form of down payments), and not simply Title Insurance (which is all that the lender will insist on, but only covers the basic mortgage itself).

You will also be required to take out hazard insurance. It is also advisable to get an all-risk policy, which includes liability cover: there are frequent claims against homeowners by people who have been injured on their property. The average premium on a $120,000 house would be $700-$800. For more information on insurance contact a real estate agent or the National Consumer Insurance Helpline ☎1-800-942-4242 (toll-free in the USA). The Insurance Information Institute (www.iii.org) can answer all your questions concerning the nature of home insurance and the options available to house buyers.

Closing costs often take people by surprise, as they are demanded upfront, and can be sizable. With mortgage points (percentage to the lender), house inspection survey and appraisal, and lawyers fees you should expect to pay $3,000 to $4,000. In some states closing costs are much higher; in Florida for example the average is $6,000 to $8,000.

Non-Resident and UK Mortgages

If you hope to buy a property with a US mortgage without being a resident, you face certain restrictions on the amount of money you can borrow. US banks will not usually lend more than 80% of market value of the desired property or a maximum of 70% for an investment property. If you want to pay less than 20% deposit you will be asked to take out a private mortgage insurance policy (PMI) which will pay off the outstanding balance on the mortgage should you be unable to continue payments. Many banks will require overseas purchasers to put down a deposit of six months mortgage payments, insurance fees, and due taxes.

It is generally not a good idea to take out a mortgage in the UK for a foreign property. Arranging a mortgage within the US may be easier because British banks need to know that if they repossess the property, they are guaranteed to recoup the loan. If you do choose this option, you may have to put your house in your home country up as security. This is unwise: it's best to arrange your US mortgage so that it poses as little threat as possible to your home lifestyle. As well as this, US rates are usually cheaper than UK rates (even though the gap is closing), so there is no saving to be gained. There can also be tax problems.

Mortgages from UK offshore banks (or from onshore banks with offshore branches) should present no problems, depending on the particular policy of the bank. Contact any major UK bank for details of their offshore accounts. The base rate in America is 2.25% compared with 4.75% in the UK.

PURCHASING AND CONVEYANCING PROCEDURES

TABLE 3	USEFUL TERMS

Amortize to make regular payments covering both the principal balance and the interest.

Binder written document binding both parties to sign sales contract, sometimes supported by a small deposit ($100-$1,000) known as 'earnest money' or 'good faith' deposit.

Certificate of Title, or *Title Insurance Document*, a document, signed by a title examiner, stating that a seller has an insurable title to the property.

Closing completing the deal.

Comparable Market Analysis (CMA) a survey of comparable houses on the market, or recently sold.

Earnest money in some states this is referred to as a binder (see above); can also be the deposit paid on signing of the contract.

Escrow a fund or account held by a third party (often a bank, or a closing agent) until all conditions of the contract are met.

Lien a security claim, usually against a debt. If a property has a lien on it, the holder of the lien has a legal claim on the property until the debt is discharged.

Title search a detailed examination of the document history of a property.

Running costs

Remember that in addition to mortgage costs and taxes, any financial calculation needs to include annual running costs. Taxation is, as one can imagine, a complicated subject and rates can vary from state to state and county to county. So if you're thinking of buying a property it's best to conduct some research about your preferred location first. Property taxes in Florida for example cost about 1% of the value of the property and are re-evaluated every three years.

Management costs for a home might cost $100 per month and utilities such as water and gas may cost $75 each per month. On top of these you might want to pay someone to clean the house and maintain a pool and a garden.

A home in Florida costing $175,000 to purchase may well cost $1,920 per annum to cover all the expenses including mortgage payments. This is a substantial figure, but to be expected. It only begins to look steep if the house functions as a second, holiday home. But if for example you are looking to buy such a second home in Florida, you are likely to offset costs by renting the house out while you are occupying your primary residence.

An owner, renting out a house in Florida valued at $175,000 for 40 weeks a year of which 20% ($34,948) was paid as a deposit, can expect to cover all running costs and make a profit of $3,050 profit assuming that the rent paid was $725 per week. Naturally this figure varies depending on the size of the mortgage.

Finding a Property

The American system of property purchase is efficient and well-organised. Most qualified real estate agents are members of Multiple Listing Services, which are local and nationwide databases of all properties for sale. This means that you do not necessarily have to contact an agent in the particular area in which you intend to buy: a member agent in New York will be able to key in your criteria and produce a list of properties in California, for example.

The Internet, with its capacity to cross refer and link to literally millions of pages of information, is the ideal vehicle for seeing what sort of property is around. You'll still want the services of an estate agent, but you could do worse than browse a few sites to see what is available. The US Home Exchange (www.ushx.com) is a free listings site with thousands of houses listed state by state. The sites listed in *Mortgages on the Web* above also have links to real estate services.

Philip Jones found accommodation difficult to find

New York real estate is impossible. Like London it is prohibitively expensive and hard to find. We were fortunate enough to buy an apartment in TriBeCa, a region near to the financial district, eight years ago. Property has gone up substantially in price since and we certainly would be unable to buy it now! We were very lucky.

Auctions are also a popular means of purchasing property in the United States.

At an auction you'll receive the particulars and conditions of sale outlining the property and terms of the auction. Once you've made the highest bid and it is accepted then you are legally obliged to buy the property. Usually, 10% of the purchase price must be paid as a deposit one to three months after signing the agreement. The best preparation for an auction is to arrange finance in advance with approval to bid up to a pre-arranged amount.

Within the UK one starting point is to visit a trade fair dedicated to buying property or emigration. At the annual Homebuyers Show at the ExCel Centre in London (www.homebuyer.co.uk) you can find estate agencies and services specialising in American property. The World of Property is a similar trade fair held in Sandown, Surrey, in March and October, and York in May. For more information contact *Outbound Publishing*, 1 Commercial Road, Eastbourne, East Sussex BN21 3XQ; ☎01323-726040; fax 01323-649249; e-mail info@outboundmedia.co.uk; www.outboundpublishing.com.

Estate Agents

Real estate agents act both as agents and as lawyers in property transactions. In order to become a member of the National Association of Realtors (NAR), or be licensed by their state regulator, they are required to take examinations in estate law, finance, surveying and other subjects. After a certain length of time in practice, and further exams, they can then qualify as a broker. There will usually be two realtors in any transaction, although the commission is charged only to the seller.

Estate Agents do not normally have high street premises with photographs of property for sale in the window. Look in the yellow pages (under Residential Real Estate Agents), contact the relevant state Chamber of Commerce (see the *Employment* chapter for contact details), or the National Association of Realtors for the address of the local Real Estate Commission. These are set up by the state government and can also be found through the state Justice Department. The Sunday newspapers are also fruitful sources of advertisements for agents, mortgage brokers and private sellers and buyers.

The NAR and state authorities guarantee the credentials of their members. The term 'realtor' is actually patented by the NAR, and anybody calling themselves a realtor must be a member and abide by a strict code of ethics.

Dealing with Estate Agents. When dealing with estate agents the usual rules of caution apply. Remember that they are usually acting for the seller, not for you, and the bigger the sale price, the bigger their commission. Some agencies will advertise themselves as operating under 'buyer's brokerage' or 'buyer's agency' principles, which means that they are supposed to act solely in the buyer's interests. It is strongly recommended to buy any property through a qualified broker, in order to be sure that they are fully conversant with the market and the regulations. This is doubly important if you are new to the country and are unsure of the mechanics of house-buying.

When looking at a property it is perfectly acceptable to go over it thoroughly. Turn on all the taps (faucets) to check the water pressure, check under the sink for drips, run the garbage disposal, the dishwasher, the jacuzzi, and any other of the electrical gadgets that may be part of the sale. Ask the seller for copies of the latest water bills and check with the water company that usage for that size of house is normal. You can also ask for gas and electricity bills to get an idea of how much it costs to maintain the house. A full structural inspection by a qualified house inspector will be a condition of the mortgage (see Professional Assistance, below). An appraisal (valuation) will also be necessary: you are entitled to a copy of this.

If you aren't disturbed by the thought of benefiting from another's misfortune it is possible to pick up foreclosed homes (repossessions), from the US Department of Housing and Urban Development (HUD – address below). These houses are often in very poor condition, but they are extremely cheap, only a small deposit is required, and the HUD will often take on the closing costs as well.

Condominiums & Co-operatives

An alternative to a detached house or an apartment is a condo or a co-op. Condominiums are effectively apartment blocks but can be housing estates, owned and run by a management company. Units can be bought directly, the owner sharing a common interest in the grounds and facilities. You are in charge of what happens inside the unit, while the owner is responsible for the communal fabric of the building and the grounds.

Co-operative apartments don't belong directly to the buyer: you buy shares in a corporation that owns the entire building. While you are still responsible for the inside of your unit, a residents' committee, or a management company, deals with the day-to-day running of the common areas.

Purchases are normally financed by a conventional mortgage (although buying shares in a co-op tends to be more complicated). There are also monthly payments, called maintenance fees, association fees or homeowners' dues, to pay for the operating costs of the building. Some condominiums can be bought in what is called a 'Turn-key' deal, which includes furniture, carpets and other elements of the 'household pack' which can be included in the mortgage.

It is important to look at the structural state of the building and grounds. If the paintwork looks tired and the common areas are a mess, leave well alone. Contracts normally specify a percentage that unit owners have to pay for major structural repairs, so you could be faced with a $50,000 bill for curing the building of dry rot.

It is equally important to check the state of the management company and the owner. This should be part of the estate agent's job: he will need to supply you with information about the cash reserves of the company, its operating budget and its legal status. If it is inefficient, or simply crooked, it will hopefully come to light.

You could also go to an owners' or shareholders' meeting, which will give you an idea of the way the operation is run. Get hold of a copy of the condo or co-op rules to make sure that there are no exclusion clauses that don't allow you to keep pets, or throw parties.

Professional Assistance

Buying a house in your own country can be a stressful experience, but the traumas are magnified when buying abroad. Although American property law is based on English common law, with emphasis on proof of title, a contract, and a closing (what in the UK is called completion), customs and practices are very different. It is absolutely essential to get the advice of a lawyer before signing anything at all. Contracts are exchanged much earlier in the deal than in the UK, and you might find yourself signed into something that you cannot back out of (see Contracts below). If you are being pushed into something and you are afraid that you might lose the house of your dreams, put in a clause saying that the contract is subject to approval by your lawyer.

US lawyers charge anything between $100 and $500 per hour. You are likely to pay around $1,500 for contract checking, looking at the abstract (the title deeds) and co-ordinating the closing. Administrative expenses will be added on as extras to the basic legal fee.

If you are intending to buy an American property from the UK it will be difficult to handle the legal aspect with a British based legal practice as there are so few solicitors working in the US property market, but if you do need help contact the *Law Society of England and Wales* (113 Chancery Lane, London WC2A 1PL; ☎020-7242 1222; fax 020-7831 0344; e-mail info.services@lawsociety. org.uk; www.lawsociety.org.uk). It is best to hire a relocation agency to find an American property attorney or find one yourself by contacting the *American Bar Association* (321 North Clark Street, Chicago, IL 60610; ☎312-988 5522; www.abanet.org) for a referral.

Title insurance is an area that can be confusing. The title of a house (title deeds in the UK) show that it belongs to who it is supposed to belong to. Title insurance does not guarantee the title, but it compensates the holder if the title is found to be defective. With this insurance Americans sometimes decide that they do not need a lawyer to do a search on the property. However, it does not insure such things as right of way, use conditions, zoning restrictions. In other words, you are covered if your house is found to belong to someone other than the person you have bought it from, but not if you discover that it cannot be used for business purposes as you thought, or has a right of way going through the back yard.

The mortgage lender will carry out a physical inspection of the property to confirm that it is safe to lend on. You should also get an inspection done yourself. Be careful of asking friends or relatives to do it, however expert they are: it is difficult, or impossible, to sue them if they fail to notice a major fault that might have stopped you from buying the house. Advice on inspections and inspectors can be had from the National Association Of Home Inspectors (address below) who are comparable to British surveyors, or contact the appraisal section of the NAR. A full inspection will start at $200 and rise according to the extent of the inspection and size of the property.

In some parts of the country a third party, called an escrow firm or a title company, will conduct the closing (completion) of the contract. It will hold the down payment, oversee all the paperwork and distribute the money when all the terms of the contract have been met.

If you are buying US property from the UK it's best to use an agency that is a member of the *Federation of Overseas Property Developers, Agents, and Consultants (FOPDAC)*, 1st Floor, 618 Newmarket Road, Cambridge CB5 8LP; ☎0870-350 1223; fax 0870-350 1233; e-mail enquiries@fopdac.com; www.fopdac.com), a trade association which regulates the overseas property market. FOPDAC can provide a list of accredited agencies and supply factsheets on buying or selling property abroad. Most British agents working in the US tend to specialise in Florida because the state is the largest market. For property purchases in other states it might be best to contact a relocation agency or a property company in the US directly.

Useful Addresses

UK & USA

National Association of Home Inspectors, 4248 Park Glen Road, Minneapolis, MN 55416; ☎800-448 3942 or ☎952-928 4641; fax 952-929 1318; e-mail info@nahi.org; www.nahi.org.

American Society of Home Inspectors, 932 Lee Street, Suite 101, Des Plaines, IL 60016; ☎847-759 2820; fax 847-759 1620; www.ashi.com. North America's largest organisation for home inspectors.

US Department of Housing and Urban Development, 451 7th Street SW, Washington, DC 20410; ☎202-708 1112; www.hud.gov.

Insurance Information Institute, 110 William Street, New York, NY 10038; ☎212-346 5500; www.iii.org. A primary source of insurance information for consumers.

www.dreamsinusa.com. A handy website published by a legal firm which has a section on buying a home in the US in addition to other information on health, education, taxation.

Florida Choice, Formosa Gardens Plaza, 7814 West Irlo Bronson Highway, Kissimmee, FL 34747; ☎407-397 3013; fax 407-397 3017; e-mail orlando@floridachoice.com; and 542 Rayleigh Road, Eastwood, Leigh-on-Sea, Essex SS9 5HX; ☎01702-529 6000; fax 01702-529616; e-mail UK@floridachoice.com.

LaVigne, Coton & Associates, 7087 Grand National Drive, Suite 100, Orlando, FL 32819; ☎407-316 9988; fax 407-316 8820; email attylavign@aol.com; www.lavignelaw.us. A law firm handling both real estate and immigration.

National Association of Realtors, 30700 Russell Ranch Road, Westlake Village, CA 91362; ☎805-557 2300; fax 805-557 2680; www.realtor.com.

Prudential Florida WCI Realty, 1306 South East 17th Street, Fort Lauderdale, FL 33316; ☎954-449 2700; fax 954-467 4142; or UK office ☎020-8257 9988; fax 020-8501 0311.

The World of Florida, St Ethelbert House, Ryelands Street, Hereford HR4 OLA; ☎01432-845645; fax 01432-845640; e-mail homes@worldofflorida.co.uk; www.worldofflorida.co.uk. Specialise in villas to buy and rent in Florida.

Useful Publications

A Place In The Sun by Fanny Blake. Channel 4 Books. Price £16.99. A companion book to a television series explaining how to buy a holiday or retirement home in a warm climate. (The series included Florida.)

Going USA. A bi-monthly newspaper which includes news and information for people who want to live, work or emigrate to the United States. Immigration law, developments for prospective emigrants. There are also many relevant advertisements for legal and relocation services. Available on subscription from Outbound Publishing, 1 Commercial Road, Eastbourne, East Sussex BN21 3XQ; ☎01323-726040; e-mail info@outboundmedia.co.uk; www. outboundpublishing.com. Six issues are £19.

World of Property Magazine. Also available from Outbound Publishing. Regularly features Florida property and buying tips.

Contracts

One of the major differences between US, English, and Welsh (though not Scottish) conveyancing procedure is in the contract. In England and Wales nothing is settled until the contract is signed, and then the buyer must complete the deal on pain of severe financial penalties. At any stage before that the seller can take a better offer and the buyer can be gazumped. Gazumping does happen in the USA because nothing is binding until the seller accepts the offer, but it is far less common, primarily because of the greater involvement of the agents and brokers, and because the contractual process is begun when an offer is made. It is in many ways a much fairer system: the contract is signed much earlier, and it is equally binding to buyer and seller, although with let-out clauses for any major problems.

Once your offer is accepted by the seller you immediately sign a contract, usually in the realtor's office. You then pay a deposit (sometimes called 'earnest money') of around 10% of the purchase price into an escrow account held by a bank or another regulated body. This ensures that if you have to pull out of the deal you will see the money again. Under Federal law you have a right when buying a residential property to have the deposit put in an escrow account, unless you agree otherwise. Most builder's contracts (if you are buying a new home) contain a clause that you *do* agree otherwise. This should be negotiated out if possible.

Standard contracts contain let out clauses for the buyer if the mortgage does not come through, or if the inspection discovers major structural problems. You may also be able to persuade the seller to allow a clause making the contract conditional on sale of your current house. A closing date will be specified: this should be realistic – it can take five to six weeks for the mortgage to come through.

Another essential clause specifies that the house conforms to all local, state and federal real estate regulations. Title insurance should also be taken out by the buyer (see *Professional Assistance*, above) When you sign the contract you give the seller a deposit (a percentage of the purchase price) which goes towards the down-payment, which in turn is handed over on completion of the purchase.

TABLE 4:	HOUSE PRICES
Median house values 2004 in selected metropolitan areas	
Northeast:	
Hartford, Connecticut	$232,800
Boston, Massachusetts	$387,800
Pittsburgh, Pennsylvania	$107,600
New York, New York	$403,600

Midwest:	
Cincinnati, Ohio	$143,000
Lansing, Michigan	$140,700
St Louis, Missouri	$129,100
Minneapolis, Minnesota	$220,600
Chicago, Illinois	$242,600
South:	
Atlanta, Georgia	$157,700
Houston, Texas	$135,500
Miami, Florida	$297,200
Nashville, Tennessee	$148,700
West:	
Denver, Colorado	$237,100
Las Vegas, Nevada	$281,400
San Francisco, California	$656,700
Phoenix, Arizona	$180,200

RENTING PROPERTY

Most apartments in the USA are rented unfurnished, although a refrigerator is normally included. Post-war apartment blocks in cities like New York and San Francisco have public basements with laundry rooms with washing and drying machines – an in-house laundrette, in short. The more modern and luxurious apartment blocks will have a swimming pool, gym and sauna. Rented furnished accommodation will have all mod cons, including air conditioning (in the older buildings the units will be window mounted). The cheapest apartments go by a variety of euphemistic names: bachelor apartments, studios, or efficiency apartments. These will be very small, a bedroom and a curtained-off cooking area (called an American kitchen in Europe, from the days when New York apartments were built without kitchens: it was assumed that every meal would be eaten out).

TABLE 5	USEFUL RENTAL TERMS
Apartment:	flat
Dormitory:	student hall of residence, often with single rooms
Duplex:	apartment on two floors
Half-bath:	room with toilet and sink but no bath
Walk-up:	studio or flat in a block without a lift
Cold-water apartment:	flat without hot water (relatively rare except in the oldest buildings)
Efficiency, bachelor:	bed-sit or studio flat
First floor:	ground floor (therefore the second floor is the same as the

	British first floor, and so on)
Roomer:	lodger
Roommate:	flatmate
Rooming house:	a house in which rooms are let
Flatware:	cutlery
Washer:	washing machine (clothes)

Local newspapers and magazines have 'Apartments for Rent' sections, and free monthly rental guides are published in most areas. These are available from chambers of commerce (see *Regional Guide* for addresses), and can also be picked up from visitor centres, supermarkets, and street racks. Most of the larger real estate agents have rental sections, and major apartment blocks and condominiums have their own rental offices. Other places to look are noticeboards in colleges, company offices, shopping malls, supermarkets, and visitor centres. One of the most fruitful sources of information will of course be friends and colleagues.

Beware of referral services and 'apartment finders', who will try to charge a commission, or demand a deposit in advance for a variety of services such as property listings, viewing fees and so on. This is illegal: you should pay nothing except to an established real estate agent, or the owner of the property.

Tenancy Agreements

Renting an apartment requires all the usual documentation and guarantees of income. You will have to complete an application form (most states have standard lease forms, available from real estate offices and stationers). Agents will not be happy finding you an apartment that is going to take up more than 25%-30% of your monthly income. The application form will include references from your employer or business, your bank, and credit and personal references. If you pay a deposit it should be put into an escrow account. Tenants in the USA do not have the same sort of security that they do in the UK, and in much of Europe. The law is generally weighted in the landlord's favour, so it is essential to read everything carefully before signing. Look out for leases with automatic renewal clauses, which will penalise you if you do not inform the landlord that you are leaving before the first term expires and the second automatically begins.

Rental periods, lease regulations, amounts of deposit, and agency (brokerage) fees vary from state to state. In Florida, two months' rent in advance is the normal rate, and the landlord will pay the agent. In Illinois, standard leases contain a transfer clause: one month's notice and a fee of $50-$100 is required to break the lease. Leases are normally for one year, with an option to renew. In some states rental periods are seasonal: most leases in Illinois, for example, expire in May or September, so it is extremely difficult to rent at any other time of year.

Some states have 'rental control' schemes, based on the Consumer Price Index, which keep rent increases within a certain limit. In Los Angeles, for example, most rented accommodation is covered by the scheme which guarantees that every 12 months rental increases of not more than 8% and not less than 3% will be allowed. This is put into effect as soon as an apartment is occupied; when it is vacated, the landlord can increase the rent as he likes. Contact local Chambers of Commerce or real estate agents for details of schemes.

Rental Costs

Again, these vary enormously from state to state and from city to city. New York City is possibly the most expensive city in the US to live in. Rents per month can range from $1,500 for a studio to $5,000 for a three-bedroom apartment. Other areas of the country will be much cheaper. Los Angeles, a city of comparable size, offers much better value. A studio, for example, will cost approximately $900 per month while you can rent a three-bedroom house for $3,000 and a four-bedroom for $4,000. Elsewhere, a two-bedroom apartment in Houston will on average cost $1,300 a month while the same apartment would cost $1,600 in Boston, $2,200 in Atlanta and Washington, and $3,000 in Miami. As any estate agent will tell you, the three most important rules of property pricing are: one, location; two, location; and three, location.

Finding rented housing in some cities can be difficult as in Europe simply because demand is high. Properties go quickly and prices can be steep. Often you'll be asked to put down a month's rent as deposit and a month's rent in advance.

In blocks of apartments there may well be a doorman who guards access to the building and provides general security. They may also provide other services, such as taking delivery of the mail, letting in repairmen, and keeping an eye on the apartment while you're away. Doorman buildings are more expensive to occupy but provide an added sense of safety in urban areas. There may well also be a building 'super' who maintains the upkeep of the building. Remember that these building employees expect generous tips, usually around the end of the year in the Christmas season. It's not unusual for tenants to give tips from $50 to $200 and upwards for the help and service they receive during the entire year.

Relocating agencies (see below) can advise on average prices within an area or you could contact a real estate agency directly. Students attending universities and colleges should approach the student advisor or housing office for assistance in finding rented accommodation.

Useful Address

The World of Florida, St Ethelbert House, Ryelands Street, Hereford HR4 OLA; ☎01432-845645; fax 01432-845640; e-mail homes@worldofflorida.co.uk; www.worldofflorida.co.uk. Specialise in villas to rent and buy in Florida.

Relocators

Relocation companies specialise in moving people to live and work in foreign countries. Many work principally with the human resource departments of large companies but can accommodate individuals if required.

Weichert Relocation Resources Inc points out that a particular issue for individuals moving to the United States from the UK is that they can sometimes underestimate the degree of adjustment needed. 'There's an assumption that because there is a shared language and a degree of cultural exchange that the move will be simpler than for example moving to India. But bear in mind that the United States is a continent encompassing wide regional differences. Moving to New York will be quite a different experience from living in Houston'.

Sometimes an assignment may actually fail if an employee is not properly prepared for the move. However, the process of adjustment may vary depending on an individual's experience of international life and to what extent a company is proactive about helping employees settle into a new life in the US. On a practical level, a relocation company will organise all the visa arrangements and smooth out any other legal and financial issues like pension planning and taxation. Similarly, they will arrange the actual shipping of households.

Relocation packages may provide a house search for temporary or more permanent housing, school searches for children, searches for specialist services such as asthma clinics, and cross-cultural training covering the culture of the country, its politics, religion, history and attitudes. Orientation days are sometimes provided which teach an individual or family how to use the local supermarket, post office, or hire a television. There's even support for what is indelicately referred to as the 'trailing spouse.' Often spouses are not allowed to work and are in most need of support.

After an initial interview, during which they will find out as much as possible about you and your family, the relocator will bring in an American firm (most of the large European relocators have sister companies or associates in the USA) which will take over the business of finding a property, schools and other essentials. Your belongings will be transported door to door, all customs formalities will be taken care of: in short, your hand will be held until you feel you can cope on your own.

Relocation is not cheap. Often though if an employee is being moved by their present employer most, if not all, of the costs will be carried. If you have been offered a job through an application process, relocation costs are also likely to be part of the employment package. Alternatively, it's something that can be negotiated before acceptance of the job offer. Because the US is so large and relocation a common fact of career progression, American employers expect to carry many of the costs. As a rough guide, a home search will cost £2,000 and a school search an extra £300.

To move the possessions of an average British household would cost approximately £5,000 but insurance will need to be added and that figure depends entirely on the value of the goods being moved. An insurance assessor will need to make a valuation of the contents being moved before giving a quote.

For individuals and small companies wanting to relocate, it is an expensive business, and the best option would be to contact a US real estate agent who deals with relocations. Most agents have access to Multiple Listing Services, local and nationwide databases of properties for sale, and they are equipped to offer a more complete service than most European agents. You can also look up relocators in the Yellow Pages, but there are a number of things to look out for.

Some of the smaller operators will not abide by any code of practice and will be taking a commission from real estate agents: they will take you round properties but will not be bargaining entirely on your behalf. In the USA, the Employee Relocation Council has 1,200 members from corporations that relocate their employees, as well as 10,000 members from the relocation, real estate and associated professions. In the UK, the Association of Relocation Agents, although dealing mainly with the UK, has US contacts and can give advice on relocating to the USA.

The company Four Corners Emigration listed below differs slightly from other relocation firms in that it concentrates on assisting with immigration and visas, although its clients do receive full support with their relocation and resettlement.

Useful Relocation Contacts and Resources

Employee Relocation Council, 1717 Pennsylvania Avenue NW, Suite 800, Washington, DC 20006; ☎202-857 0857; fax 202-659 8631; www.erc.org.

Association of Relocation Agents, PO Box 189, Diss IP22 1PE; ☎08700-737475; fax 08700-718719; e-mail info@relocationagents.com; www.relocationagents. com. This UK based trade association lists many companies specialising in international relocation on its website.

Anglo-Domus, 64 Islip Road, Oxford OX2 7SW; ☎01865-514458; fax 01865-516390; e-mail info@anglo-domus.com; www.anglo-domus.com.

Avalon Overseas Movers, Drury Way, London NW10 0JN; ☎020-8451 6336; fax 020-8451 6419; www.avalon-overseas.com.

Community Connections, PO Box 1236, Menlo Park, CA 94026; ☎650-327 0577; fax 650-327 6804; e-mail cci@communityconn.com; www. communityconn.com.

www.directmoving.com. An international relocation web portal. Contents include information about jobs, health and insurance, immigration and expatriate contacts.

Four Corners Emigration, Strathblane House, Ashfield Road, Cheadle, Cheshire SK8 1BB; ☎0161-608 1608; fax 0161-608 1616; e-mail info@fourcorners.

net; www.4-corners.net.

North American International, Sirva House, 345 Southbury Road, Enfield, Middlesex EN1 1UP; ☎020-8219 8100; fax 020-8219 8183; www. nalworldwide.com.

Moves International Relocations, Moves House, 141 Acton Lane, London NW10 7PB; ☎0870-010 4410; fax 020-8267 6003; e-mail enquiries@moves.co.uk; www.moves.co.uk

Pricoa Relocations UK, Plaza, 353 Kings Road, London SW10 0SZ; ☎020-7838 5102; fax 020-7352 1440; www.pricoarelocation.com.

Weichert Relocation Resources Inc, 1st Floor, 56 Buckingham Gate, London SW1E 6AE; ☎020-7802 2500; fax 020-7802 2525; e-mail info@wrri.com; www.wrri.com.

Runzheimer International, Runzheimer Park, Rochester, WI 53167; ☎262-971 2200; fax 262-971 2254; www.runzheimer.com. International relocation specialists.

www.homestore.com. This site is principally concerned with real estate but has sections dedicated to moving, home improvement, and decorating.

www.monstermoving.com. American information listings for anyone needing assistance with moving and relocation.

Income from Holiday Homes

Florida and to a lesser extent Arizona and Colorado, are the most popular states for Europeans to buy holiday homes, and real estate agents there are experienced in buying, selling and managing homes for expatriates and summer visitors.

Holiday homes can be less of an expense if you rent them out for the months that you are not there. Income derived from this should normally be taxed at the standard 30% rate of federal income tax, as income not effectively connected with a US business. However, because this would deter foreigners from investing in US real estate, you can choose to have the income taxed as effectively connected with a US business. It is then taxed on a net basis (after deducting all expenses), and at a graduated rate.

Renting out your property can be a headache. Many management companies guarantee a certain rental income, but once you've paid the purchase price and the various commissions, such a guarantee will almost certainly fail to live up to its promise. Remember that management of your home will make a decent profit for builders and management companies, so don't feel you are doing them a favour by letting them handle it. If you are dependent on rental income to support the property, make sure that there are no zoning (local property regulation) or other restrictions on short-term rentals, and that you will be able to recoup enough to cover the mortgage at a 75% occupancy rate – probably the most you can hope for. You must also take into account maintenance costs. Depending on the state, the income will also be subject to state taxation (state income tax or sales tax), and licence fees of some sort. Most importantly, your income will also be taxable in your country of residence, subject to any available double taxation relief.

Contact a real estate agent, a solicitor, or an accountant for advice. Alternatively, you can download the relevant forms (non-resident alien) from the Internal Revenue Service at www.irs.gov or call 1- 800-829 1040 within the US.

INSURANCE AND WILLS

Insurance

Americans like to insure themselves against all eventualities, which is arguably sensible in such a highly litigious society. As a consequence the insurance industry is huge. More life insurance is written in the state of New York than in the whole of the UK: $79 billion annually. $1,800 per head is spent on insurance every year. One of the reasons for this is that there is far less mandatory insurance, in the form of social security deductions and payments, than in most European countries. Health insurance is essential. Most people in employment will be covered by a company policy but the self-employed must take out their own policies.

A homeowner's insurance policy usually consists of casualty insurance and liability insurance. The first covers the fabric of the house and your possessions, and the second insures against an injury sustained by a third party while on your property. It is not unknown for friends to sue friends, and for families to meet in court over an ankle sprained on the porch steps. It is recommended that your liability insurance covers you for at least $300,000: check the policy for this, as the basic sum is usually $100,000.

Policies come in basic and more comprehensive packages. The basic (HO – 1) policy insures the home and possessions against 'common perils' such as fire, lightning and other natural disasters. Broad policies and all-risk policies cover many more eventualities, and it is wise to pay the extra on the premium to be covered for damage from smoke, sprinkler systems, or leaking air conditioners. Earthquake insurance is (obviously) expensive in high-risk areas like California, but only a small percentage take it out.

It is also a good idea to take out guaranteed replacement cost coverage on the house. This can be as little as $10 a year, and insures against an agent's underestimate of the value of the house. There are often policy limits ($1,000 to $2,500) on certain items such as silver and gold, money, firearms and furs, and special responsibilities for safeguarding them.

Condominium and co-operative buyers need to take out different types of insurance. A master policy, held by the owners, will cover the basic building, but will not cover such things as refrigerators and kitchen units, and any decorating or improvements. You must also be insured in case the master policy is inadequate after a loss, in which case individual owners will have to make up the difference.

In the UK, advice is available from the Association of British Insurers (51 Gresham Street, London EC2V 7HQ; ☎020-7600 3333; fax 020-7696 8999; e-mail info@abi.org.uk; www.abi.org.uk); and in the USA from the National Consumer Insurance Helpline (☎1-800-942-4242) or from the Insurance Information Institute (110 William Street, New York, NY 10038; ☎212-346 5500; www.iii.org).

Wills

All adults should make a will no matter how large or small their assets. In the USA, the process is more or less the same as in most of Europe. If you are a non-resident you can specify that your estate be subject to non-US inheritance laws. If this is not specified in the will, US law automatically applies. It is possible to make tax-free bequests to charities. If you have assets of more than $625,000 (an exemption that will gradually increase to $1 million in 2006) you will be liable to estate tax and you should consult an attorney about your will. Otherwise, most states have standard will forms that provide for you to leave your possessions and money to your spouse and children, and to a charity if you wish. A will must still be drawn up and witnessed using the proper legal process.

You may also want to look into the possibility of creating a trust, which is a way of bequeathing your money before death. This has valuable taxation implications: a trust can be used to shift income to a beneficiary (usually a close relative or child) who is in a lower taxation bracket. An attorney or accountant should be consulted about the various options open to foreigners; see also *Understanding Living Trusts* by Vickie and Jim Schumacher, published in the USA; also check the wills and probate section of FindLaw at www.findlaw.com for lawyers countrywide specialising in wills.

UTILITIES

Utility companies in the USA are usually state owned, and are regulated by public utility or public service commissions. Utilities are sometimes run by the same organisation, so it is not unusual to be billed for electricity, gas and water on the same bill. Most states have utility consumer advocates, which deal with problems and complaints. Contact the National Association of State Utility Consumer Advocates (8380 Colesville Road, Suite 101, Silver Spring, MD 20910; ☎301-589 6313; fax 301-589 6380; e-mail nasuca@nasuca.org; www. nasuca.org) for details of the service in individual states. As in most European countries, when you move into a property, you must apply to have the utilities changed over to your name, or switched back on. Costs for this vary, and you may have to pay a deposit of between $50 and $300, which is returnable.

Electricity

The electricity supply is generally 110-120 volts, AC 60 cycles, single phase. Flat two-point fittings are normal for most appliances. European appliances rated at 240 volts AC can be used with an adaptor, although this is not always the case: check that your favourite curling tongs are usable on the US current before you go. Electrical goods are considerably cheaper in the USA than in Europe, and most people decide to buy new radios, razors and so on when they arrive. Check your electrical devices to see if they have a 110\240 volt switch, in which case they will work in the USA. All light bulbs have screw-type fittings.

Gas

Gas is available in all cities and in most apartments. In rural areas it may not be piped, but will be delivered in bottles. In some rented apartments the gas supply may be included in the rent. There is no need to shop around for the cheapest supplier of bottled gas: in most areas there will be only be one company.

Water

The water supply is entirely safe to drink. In the west and south there are often restrictions on the use of water, particularly after snow-free or dry winters. In many areas the cost of the water is included in the local property taxes, in other areas each apartment or building has its own water meter, and you are billed by the municipality. Water rates are generally low.

Refuse & Snow Clearing

Most districts have regular refuse collection, and in areas where there is regular and heavy snowfall it is possible to arrange for snow to be cleared from your entrance and driveway.

Telephones

The American telephone system is entirely deregulated into regional companies and consumers have a number of different choices of line and apparatus. You can buy your own phone from a retailer – regional telephone companies are not allowed to manufacture or sell telephone equipment. Connection costs are between $50 and $100 depending on the area; it normally takes only a few days to be connected. All telephones should be approved by the Federal Communications Commission. You will be billed monthly; different companies have varying charges for local, long distance and on and off peak calls: the average charge for a local call is 10 cents, but in some states all local calls are free. In some areas you are allowed a local free call allocation (between 20 and 75 a month), after which you will be charged a basic rate. Monthly line charges are between $10 and $15. More than 500 companies now compete in the long-distance call market, so it is a good idea to contact a number of companies, and ask colleagues and friends, before deciding which one to choose. The major long-distance carriers are AT&T, MCI, and Sprint.

REMOVALS

Removals firms should be affiliated either to the Association of International Removers, or to the British Association of Removers (addresses below). Removal companies are not regulated by law in any case, and this is the best guarantee of protection. Affiliated companies are inspected for their business practices and for their financial security, and they are also covered by shipping guarantees and bonds in case they go out of business while your goods are in mid-Atlantic.

> **James Dasey, International Manager at Doree Bonner International, gives the following advice**
> *For any international removal, the costs involved are based specifically upon the volume of goods an individual is looking to ship. Generally speaking, the larger volume of goods shipped, proportionately, the more cost effective the shipment becomes. It is not advisable to ship electrical items into the USA as problems will be encountered because of the voltage differences between the UK and the US. Problems will also be encountered with the shipment of vehicles and this is not advisable. However, other than this, if an item has a useful and usable life span upon arrival in America, it is generally worth sending.*

Most companies will offer a certain number of weeks' free storage and will undertake to move absolutely anything door to door, including motorbikes, cars and pets. Costs vary widely depending on the destination: shipping to a port in the USA is generally reasonable, but as soon as the goods have to be transported any distance inland, the price escalates. It is therefore a good deal cheaper to ship to Los Angeles or New York than to Las Vegas or Texas.

Moving the average family home of three to four bedrooms from the UK to the US will cost on average £5,000. Air freight is usually not considered an option because of the expense: household goods are priced by bulk rather than by weight. Shipping then is the common option. An average family home will fit into a 20-foot (6 m) container, but it is possible to use a 40-foot (12 m) alternative.

Employers are not required to report to the Internal Revenue Service moving

expenses paid directly to a third party on behalf of an employee. Therefore for US tax purposes your employer should pay your moving expenses directly to the removal firm rather than reimburse you for the cost of moving.

Useful Addresses

The British Association of Removers, 3 Churchill Court, 58 Station Road, North Harrow, Middlesex HA2 7SA; ☎020-8861 3331; fax 020-8861 3332; e-mail info@bar.co.uk; www.removers.org.uk.

Avalon Overseas Movers, Drury Lane, London NW10 0JN; ☎020-8451 6336; fax 020-8451 6419; www.avalon-overseas.com.

Bishop's Move Group, 102/104 Stewarts Road, London SW8 4UF; ☎020-7489 0300; fax 020-7627 1173; e-mail london@bishopsmove.com; www.bishopsmove.com. Offices across the UK.

Davies Turner Worldwide Movers, 49 Wates Way, Mitcham CR4 4HR; ☎020-7622 4393; fax 020-7720 3897; e-mail T.Hutchison@daviesturner.co.uk; www.daviesturner.co.uk/movers

Doree Bonner International, Head Quarters, International House, 18 Kennet Road, Dartford, Kent DA1 4QN; ☎0800-289541; e-mail moving@dbonner.co.uk; www.doreebonner.co.uk. Also branches in London, Dartford, Dunstable, Swindon, Bath, High Wycombe, Ashford, Canterbury, Nottingham, Glasgow and Edinburgh.

International Federation of International Removers, 69 Rue Picard B5, 1080 Brussels, Belgium; ☎32-2-426 5160; fax 32-2-426 5523; e-mail fidi@fidi.com; www.fidi.com.

John Mason International, 5 Mill Lane Trading Estate, Croydon, Surrey CR0 4AA; ☎020-8667 1133; fax 020-8666 0567; www.johnmason.com. Offices also in Liverpool and Manchester.

Oceanair, Locksfield Avenue, Enfield, Middlesex EN3 7PX; ☎020-8805 1221; fax 020-8805 1114; e-mail sales@oceanair-int.co.uk; www.oceanairinternational.com. International removals.

PSS International Removals, Head Office 1-3 Pegasus Road, Croydon, Surrey CR9 4PS; ☎020-8686 7733; fax 020-8686 7799; e-mail sales@p-s-s.co.uk; www.pss.uk.com. UK-wide; main depots London, Colchester and York.

Customs

US customs regulations are liberal for those moving house. Almost all household and personal effects that are more than one year old can be taken in, except for certain spices, meat products, seeds and plants, fruits, ivory, crocodile and alligator skin products, switchblades (flick-knives) and the obvious things such as drugs and firearms. If you are on prescriptive drugs you will need a doctor's letter. A duty will be levied on goods that have not been used, or were bought less than one year before. If you have anything that looks very new, take proof that it is more than a year old. Unaccompanied baggage can be sent, but it should arrive within five days of the passenger to avoid storage charges, and it must be declared when you arrive to be eligible for customs exemptions.

Returning US residents are allowed to import duty free up to $400 worth of goods bought abroad, as well as 200 cigarettes, one litre of spirits, and reasonable quantities of perfume. Non-residents are allowed to import duty free gifts of up to $100 in value, plus alcohol and cigarettes as above. If you need more information on import procedures, contact the Customs Attaché at the US Embassy (☎020-7499 9000, ext 2771/2772) or write for an information packet: US Customs Service, London Attaché Office, American Embassy, 24 Grosvenor Square, London W1A 1AE; www.usembassy.org.uk.

Import Procedures

Imported goods must be entered on US Customs form 3299, and submitted to the customs office at the port of entry. All goods must be listed on the form, with particular detail given to goods that are less than a year old, as duty will be charged on these at a rate of four per cent to 10% of their value. On arrival in the USA you must provide an address to the customs office, which will then contact you when your shipment arrives. All shipping firms are fully aware of import procedures, and you will find that everything is taken care of, unless you are shipping independently. In the USA, contact the local customs office for your port of entry, listed in the telephone directory under US Customs.

IMPORTING VS BUYING A CAR

There is no import duty for non-residents importing foreign-made cars. For residents, the duty is 2.5% of the price for cars, and 1.5% to 2.9% (depending on cylinder capacity) for motorcycles. (If you are bringing in a car for less than a year you will be exempt from US emission control and safety standards but you will need to take the registration document.) But there is little point in importing your car to the United States, as the cost of buying a new one and selling it when you leave would certainly work out cheaper.

Buying a new car can be a good deal cheaper in the States than in Europe. Many dealers will offer to take care of insurance, and finance in the form of a loan, but it would be advisable to arrange this for yourself – the dealer will be going to the same sort of bank or insurance company as you, and will be taking a commission himself.

Buying a used car comes with many attendant problems. Try to find a dealership outside the city limits to avoid city sales taxes. If you are buying privately, try to buy in a wealthy area: the car may cost more, but it will be in better condition. There is a publication called the *Blue Book* available at most bookstores, giving information on standard values for new and used cars.

IMPORTING PETS

In order to bring in a dog or cat to the US you will need to present a health certificate from a vet. As the UK is free of rabies there will be no quarantine requirement when you arrive in the US. However all other animals and birds are subject to strict customs regulations and quarantine. The exceptions are the states of Hawaii and Alaska which have additional regulations: to take a dog, cat, or bird into these states you have to have an Interstate Health Certificate from a vet, issued no more than 10 days prior to shipping. Hawaii is rabies-free, and all dogs and cats (except those coming from continental USA or Australia, New Zealand or Britain) must be quarantined for 120 days.

The US Embassy will supply current regulations concerning import of pets, or write to the *US Public Health Service* (Centers for Disease Control and Prevention, Public Inquiries/MASO, Mailstop F07, 1600 Clifton Road, Atlanta, GA 30333; ☎404-639 3534 or 1-800-311 3435 within the US; www. cdc.gov). The *American Society for the Prevention of Cruelty to Animals* (424 East 92nd Street, New York, NY 10128; ☎212-876 7700; www.aspca.org) also has useful information about the keeping of pets in the USA.

The UK has now introduced the Passports for Pets scheme (to avoid the six month quarantine process for bringing a pet back into the country) but the United States does not yet qualify to participate because it is not classified as rabies-free. Information on exporting pets from the UK to outside the EU is available from local Animal Health Divisional Offices. A list of these offices can be found at www.defra.gov.uk/corporate/contacts/ahdo.htm. The only exception is the state of Hawaii because it is free of rabies.

DAILY LIFE

CHAPTER SUMMARY

○ Although English is the main language spoken in the US nearly a quarter of the population does not speak it at home.

○ **Education.** Children are graded at school by continual assessment rather than formal exams.

○ University and college courses tend to be more general than in the UK.

○ **Media.** Americans tend to get their national and international news from the broadcast media: newspapers are more local in focus.

○ The US love of tv is shown by the highest proportion of tv ownership in the world, with more than one set for every two people.

○ **Transport.** The US has 145 million cars, 42,000 miles of freeways and 4 million miles of secondary roads.

○ You can only drive in the US for up to a year on a foreign licence: after that you need a state licence that may involve taking a test.

○ The cost of air travel is governed more by the popularity of the route than the distance travelled.

○ **Health.** The US has some of the most expensive health care in the world and private health insurance is essential.

○ **The way of life.** The prevalence of firearms makes America a potentially dangerous place, but exercising a little common sense can minimise the risk.

○ America has a fluid society, and Americans tend to be more open and gregarious than Europeans.

○ The international dominance of Hollywood in film is well known, but standards in most other arts also tend to be world-class.

THE LANGUAGES

English is the principal language of the United States by virtue of the fact that it is the first language of the majority of the population, but it has no constitutional status as the official language. Of the 286 million inhabitants of the country about 237 million speak English at home. For the rest of the population, English is a second language, and many people hardly speak it at all. There are 17 million people who speak Spanish as a first language. Surprisingly, French is spoken by 1.7 million people at home, the largest foreign language after Spanish. French has official standing in Louisiana (which was a French possession until 1803), and has evolved into two main branches: Cajun Acadian, spoken by the descendants of Canadian refugees, and Creole French, spoken by the descendants of slaves from Southern Louisiana. Significant minorities speak Italian, German, Chinese, Korean, Greek, and Japanese. Spanish is an official language in New Mexico. California, Texas and New York State have the greatest concentration of Hispanic immigrants.

There are very few languages that are not spoken somewhere in the United States, and there are a few that are not spoken anywhere else in the world. In eastern Pennsylvania, around 100,000 people speak Pennsylvania Dutch, a mixture of German and Dutch dialects; there are no records showing how many of them speak it as a first language. On the coast of Georgia and South Carolina some people still speak a language called Gullah, a dialect of the original African language brought to the US by slaves. There are also speakers of Yiddish, Hungarian, Russian, Polish, Serbo-Croat, Ukrainian, Czech, Arabic, Eskimo, Aleut, and Tagalog, the official language of the Philippines. There are 300,000 Gypsies who use Romany as their first language.

Native Languages

Of the 1.5 million Native Americans (American Indians) 300,000 speak an Amerindian language at home. The biggest group is Navajo, with 100,000 speakers living in Arizona, Utah and New Mexico; there are around 10,000 Apache, Cherokee, Choctaw, Dakota and Ojibwa speakers. The many other Indian languages are spoken by a diminishing number: 5,000 speak Blackfoot, Creek, Keres or Passamaquoddy; around the same number speak Arapaho, Cheyenne, Chickasaw, Comanche and Crow; 2,000 Flathead; less than a thousand Mohave, Seminole and Pawnee. It is likely that many of these ancient languages will be extinct within the next two generations, as English continues its relentless advance.

SCHOOLS AND EDUCATION

The Structure of the Education System

There is no Federal Government control over the education system in the United States. Each state's department of education is controlled by an elected board and is divided into local areas. The public (state) schools system is funded by state and local governments, and receives only marginal funds from the federal government. The state board is responsible for setting educational policy and for deciding compulsory attendance ages, which in most states are between six and 16. Working within policies established at state level, the school districts build schools, employ teachers, buy equipment, arrange dates of terms and holidays and generally oversee the daily operation of the schools.

Elementary and secondary education normally takes a child through school from the age of six to 18, moving up the system from Grade 1 to Grade 12. Most children, in fact, start their schooling at the age of five at kindergarten, where they learn basic numeracy and literacy. It is considered important for a child to attend kindergarten: entering Grade 1 without having done so can put a child at a disadvantage. Private nursery schools for four-year-olds have become very popular.

Although it is legal to leave school at 16, in practice it is very uncommon. In most states those who have left school without completing Grade 12 would find it difficult to get a decently-paid job.

Grades one to six are spent in elementary school, seven to nine in junior high school, and the final grades 10 to 12 are spent in senior high school. There are variations from state to state, but the system is more or less the same throughout the country.

Education in the state system is co-educational and comprehensive. Students are obliged to take a certain number of courses depending on their age and grade – courses are usually mathematics, English, health, physical education, general science and social science. Students specialise and choose extra subjects according to their individual interests and career choices.

Students do not sit formal exams like GCSEs or A levels, but are continually assessed throughout their 12 years of education. When they start in a school a folder is opened for them and they are given grades from A to F in each subject that they take, depending on performance in tests that are set each term, on homework and participation in class discussions and so on.

There is an exam similar to the A level which is increasingly being recognised by UK universities. This is the Advanced Placement test, which is taken in the final grade. A good mark generally means that the student will be able to skip some of the general education requirements that are compulsory for the first year at university.

On graduation from high school students are given a 'high school diploma'.

Those that wish to go to university are assessed on a summary of their grades and also on the results of national college aptitude tests which are taken in the last two years of high school. These tests are designed to measure ability in verbal and mathematical skills and are not based on any specific course work.

The most well-known of these are the Scholastic Aptitude Test (the SAT) and the Achievement Tests administered by the Educational Testing Service (Rosedale Road, Princeton, NJ 08541; ☎609-921 9000; fax 609-734 5410). From www.ets.org it's possible to consult a database of tests or order them for student practice.

Foreign Students

The procedure for foreign nationals to gain admission to the American public (that is, state) school system is fairly straightforward. If parents are studying, working or on diplomatic service in the USA then their children will be able to attend school on the basis of the parents' visas, without paying tuition fees.

A zoning system exists for public schools and children can only attend a school if it is in the area in which they live. Many parents, if they have the means, will make sure that they move to an area in which they like the schools. Children will be assigned to a school which will usually be the one nearest the home. Parents should enquire at the central office of the local school district for details of what documentation – such as records of immunisation and academic records – will be necessary.

The student's academic performance record is important and should be as detailed as possible as this will be used to place him or her in a suitable class.

If the student is planning to live with anyone other than his or her parents, an F-1 student visa will be necessary. It is best to ask about visas in the US Consulate in your home country. Students whose ambition is to live and work in the USA can get a foretaste of life in the States through the EIL programme, which offers homestays abroad with or without language courses, for individuals, couples and families (though not in the same home). There is also the US High School plus Homestay programme, which lasts for five months. Contact Experiment in International Living (address in *Contacts*) for details.

Parents should contact the school in question to see if it is eligible to meet visa requirements and admit foreign students. The school must be able to issue the form I-20 which must be used to apply for an F-1 visa.

Students attending a school on an F-1 visa can be charged for their tuition. This is up to the individual school and there is no central regulation (or any information available), so it is simply a matter of getting in touch with the school or education district in question and finding out what their policy is.

Foreign Students and the Private School System

American private schools are different to those in the UK, in that they have been established to fulfil a multitude of particular educational needs. There is no 'typical' private school: some will cater for a religious minority, others will be expressly for the purpose of pushing their pupils on to university, others will be for students with learning difficulties.

Private school fees range from $20,000 to $26,000 per year for boarders and between $10,000 and $15,000 for day pupils. The decision on whether or not to send your child to private school is quite often based on the area you live in rather than personal (or political) choice. There are elite private schools – particularly in Connecticut and Massachusetts – but private education is not generally a question of elitism: some parents will meet the fees of a private day school because they consider that the public schools in their area are not safe. When considering a private school it is essential to examine the particular goals of the school to decide if they are what you need.

The application process for day and boarding private schools is much the same as for the public schools. You must first establish that the school is eligible to issue the form I-20, and then apply to the school itself for details of academic requirements.

Many private secondary schools require the SSAT, the Secondary Schools Admissions Test. This is administered by the Educational Testing Service. It is held internationally in December and April: for more information and for application forms contact the Educational Advisory Service at the Fulbright Commission (see *Contacts* below). It is advisable to begin the application process well in advance of the enrolment date in order to meet the school's application deadlines.

The International Baccalaureate

If you are at secondary school in the States but will eventually return to Europe in order to go to university, it would be worth considering the International Baccalaureate. This exam is designed to meet university entrance requirements of most countries, and covers a broad range of subjects. It is taken in the final two years of secondary school.

For more information contact the International Baccalaureate Organization (Route des Morillons 15, Grand-Saconnex, Geneva CH-1218; ☎41-22-791 7740; fax 41-22-791 0277; e-mail ibhq@ibo.org; www.ibo.org).

International Schools

The European Council of International Schools (ECIS) is the oldest and largest of the associations that assess and grade international schools. The ECIS is responsible for school accreditation, teacher and executive recruitment, professional development, fellowships in international education, and entry into Higher Education. Most ECIS colleges in the United States prepare students for college or university on the basic US preparatory school programme, also teaching the standard UK GCSE, German Arbitur, French Baccalaureate, Swiss Maturité, and the Spanish Bachillerato. More and more also do the International Baccalaureate Organisation.

International Schools are usually private, though ECIS members also include state schools. Instruction is mainly in English, and the majority of students will be the children of US or British citizens.

The following schools are ECIS associate members. For further information see the ECIS Directory of International Schools, or contact them direct (address below).

European Council of International Schools (ECIS), 21B Lavant Street, Petersfield, Hampshire GU32 3EL; ☎01730-268244; fax 01730-267914; e-mail ecis@ecis.org; www.ecis.org: and at 105 Tuxford Terrace, Basking Ridge, NJ 07920; ☎908-903 0552.

Atlanta International School, 2890 North Fulton Drive, Atlanta, GA 30305; ☎404-841 3840; fax 404-841 3873; e-mail info@aischool.org; www.aischool. org. French, German and Spanish taught as second languages; 54 nationalities attend; co-ed.

Ecole Bilingue de Berkeley, 1009 Heinz Avenue, Berkeley, CA 94710; ☎510-549 3867; fax 510-549 2067; www.ebfas.org. French taught as a second language; 44 nationalities; co-ed.

The Masters School, 49 Clinton Avenue, Dobbs Ferry, NY 10522; ☎914-479 6400; fax 914-693 1230; e-mail info@themastersschool.com; www. themastersschool.com. Fourteen nationalities; co-ed.

The Awty International School of Houston, 7455 Awty School Lane, Houston, TX 77055; ☎713-686 4850; fax 713-686 4956; www.awty.org. Arabic, English, French, German, Italian, Spanish taught as second language; 35 nationalities (40% US, 30% French); co-ed.

Lycée Français de New York, 505 East 75th Street, New York, NY 10021; ☎212-369 1400; www.lfny.org.

Lycée Français de Los Angeles, 3261 Overland Avenue, Los Angeles, CA 90034 ; ☎310-836 3464.

United Nations International School, 25-50 Franklin D Roosevelt Drive, New York, NY 10010; ☎212-684 7400; fax 212-684 1382; www.unis.org. Strong liberal arts tradition; 1450 students from 115 countries.

French-American International School, 150 Oak Street, San Francisco, CA 94102; ☎415-558 2000; fax 415-558 2024; www.fais-his.org. 52 nationalities, mainly French; co-ed.

Washington International School, 3100 Macomb Street NW, Washington, DC 20008; ☎202-243 1800; fax 202-243 1802; e-mail advancements@wis.edu; www.wis.edu. French, Spanish and Dutch taught as a second language; other languages taken if necessary; co-ed; 80 nationalities.

HIGHER EDUCATION

There are more than 3,000 universities and higher education colleges in the United States, many of them internationally renowned. The best-known are the Ivy League schools which include the most famous names in American higher education, Brown, Columbia, Cornell, Dartmouth, Harvard, Pennsylvania, Princeton, and Yale. The term *Ivy League* was first used by a sports writer to describe a sports league restricted to the eight oldest universities in the country plus the army and navy who formed their own sports league and simply alludes to the college buildings covered in ivy. These prestigious 'schools' have their own entrance requirements, but others like the University of California at Los Angeles (UCLA), the Massachusetts Institute of Technology (MIT) have excellent international reputations. For details of 2,790 institutions in the USA that actively seek applicants from other countries see the *College and University Almanac* ($12.95) which is published by Peterson's in the US (www.petersons. com).

Each state administers its own university system, and each has an official state university. There are also private universities. Degrees are either four-year (the standard BA, BSc), or two-year (an Associate degree, after which it is possible to move on to a four-year degree – see below).

American students tend to go to college near their hometown. Although this is of course not compulsory, the size of the United States and the difference in cultures across the country means that it is unusual to find students at university far from their home state.

An American degree is much more general than a UK degree. In the USA, a degree consists of a four-year programme of four courses taken simultaneously: a major, concentrated field of study, general education courses in a wide range of subjects, supporting courses for the subject majored in, and 'electives', chosen areas of particular interest to the student.

As in the secondary education system, assessment is continuous, and each course (or 'class') per term is awarded a number of credits that go to make up the final degree.

Law and medicine cannot be studied at undergraduate level in the United States: these are taken at graduate school.

Foreigners at American Universities

American colleges expect you to have qualifications that would admit you to higher education in your own country. Students from the UK should have at least two A levels and five GCSE's in academic subjects. It is usually also necessary to sit the Scholastic Aptitude Test (SAT), which is held in Britain every year in October, November, December, January, April, May and June. American universities require SAT 1 and possibly up to 3 SAT II's. The SAT is administered by the College Board (www.collegeboard.com) and students can go to this site, register for the test, choose the date they want to sit it and pay online. The official SAT test prep book and more information is available from the Fulbright Commission's Educational Advisory Service (address below) which offers advice and scholarships to UK students. For more detailed information you can read *Applying to Colleges and Universities in the United States* (www.petersons.com) or the Fulbright Commission's *Undergraduate Study in the United States* price £4. In 2003, about 8,000 Brits were studying in US universities.

Financial Costs and Aid

State universities do not give financial aid to students; private colleges sometimes give partial scholarships. A list of colleges giving substantial financial aid is contained in *Scholarships for Study in the USA and Canada* published in the US by Petersons (www.petersons.com). The Fulbright Commission's Education Advisory Service can supply *Study Abroad*, published by UNESCO.

Tuition fees vary widely in the USA: generally, fees in state universities range from $7,000 to $15,000, and in private universities from $13,000 to $29,000. Remember you will need to provide for living expenses and course materials too. As a foreigner you will not be able to get financial aid from the state, but the universities themselves offer scholarships. Another useful starting point is www.studyusa.com aimed at foreign students which publishes a section called financing your education.

Living costs also vary from state to state. They are highest in the big cities in the Northeast and in California. You should expect to meet living expenses of between $7,500 and $12,000 for an academic year, unless you live at home.

Which College

It is advisable to start thinking about which colleges you would like to apply to at least 18 months before you want to enrol. It is also essential to meet the various deadlines for fees, financial aid and other parts of the application process. There is no clearing system in the USA and a missed deadline could mean having to wait another year to enrol.

When choosing a college, some of the things that you need to take into account are the location and size of the university – do you want to be in the centre of New York or in Mississippi, on a state university campus with thousands of new intakes each year or in a small private liberal arts college? You also need to be sure that you can meet the costs, and that the university offers exactly the subjects that you want to study.

The SAT tests should be taken before applying: find out the application deadlines of the colleges of your choice, then contact the Fulbright Commission for information on taking the tests.

A timetable for applications would run roughly as follows: you should send off for application forms and prospectuses 12 months before enrolment – probably in August. By the autumn of the year before enrolment you should have submitted the completed application forms. Letters of rejection or acceptance will arrive in the following January. Finances can be sorted out in the next couple of months, visas arranged, and final arrangements made to set off at the end of the summer.

It is impossible to give here all the information necessary for applying to an American college. The Fulbright Commission has an Educational Advisory Service which provides comprehensive information on all aspects of education in the United States. They have qualified advisors, and organise lectures and information sessions, and also have a comprehensive reference library with information on all aspects of the American secondary and higher education system. A useful publication is the annual *College and University Almanac* (see above).

Athletic Scholarships

Many colleges offer scholarships to students who are gifted in a particular sport. There is usually an upper age limit of 25, and postgraduate students are not eligible. Students must fulfil the normal entry requirements of the college. There is a UK placement service, College Prospects of America (address below) which will put together a resumé of your sporting achievements and send them to US colleges. The alternative is to contact colleges direct. A useful publication is *Sports Scholarships and Athletic Programs in the USA* (available from www. petersons.com) which lists thousands of scholarships worth millions of dollars, and the names of individual coaches for specific sports at more than 1,000 US colleges. Expert advice on how to apply is given.

Two-Year Colleges

Community, Technical and Junior Colleges – called two-year colleges because of the length of their courses – offer Associate Degrees which are associate of arts, science or applied science. These can be used as a basis for entering university in the third year of a four-year course, although this option is not always open to foreigners. There are about 1,500 two-year colleges: they are becoming more popular because of their reasonable fees – they are state and locally supported and tuition can be less than $4,000 per year. In order to enter, UK students should have completed their GCSE's with passes in English and maths; some colleges also require students sit the SATS. American students normally live at home and commute, and there are opportunities for foreign students to arrange home-stay with families on a term-by-term basis. Contact the Fulbright Commission for details.

TABLE 6   TUITION FEES

20 largest four-year colleges and undergraduate tuition fees for out-of-state residents (for state-run universities):

University of Austin, Texas	$10,096
Ohio State University, Columbus	$12,698
Texas A&M University	$8,929
Penn State University, PA	$14,394
Arizona State University	$10,352
University of Florida	$9,771
Michigan State University	$13,641
University of Illinois, Urbana	$4,168
University of Wisconsin, Madison	$13,920
Purdue University, Indiana	$13,114
University of Michigan	$20, 973
University of California, Los Angeles	$15,267
University of Washington, WA	$13,257
University of Minnesota, Twin Cities	$13,463
Indiana University, Bloomington	$14,469
University of Arizona	$9,804
San Diego State University, CA	$7,758
New York University, NY	$25,380
University of Maryland, College Park	$13,413
Wayne State University, Michigan	$8,578

Contacts

The Fulbright Commission, Educational Advisory Service, Fulbright House, 62 Doughty Street, London WC1N 2LS; ☎020-7404 6880; fax 020-7404 6834; e-mail education@fulbright.co.uk; www.fulbright.co.uk.

Experiment in International Living (EIL), 287 Worcester Road, Malvern, Worcestershire WR14 1AB; ☎0168-456 2577; fax 0168-456 2212; e-mail info@eiluk.org; www.experiment.org.

International Baccalaureate Organization, Route des Morillons 15, Grand-Saconnes, Geneva CH-1218; ☎41-22-791 0277; www.ibo.org.

International Baccalaureate Organization North America, 475 Riverside Drive, 16th Floor, New York, NY 10115; ☎212-696 4464; fax 212-889 9242; e-mail ibna@ibo.org.

International Baccalaureate Organization UK, Peterson House, Malthouse Avenue, Cardiff Gate, Cardiff CF23 8GL; ☎029-2054 7777; fax 029-2054 7778; e-mail ibca@ibo.org.

ECIS, 21B Lavant Street, Petersfield, Hampshire GU32 3EL; ☎01730-268244; fax 01730-267914; e-mail ecis@ecis.org; www.ecis.org.

College Prospects of America, 5 Manland Avenue, Harpenden, Hertfordshire AL5 4RE; ☎01582-712364; fax 01582-468091; www.cpoauk.com; and PO Box 269, Logan, OH 43138; ☎740-385 6624; fax 740-385 9065; e-mail homeoffice@cpoa.com; www.cpoa.com. An organisation dedicated to placing talented athletes in college and finding scholarships.

MEDIA AND COMMUNICATIONS

Newspapers

There are more than 3,000 daily, weekly and monthly newspapers published in the USA. Some of them are among the oldest newspapers in the world: the *Philadelphia Inquirer* was established in 1771, for example. All the larger cities support several newspapers, and even small towns have their own free journal. Only a handful of titles like *USA Today*, *The Wall Street Journal*, and the *New York Times* are distributed nationally. But they do not compare to European titles, which have a genuine national readership and wide demographic appeal. American's tend to rely on the news broadcasters for national and international news. The American newspaper market is much more regional in nature because of the country's vast size. Even in a city the size of New York or Los Angeles the political and cultural establishment are usually obtaining comment and analysis from a single broadsheet. Other papers with a national readership are the *Los Angeles Times*, and the *Washington Post*.

Foreign newspapers such as *The Financial Times*, which prints an American edition, are of course available in all big cities. Another widely available international edition is *The International Express* and *The Guardian Weekly*, which produce editions summarising British news, politics and sport over the previous week. They are available from newsagents and on subscription. In the USA, contact Speedimpex (35-02 48th Avenue, Long Island City, NY 11101; ☎718-392 7477; fax 718-361 0815; e-mail infony@speedimpex.com; www.speedimpex.com) for information about local distributors.

US newspaper publishing is dominated by a handful of large corporations including Dow Jones, Gannett and Co, Hearst Corporation, Knight-Ridder, Newhouse, EW Scripps and Thomson, which between them account for 60% of the circulation.

Almost all newspapers of any size now have their own websites which publish most of that day's edition online with other supplementary information like entertainment guides and classified advertising. Many large cities publish local interest magazines like *Time Out New York* or *Los Angeles Magazine*. Citysearch (www.citysearch.com) runs a network of 105 national city guides which allow users to interact with the local community whether it's buying tickets online, searching for a movie or finding a house to rent. Digitalcity (www.digitalcity.com) runs a similar network of local information. For lists of all American newspapers and publications consult www.newslink.org, which lists more than 4,000 with an online presence and the media section of www.yahoo.com.

Contact details for two major publications with national distribution are as follows:

USA Today, Gannett Co Inc, 7950 Jones Branch Drive, Mclean, VA 22108; ☎703-276 3400; www.usatoday.com.

The Wall Street Journal, Customer service telephone within the US ☎1-800-369 2834; within the UK ☎020-7842 9609; www.wsj.com.

The following is a list of newspapers published in selected states:

Arizona

Arizona Republic, 200 E Van Buren Street, Phoenix, AZ 85004; ☎602-444 8000; www.arizonarepublic.com

California

San Francisco Chronicle, Chronicle Publishing Co, 901 Mission Street, San Francisco, CA 94103; ☎415-777 1111; www.sfgate.com.

Los Angeles Times, 202 W 1st Street, Los Angeles, CA 90012; ☎213-237 5000; www.latimes.com.

Colorado

Denver Post, 1560 Broadway, Denver, CO 80202; ☎303-820 1010; www.denverpost.com.

Connecticut

Hartford Courant, 285 Broad Street, Hartford, CT 06115; ☎860-241 6200; www.ctnow.com.

District of Columbia

Washington Post, 1150 15th Street NW, Washington, DC 20071; ☎202-334 4623; www.washingtonpost.com.

Florida

Miami Herald, Knight-Ridder Newspapers, 1 Herald Plaza, Miami, FL 33132; ☎305-350 2111; www.herald.com.

Georgia

Atlanta Journal-Constitution, Atlanta Newspapers, PO Box 4689, Atlanta, GA 30302; ☎404-526 5151; www.ajc.com.

Illinois

Chicago Tribune, Tribune Co, 435 N Michigan Avenue, Chicago, IL 60611; ☎1-800-874 2863; www.chicagotribune.com.

Indiana

Indianapolis Star, PO Box 307 N, Pennsylvania Street, Indianapolis, IN 46204; ☎317-444 4000; www.indystar.com.

Louisiana

Times-Picayune, Newhouse Newspaper Group, 3800 Howard Avenue, New Orleans 70125; ☎504-299 3500.

Massachusetts

Boston Globe, Globe Newspaper Co, 135 Morrissey Boulevard, Boston, MA

02125; ☎617-929 7900; www.bostonglobe.com.

Michigan

Detroit Free Press, Knight-Ridder Newspapers, 600 W Fort Street, Detroit, MI 48226; ☎313-222 6400; www.freep.com.

Nevada

Las Vegas Review-Journal, 1111 W Bonanza Road, Las Vegas, NV 89125; ☎702-383 0211; www.reviewjournal.com.

New Jersey

Star-Ledger, 1 Star Ledger Plaza, Court and University Avenue, Newark, NJ 07102; ☎1-888-782 7533; www.nj.com/starledger.

New York

Financial Times, 1330 Avenue of the Americas, New York, NY 10019; ☎212-641 6500; www.ft.com.

New York Post, New York Post Corporation, 1211 Avenue of the Americas, New York, NY 10036; ☎212-930 8000; www.newyorkpost.com.

New York Times, 229 W 43rd Street, New York, NY 10036; ☎212-354 3900; www.nytimes.com.

Village Voice, Village Voice Inc, 36 Cooper Square, New York, NY 10003; ☎212-475 3300; www.villagevoice.com.

Wall Street Journal Eastern Edition, Dow Jones Inc, 420 Lexington Avenue, New York, NY 10170; ☎1-800-369 2834; www.wsj.com.

Irish Echo, Irish Echo Newspaper Corp, 14 East 47th Street, New York, NY 10017; ☎212-686 1266; fax 212-683 6455; www.irishecho.com.

Pennsylvania

Philadelphia Inquirer, Knight-Ridder Group, 400 North Broad Street, Philadelphia, PA 19130; ☎215-665 1234; www.philly.com.

Texas

Dallas Morning News, 400 S Record Street, Dallas, TX 75202; ☎214-977 7140; www.dallsnews.com.

Washington

Seattle Post-Intelligencer, Hearst Corporation, 101 Elliot Avenue W, Seattle, WA 98119; ☎206-448 8000; http://seattlep-i.nwsource.com.

Magazines and Periodicals

Of the 10,000 magazines published in the USA, the most popular achieve circulations that newspaper editors can only dream of. A study of the most popular magazines would show that Americans are most concerned with how to fill their free time (the *TV Guide* is one of the top 10, as well as other leisure magazines like *Friendly Exchange*), and that the massed ranks of the retired are poised to take over the country. The two best sellers are the *American Association of Retired Persons (AARP) Bulletin* (circulation 21 million) and *Modern Maturity* a close second at 20 million. Other top sellers are the *Reader's Digest*, and *TV*

Guide (16 million each), *USA Weekend, National Geographic, Better Homes and Gardens, Friendly Exchange* (travel and leisure), *Family Circle, Good Housekeeping,* and the *Ladies' Home Journal.* Among the most entertaining periodicals are the 'schlock' magazines such as the *National Enquirer* and the *National Examiner* (also available in many UK newsagents). Headlines such as 'Woman Gives Birth to 200lb Baby', and stories about children that are half-bat and half-boy, can enliven a dull day.

Television

The US has the greatest number of TV sets per head of any country in the world – 193 million, which is more than one set for every two people. The average family has 2.1 televisions, and watches around seven hours a day. There are several main TV networks of which the best known are CBS, NBC, ABC, and Fox. Unlike in Europe, these networks operate much like a franchise whereby locally owned stations act as affiliates and broadcast the network's content. In addition to these network stations are literally hundreds of cable networks broadcasting specialised content like sports or movies.

Anyone remotely conversant with TV in the UK will be no stranger to the best – and worst – of American television. Shows such as the various strands of the *CSI* and *Law & Order* crime series, the hospital drama *ER* and *24* are massive popular and critical hits in the UK. *Friends, Seinfeld, Frasier, Will and Grace, Larry Sanders,* and *Ally McBeal* have achieved cult status, and many of them are still repeated over here long after they ceased production in the US. Add to that cartoons like *The Simpsons, King of the Hill, Beavis and Butthead,* and *South Park,* and it's easy to see why British TV bosses are constantly looking across the Atlantic for top-grossing American shows to buy. Much of the success of comic writing in the US is attributed to the fact that they are made by teams of writers numbering as much as 15. These writers sit around large tables each week bouncing comic ideas off each other in contrast to the traditional image of a writer struggling alone to come up with the gags.

Naturally, with such a huge market and proliferation of channels, the best is hedged around with the worst. American TV can be very bad indeed – channels have to appeal to as wide an audience as possible and often serials and sitcoms become an indistinguishable blur. There is also a craze for distasteful real-life TV, with 'confessional' hosts such as Jerry Springer inviting misfits and inadequates to work out their domestic quarrels on screen, sometimes with extreme – and often choreographed – violence.

The Public Broadcasting Service (PBS) is a non-commercial station that does not carry advertising and shows a mixture of documentaries, discussion programmes and quality foreign drama. It is non-profit-making, and is financed by public subscriptions and federal government funds.

America's – and the world's – love affair with television was brought to a climax by the trials of O. J. Simpson, British nanny Louise Woodward, the televised Grand Jury hearing of President Clinton and, more recently, the trial of Michael Jackson. These real-life dramas were watched not only by the majority of the adult population of the USA, but by hundreds of millions more around the world.

One distinctly bizarre, but characteristically democratic feature of American television is the presence of local cable stations which allow individuals and groups to broadcast 'home-made' shows. These can range from an amateur musician performing cabaret in their own home to mediums taking calls from anxious viewers hoping to find reassurance about their love lives.

Radio

There are around 10,000 commercial radio stations in the US: 5,000 AM, 5,000 FM, and any number of tiny local stations that you will find by twiddling the dial. Depending on where you are you will get rock and roll or country and western (the late Tammy Wynette is bigger than Bruce Springsteen in the USA) on the music stations, and the usual assortment of talk shows and religious broadcasts elsewhere.

The radio is a much more satisfying medium than the TV for all sorts of reasons: it requires more concentration for a start, but more importantly it is not dominated by powerful networks, and so it is more intimate and idiosyncratic. If you are driving, there is no better way of getting the feel of the locality you are entering than to start picking up the local stations.

The BBC World Service is also available in the USA on many stations, or can be listened to on the Internet. For full details of names, frequencies and times log on to the World Service at www.bbc.co.uk/worldservice/americas or telephone the BBC in London on ☎020-7557 2211.

Books and Bookshops

Books are cheap in the USA. They are more or less all discounted, and the usual, undiscounted, price of $8.99 for a paperback is less than we are used to in Europe. Bookshops are huge and well-stocked, although for more academic or literary works it is best to look for smaller specialist bookshops. These are common in university towns. The biggest chains are Doubleday, B Dalton, and Walden books, and the discount chain Barnes and Noble. In the major cities bookstores are open late, often until midnight, and many are open on Sundays. During the 1990s, the larger urban stores began adding cafes to create a place where book lovers could 'hang-out' over a coffee, a trend that has now also crossed over to the UK. Book stores have now begun to resemble libraries and clubs where you can spend a snug afternoon in an armchair or as a place to meet friends.

Post

'Send me dead flowers every morning
Send me dead flowers by the US Mail'
(Mick Jagger and Keith Richards)

The Federal Mail has a mixed reputation. Letters can go missing, but like earthquakes and tornadoes, it is a risk that you have to take. Next day delivery can seldom be guaranteed: at standard rates letters can take up to seven days to arrive. For some reason, New York delivery times are always longer. All long-distance internal mail is sent by air without a surcharge, and overnight express for guaranteed delivery next day is available at extra cost. Air mail between northern Europe and the United States usually takes five to six days but varies according to destination and can take a week or more to reach the West Coast, Alaska and Hawaii. Surface mail takes approximately six weeks. Post Offices are open Monday to Friday from 8am to 5.30pm, and until midday on Saturday; main post offices in larger cities are open 24 hours. Stamps can be bought in drugstores, hotels, bus and train stations and many other places: they are 25% more expensive anywhere other than in a post office. Mail boxes in the street are dark blue and stamped US Mail. They can also be found in the sides of major buildings and in hotel lobbies, in which case there will be a flap, also marked US Mail. Addresses consist of the name of the person, the street number and street (or PO Box number), the city, state and zip-code. Zipcodes (post codes) refer to a specific district in the country. They are always five digits, with the lower numbers in the north-east and the higher ones in the west. For example, a Boston zipcode might be 02116, a Hawaii one might be 96815. Some zipcodes are followed by a second sequence of four digits: this is not essential but might speed up delivery. Table 7 lists the two-character abbreviations of state names that precede the zipcode.

An alternative to the federal postal service is to use one of the many express delivery services which promise overnight delivery at a price. The most extensive networks belong to FedEx and UPS which own a fleet of aircraft on the scale of a passenger airline to take parcels and mail rapidly across the country. Most towns and cities have offices belonging to these services and they also offer home collection. Setting up an account will produce discounted rates.

Telephones

Telephone numbers consist of a three-digit area code and the seven-digit main number, and are written thus: 000-000 0000. If you are calling from outside the area, use the area code (most cities are also divided into different areas, so calling from Manhattan to Brooklyn, for example, you would have to use the area code). Many large public companies and offices will also have a toll-free number which is denoted by 1-800 instead of the area code. These numbers cannot be called from outside the US. 900 numbers will get you the latest sports results or your horoscope but charge premium rates.

Payphones take nickels, dimes and quarters, and also credit cards and phone cards. You can charge any call to your credit card by ringing the operator and giving them the credit card number, or by punching in the number, if the phone will allow you to.

The operator, reached by dialing 0, will help you in a variety of ways from telling you the weather forecast to information on dental and health services. Other telephone information is available on 411, and directory enquiries for toll-free numbers is on 800-874 4000 . Directory enquiries can be reached in any area by dialling the three-digit area code plus 555 1212: if you are outside Manhattan and need a number there, dial 212-555 1212. Some numbers are expressed as letters 1-800-CALL-ATT. The letters on the dialling buttons correspond to numbers on the telephone and many companies advertise their numbers in this way as a marketing gimmick and as a way of helping you remember a number.

For information on domestic telephones, installation, see *Setting Up Home*. For emergencies see the appropriate paragraph later in this chapter.

Mobile (cellular) phones are popular and operate using the GSM 1900 network. UK mobile phones, other than tri-band phones, are not compatible in the USA. Service providers offering nationwide coverage include Cingular (www.cingular.com), T-Mobile (www.t-mobile.com), and Verizon (www.verizonwireless.com).

America is the home of the Internet with 67% of Americans online. Internet service providers include America Online (www.aol.com), AT&T Business Internet Services (www.attbusiness.net), Cable & Wireless (www.cw.com), and MSN (www.msn.com).

TABLE 7	STATE POSTAL ABBREVIATIONS
Alabama AL	Montana MT
Alaska AK	Nebraska NB
Arizona AZ	Nevada NV
Arkansas AR	New Hampshire NH
California CA	New Jersey NJ
Colorado CO	New Mexico NM
Connecticut CT	New York NY
Delaware DE	North Carolina NC
Florida FL	North Dakota ND
Georgia GA	Ohio OH
Hawaii HI	Oklahoma OK
Idaho ID	Oregon OR
Illinois IL	Pennsylvania PA
Indiana IN	Rhode Island RI
Iowa IA	South Carolina SC
Kansas KS	South Dakota SD

Kentucky KY	Tennessee TN
Louisiana LA	Texas TX
Maine ME	Utah UT
Maryland MD	Vermont VT
Massachusetts MA	Virginia VA
Michigan MI	Washington WA
Minnesota MN	West Virginia WV
Mississippi MS	Wisconsin WI
Missouri MO	Wyoming WY

CARS AND MOTORING

'*All alone in the night I had my own thoughts and held the car to the white line in the holy road. What was I doing? Where was I going?*' (Jack Kerouac, *On The Road*)

America is a land of rootless dreamers, forever shifting back and forth, north and south, east and west. Kerouac wrote his great road novel in 1957, but in films, in books and in everyday life, the vision is still the same. From *Bonnie and Clyde* in 1967, through *Easy Rider* to *Thelma and Louise*, the road movie is as much a part of the American dream as Thanksgiving Day. It's usually an illusion – frustrated by dull lives its heroes (or anti-heroes) take to the road and usually head west, in search of adventure and the unknown. The films often end in disaster – Peter Fonda and Dennis Hopper blown off their choppers by savage rednecks in *Easy Rider*, Thelma and Louise driving off a cliff – but still for most Americans the car and the open road represent the ultimate freedom. For a country founded on emigration, the idea that finding the end of the rainbow involves one more journey remains irresistible. The pioneering movement of people to settle the 'wild west' is still an important aspect of the American mythology. Remember that today Americans will frequently leave their home towns to relocate for new jobs or to improve their career prospects. In a country the size of a continent, movement and travel are an ingrained aspect of life.

In the United States, cars and petrol are cheap, and only the poorest do not own a car, which partly explains why public bus services can be so rudimentary. Americans own 145 million cars, one for every two people and use a billion gallons of petrol each year. As Britain invented the railway, so in the following century the US created the first automobile society. America today has 42,500 miles of freeway, and four million miles of secondary roads. In some cities the vast majority of people, even those on low incomes owns a car: in Los Angeles, for example, a city without extensive public transport, it would simply be difficult to travel anywhere without one.

The government is aware of the environmental problems caused by the volume of traffic in cities (in LA, pollution makes the sunset a brilliant toxic pink), and is introducing legislation to try to restrict car use. In most states there is a special freeway lane, called the carpool or HOV lane (for High Occupancy Vehicles) which is reserved for buses and cars with more than three occupants. These are heavily policed and using one without the requisite number of passengers (or blow-up dolls) as passengers in your car will incur a heavy fine.

The highway system consists of a bewildering variety of differently-named roads, ranging from 'super-highways' with six lanes each way, to single-lane country roads. The freeway system is linked by the national arterial Interstates, which connect cities and states, and are designated by the prefix I-, and a red, white and blue shield. Many of the old and famous roads, such as Route 101 from Los Angeles through San Francisco to northern California, have been supplanted by the fast but characterless Interstates, but are well worth taking if you have the time. National and local maps will show 'scenic routes', which can also be worth the trouble to investigate. Freeways can be controlled-access, and may be known as turnpikes, expressways or toll-roads: they have all the characteristics of motorways – a central barrier and no cross traffic. Tolls are usually two to three cents a mile. As with motorways, plan your journey on the freeways and interstates: you cannot stop or turn around, and service areas for petrol and food are limited to 'truck-stops', not literally for truckers, but often not the most salubrious of places.

Driving Regulations

These vary from state to state, so it is best to check with the local branch of the American Automobile Association (known as 'Triple A') if you want to be sure of speed limits, seat belt rules and so on in the state that you are driving in. If you are staying for any length of time in the States and are planning on driving a lot it would be worth joining the AAA, which provides breakdown service, and also maps and travel information. Basic membership costs $55 a year for breakdown service, tyre change and to the nearest repair facility regardless of distance. There's also assistance for being locked out of your car and AAA Club guarantees for a personal cheque for up to $350 of repairs. There are two other motoring organisations, the *BP Motor Club* and the *Mobil Auto Club* (addresses below).

> *The basic rules of the road throughout the USA are: drive on the right, never drink and drive or have an open container of alcohol in the car, never overtake on corners or on the brow of a hill, never pass a school bus that has stopped to unload children, and always give way to pedestrians.*

Speed limits in congested city areas are usually 20-25 mph (32-40 km/h), and on highways 55-65 mph (88-104 km/h). Highway police have all the usual tricks for detecting speeds over the limit, from radar to automatic cameras that are triggered when your car passes the limit. Speed limits are often rigorously enforced, and tickets can be very expensive.

In most states you are allowed to turn right at red traffic lights provided it is not explicitly forbidden at a particular junction. Motoring laws, much like other areas of daily life, do vary from state to state so it's best to check when you move to California or Florida for example.

Parking rules are also enforced with varying strictness in different states and towns. Never park in front of a fire hydrant or on a bus stop; look out for signs warning of street cleaning, between 7am and 11am on certain days of the week, and move your car the night before; learn what different coloured kerbs mean: generally, red is no parking at any time, yellow denotes a limited truck loading zone, green a limited waiting period, blue is for handicapped drivers, and white means set down only. These colours will vary from state to state. In some states there will be designated snow streets, which have to be left free for snow ploughs in winter. Parking on highways in rural areas is generally forbidden, and camping, apart from designated areas, is often prohibited. Parking in cities and towns is often controlled by private companies as well as the city police, who will tow away or clamp illegally parked cars. To get your car back you will have to pay a fine, and show proof of ownership, ID, insurance, registration and licence. Private and municipal parking lots charge from $10-$30 a day; you will also find private outdoor parking lots, where you pay by stuffing notes into a slot corresponding to your parking space. In some places, such as Manhattan in New York City, garage space is extremely expensive at around $300 per month. As it is essential to keep the car under cover to avoid losing it, most New Yorkers forgo the luxury of owning a car.

Driving while under the influence of alcohol is taken very seriously in the USA. In some states (such as Utah) you are not allowed to carry alcohol anywhere in the car, and in other states it must be carried, unopened, in the trunk (the boot).

Useful Addresses

AAA Foundation for Traffic Safety, 607 14th Street NW, Suite 201, Washington, DC 20005; ☎202-638 5944; fax 202-638 5943; e-mail info@aaafoundation. org; www.aaafoundation.org. For the useful publications: *How To Help An Older Driver* and *Road Rage: How To Avoid Aggressive Driving* and safety leaflets.

Department of Transportation, Office of Vehicle Safety Compliance, 400 7th Street SW, Washington, DC 20590; ☎202-366 4000; www.dot.gov.

American Automobile Association, 1000 AAA Drive, Heathrow, FL 32746; ☎407-444 7000; www.aaa.com. The AAA is organised by clubs at a state level or within a state. You can use the website which will direct you to the nearest AAA club. Alternatively, if you don't have access to the Internet, call directory enquiries within each state for contact information.

BP Motor Club, PO Box 4441, Carol Stream, IL 60197; ☎1-800-732 9600; www.bpmotorclub.com.

Mobil Auto Club, 300C Lawrence Drive, West Chester, PA 19380; ☎1-888-258 2869; www.lubeoils.com/mobautoclub.

Breakdowns and Accidents

Accidents should be reported to the nearest police station immediately, especially if personal injury or property damage is involved. If you are driving a hired car you should follow the accident procedure laid out in the rental agreement. Almost all car rental companies are full members of the AAA, which means that when you do break down you will be taken to your destination free of charge. If you break down on a freeway, raise your hood (bonnet) and wait for a state trooper. You may be advised to hang a white cloth on the driver's side, but this can look like too much of a distress signal and imply vulnerability. Interstates have emergency roadside telephones: note your location by the small green mileage markers on the side of the road. On a long journey, especially across the remote mountainous and desert areas of the west, it's advisable to take a mobile phone otherwise you might be stranded after a break down.

Insurance

Insurance varies between states, but it is usually necessary to be resident in the state in which you take out a policy, unless you are buying a short-term tourist policy, but these can be double the price of the basic policy. It is essential to check that the policy comes with collision damage waiver (CDW) and theft waiver (TW). This corresponds to the mandatory UK third-party insurance. It is not compulsory in the USA, but if you do not have it you will be fully liable for any collision, and will not be covered if the other offending car is stolen. These waivers are expensive but it's worth checking to see if your credit card company offers special deals on car rentals and corresponding insurance. American Express is one company offering better prices for collision damage waiver insurance.

For a full resident's policy you must have a state driving licence, for which you must usually surrender any other driving licence you hold. You must also be resident in the state for a certain amount of time each year – this may be from six to 10 months. The average person pays $870 for insurance but varies considerably depending on where you are resident and the corresponding rates of crime and traffic collisions. In New Jersey, at the top end, residents pay an average figure of $1,112. Road tax is included in the price of the licence plate and cost of petrol, but there is an annual registration fee, which varies too according to the state of residence. The cost of a routine service is about US$100-$200, excluding replacement parts.

A good place to start for information on car insurance is the Insurance Information Institute, 110 William Street, New York, NY 10038; ☎212-346 5500; www.iii.org.

Licences

You can drive legally in the USA on a UK full driver's licence, or international licence, for up to one year. After that you will need to get a licence issued by the state authorities. You can apply for this at the State Highway Department; you may have to take a driving test before being issued one.

The driving test varies from state to state, but is generally very easy and can be arranged at short notice. It is usually taken in two sections, written and practical. Licences are valid for between two and five years, and are automatically renewable on payment of a fee of around $10.

In most states the legal age at which you are allowed to drive is sixteen, and there is a mandatory re-test at 70 or 75.

Car Registration

Every car must have a Certificate of Title, or a Certificate of Ownership (the equivalent of a log book in the UK), which includes the driver's name and address and the vehicle licence plate number. A new Certificate is issued each time the vehicle changes hands. If you are buying a second-hand car, the seller will endorse the old certificate to say that he has sold the car, and it is then up to you to register it, by sending the certificate to the Department of Transportation (www.dot.gov) or the Registry of Motor Vehicles (www.dmv.org) in your state. It will cost between $10 and $50 depending on the State. You will need proof of ownership, ID, proof of insurance and financial responsibility, and a current registration card.

Some owners like to keep their licence plates, especially if they are personalised (see below). When you are issued the new registration certificate the plates will be transferred to your name, or you will be able to buy new ones. They cost between $8 and $48 per year: the price is often dependent on the weight or age of the car. An out-of-state car must be registered immediately, or within 10 to 60 days, depending on the state. If your children have just started in a state school or you have taken up employment, your car must be state registered.

In some states money for personalised ('vanity') plates is allotted to agencies involved in civic projects such as ecological reserves and wildlife parks: in California you will see plates displaying a variety of sentiments: IMMACHO, MAAHVLUS, SOLONG, or, typically, ALAPLAYA ('To the Beach!'). It is sometimes possible to claim a refund on your licence plates if your car is scrapped or you leave the state.

Car Rental

You have to be at least 18 to hire a car, and some rental companies insist on a lower age limit of 25. Most of the larger companies require you to possess a major credit card as well, although they may waive that requirement if you can put down a large deposit (usually about 160% of the hire charge). Rental companies come in a variety of forms, from the outfits that hire out a couple of war-weary saloons (despite it's ominous name, Rent A Wreck is an established company in this market), to the international and countrywide firms like Hertz, Budget, or National Car Rental. If in doubt, go with the big firms: their cars will be newer and in better condition, and if they cost slightly more at least you have the peace of mind that the car is less likely to blow up. If it does, the agency has thousands of offices for you to get redress. It's normally cheaper to hire from an airport than from a city-centre office. Remember most hire cars have automatic gearboxes – if you want manual (stick shift) you must ask for it.

The average price for a car ranges from $32 to $62 per day, including all insurance and unlimited mileage. Before you hire make quite sure that there is no drop-off fee if you want to take the car back to a different office. Sometimes in cross continental journeys the drop-off fee may be as high as $1,000. Check too that the insurance comes with collision damage and theft waiver (see Insurance above). You will normally be covered for up to $50,000, and can ask for extra cover if necessary. When hiring it's essential to check for hidden extras: Collision Damage Waiver is usually payable, even when a package contains 'free' car hire; additional charges include State Tax and compulsory Personal Accident and Personal Effects Insurance as well as gasoline. If a car is not returned by the appointed time, high additional hourly charges are payable plus an additional day CDW and insurance. The USA Travel Guide at www.usatourist.com provides a helpful comparative guide for car rental costs and tips on renting cars. For information on importing and buying a car, see *Setting Up Home.*

TRANSPORT

Air

Air travel in the USA is cheap and efficient. The alternatives of car, bus or train, usually take days rather than hours. A plane ticket hardly ever costs much more than the cheapest train fare. In Alaska air travel is the norm, even by light aircraft between smaller towns. Another advantage of air travel for non-residents is that there are several different discount packages, coupons and standby passes available only to foreigners.

Domestic airfares are determined by the popularity of the route and not by distance. It is cheaper to fly the 2,700 miles (4,345 km) from Los Angeles to New York than it would be to fly many much shorter distances (though New York to LA is nearly twice as expensive). The most popular and therefore cheapest routes are along the eastern seaboard (Boston, New York, Washington, Miami), the west coast, and coast to coast.

Cheap deals available before you go. Visit USA fares (VUSA) are air passes offered by different American airlines allowing several stops within the country on one visit. You can opt to buy between three and 12 coupons, depending on the airline, for separate flights. But these deals are only available to residents of other countries so are not really applicable to this guide except as an opportunity to scout out potential cities and towns before relocating to the States. VUSA Air Pass Fares cannot, currently, be booked online. For American airline numbers in the UK see *Getting There* in the *General Introduction*.

Cheap deals on the spot. For the cheaper flights see the weekend travel sections of the major newspapers, look up discount travel agencies in the Yellow Pages, or check the websites of the major airlines. In the big cities you will be able to find ticket consolidators for unbooked charter and commercial tickets. These are unofficial clubs with a membership fee of around $40. Consult www.airhitch. org for a detailed description of the process and local contacts. Southwest Airlines (www.southwest.com) is the best-known low-cost airline in America. It serves 60 airports in 59 cities across the country. One-way tickets from LA to Las Vegas start at about £27; the best fares go to those willing to take less busy days (Tuesdays, Wednesdays, and Saturdays) and less popular departure times (before 7am or after 7pm). JetBlue (www.JetBlue.com) is another no-frills airline with flights from New York to Florida (one-way) from £43. A number of full-service airlines have launched low-cost subsidiaries, such as United's Ted (www.flyted.com) and Delta's Song Air (www.flysong.com). All the main cheaper American airlines are listed at www.etn.nl/lcostusa.htm with links to each carrier's website.

Courier travel. Another way to get discounted tickets is to fly as a courier. Once such flights provided the cheapest tickets, now their prices compare with other discounted fares. The advantage of couriering is that you get a scheduled flight and so there are no funny timings or roundabout routes to cope with. Your baggage is restricted to cabin baggage only, but some courier flights now allow more luggage. Most US courier flights start from New York.

*Courier Travel (*www.couriertravel.org) is an online courier service requiring a $50 joining fee for a one-year single membership. The service also provides information about American consolidators (bucket shops) offering discounted flights. The International Association of Air Travel Couriers (PO Box 980, Keystone Heights, FL 32656; ☎352-475 1584; www.courier.org) is a valuable source of information and contacts.

Trains

Although there are high-speed commuter links in and around the big cities, and the Acela Express trains which run between Boston, New York and Washington are much used, most Americans don't choose trains for long-distance journeys. But travelling by rail on Amtrak's stately and luxurious trains can be a delight. So keen is Amtrak, the National Railroad Passenger Corporation, to get people on to trains that they deny you no luxury. The trains are luxurious, with the best cabins equipped with sofas, armchairs and private bathroom and shower. With such high-quality care offered to passengers, it is hardly surprising to learn that Amtrak has been forced to scale down its operations during the past decade yet again and axe several major routes while reducing frequency in others. But Amtrak routes still crisscross the country from Seattle to San Diego, Sacramento to Chicago, New Orleans to Boston. Several of these routes are legendary rail journeys such as the Sunset Limited between Orlando and Los Angeles or the City of New Orleans running from that city to Chicago. There is a wide variety of passes which allow unlimited travel valid for 15- or 30-day periods. Prices vary depending on time of travel and where you are travelling. At the top end, a 30-day North American pass (includes Canada) costs $475. Travel agents can supply these passes and advise you on the availability of special tours. Frequent users of the service may qualify for the Amtrak Guest Rewards Program which award points to be redeemed for travel, car rental and hotels.

The following UK outlets can supply details and tickets:
International Rail: ☎0870-751 5000; www.international-rail.com.
Destination Marketing: ☎020-7253 9009.
Trailfinders: ☎020-7938 3939 (London); 0161-839 6969 (Manchester); 0117-929 9000 (Bristol); 0121-236 1234 (Birmingham); 0141-353 2224 (Glasgow); www.trailfinders.co.uk

In the USA, call 1-800-872 7245 for 24-hour recorded timetable information and reservations. The Amtrak website www.amtrak.com offers a comprehensive means of researching routes and prices. There you'll find details of special deals and rail passes allowing unlimited travel within set periods and regions of the country. The site enables you to apply for brochures which are stocked too by most travel agents.

Bus Travel

Buses are the cheapest form of travel in America. Cynics believe that as only the terminally poor – those able to afford neither car nor air travel – go by long-distance bus. However, when you climb aboard a Greyhound you'll see exactly what they mean by their slogan 'Leave the driving to us.' Taking a bus can be a romantic experience, and it is also the cheapest way of getting around. Greyhound is the largest operator, offering the cheapest fares, and a comprehensive network serving practically every city in the country, except within national parks. You are allowed two pieces of luggage in the cabin, and each must be able to fit under the seat or in the overhead compartment. You can check in two pieces weighing a total of 100 lbs (45 kg) and one item may not weigh more than 50 lbs (22 kg). For information on other bus companies, *Russell's Official National Motor Coach Guide* has countrywide timetables and route information for all companies apart from Greyhound. It is available at bookstores (price $25) and libraries.

Greyhound's UK distributor, STA Travel (6 Wrights Lane, London W8 6TA; ☎0870-160 5990; www.statravel.co.uk) sells the Ameripass, which can be used with another 54 participating bus lines for periods of 7, 10, 15, 21, 30, 40 or 60 days. A seven-day adult pass in high season is $219, 15 days $319, 30 days $419. These passes are available from Greyhound distributors worldwide. They are more expensive if bought within the USA. Call 1-888-454 7277 within the US or from another country call 212-971 0492. Further details are available from Greyhound Lines (PO Box 660362, Dallas, TX 75266; ☎1-800-231 2222; e-mail ifsr@greyhound.com; www.greyhound.com). Information on the North America Discovery Pass, for travel on both sides of the US/Canada border, can be found at www.discoverypass.com.

Two other companies run coach tours across the USA. Tauck Tours (5114 Okeechobee Boulevard, Suite 201, West Palm Beach, FL 33417; ☎561-687 3301; e-mail tours@atlastravelweb.com; www.taucktour.com) are a high class operation doing 'all expenses' tours in the USA and Canada, including helicopter and boat trips to the less accessible parts of Alaska, and steamboat excursions in Louisiana.

For a more 'alternative' and leisurely way of seeing the country, Green Tortoise, based in California, operates reconditioned buses – 'hostels on wheels' – complete with sofa seats, stereos and dinettes. All meals are communal. The journey from San Francisco to Boston takes ten to 14 days and costs around $469, with an extra $121 for food. They also do 'loop' tours, which include days on the beach and kayaking, going to National Parks, Baja California, Grand Canyon and Alaska. Book a good two months in advance, at a regional office (see Yellow Pages) or at *Green Tortoise Adventure Travel* (494 Broadway, San Francisco, CA 94133; ☎415-956 7500; e-mail tortoise@greentortoise.com; www.greentortoise.com).

City Transport

Transport within cities usually consists of buses, subways (underground railways), streetcars (trams) in a few cities such as San Francisco and New Orleans, and taxis. In some cities (notoriously, Los Angeles), public transport is limited and unreliable so a private car is recommended. Some southern cities are so hot that taking any public transportation apart from air conditioned subways is out of the question.

The big cities, of course, have sophisticated subways, and commuter rail networks. Taxis are always common and good value compared to Europe: a 1.8-mile (3-km) taxi ride in New York should cost around $10. Except in New York and Chicago, taxi-sharing is common, although each passenger has to pay the full fare. Don't be surprised if your taxi driver does not speak very good English (especially in New York, Los Angeles, Washington and other big cities) and doesn't know his way about very well: have a map handy to help him out. New York cabbies often live up to their reputation as being rude, obstreperous and surly, but don't let it disappoint you if they are helpful, polite and charming. Indeed, the late 1990s has seen an unprecedented rise in politeness among New Yorkers in general. This phenomenon is laid at the door of the amazingly popular ex-Mayor Rudy Giuliani, who first introduced zero tolerance policing, and then set out to clean up the manners of the most ill-mannered city in America.

Getting Around Cities. American cities are often laid out on a grid pattern, with numbered streets and the spaces between streets called 'blocks'. This makes orientation slightly easier, but you must be sure that you understand the address. Americans do not usually bother with putting 'street' when writing an address, so '5th and 18th' in Manhattan means the junction of 5th Avenue and 18th Street. You will normally be able to pinpoint a block by this method. Pay attention to compass points in an address. In Washington DC, for example, street addresses are followed by NW, NE, SW, or SE, which are essential to get to the right district and the right end of what might be a very long street. Brooklyn (NY) addresses use E and W in a similar fashion.

Getting around cities in the States is no more easy or difficult than in any foreign country: make sure that you go to the tourist office on arrival, or get a decent map, and don't stray into areas that you are not sure of, especially at night. If in doubt, always take a taxi.

Except for a few of the older cities with condensed centres like Boston and New York, walking within major urban areas is unusual and may even prompt suspicion. Remember too that in cities like LA and Houston, which are essentially designed to accommodate the car, distances can be great and walking a 'couple of blocks' may take you on a prolonged hike for a mile or more. This may be inadvisable in extreme temperatures or in the dark.

BANKS AND FINANCE

Bank Accounts

American banks tend to operate on a regional or state basis. They offer the same sorts of facilities as UK banks with a few differences. The standard high street bank or building society is called a Savings and Loan, or 'thrift' bank. Individuals may open current ('checking') or deposit ('savings') accounts, money may be transferred, banker's drafts can be ordered. American banks do not usually have foreign exchange facilities, although with an international credit card such as Visa or American Express, dollars can be withdrawn and charged to your account in your own currency. This is of course an expensive way to get cash, as the commission is usually high.

It is important to remember the local nature of all banks. This means that most shops will not accept cheques from an out-of-state bank, and it may be difficult to cash cheques with banks in other states. For this reason when opening an account make sure that you choose a large, well-established bank such as the Bank of America (www.bankofamerica.com) in California, or Chase (www.chase.com) in New York.

You should have no difficulty opening a bank account. Most banks will require a minimum opening balance of between $100 and $200, and in some banks it is necessary to keep a minimum balance in your account. Falling below this may result in harsh charges being levied. Average banking charges can cost more than $200 per year.

It is advisable to check what identification is required to open an account. Some banks will require a Social Security number: these are available from the local Social Security office if you are resident or have a working visa. If you need a credit rating, open an account with a major department store such as Sears. This will automatically give you a credit rating which will be accepted by the bank.

There is a network of Automatic Telling Machines (ATMs) across the country. Most accounts include cashcards, and networks such as Cirrus and Plus are interstate and countrywide. There are also local networks in the major cities, such as the New York Cash Exchange. It would be worth opening an account with a bank that is a member of one of these networks. Banks usually charge non account-holders commission for withdrawing cash from their ATM, which is another good reason for banking with one of the larger banks. Link Cashcards, issued by many UK building societies, can be used in Plus machines to withdraw cash from the holder's UK current account. Cards issued by the Nationwide, Halifax and Woolwich building societies will be accepted. If you intend to return to the UK after a period in the USA, it would be worth opening an account at one of the building societies that participate in the Link\Plus network, as your current account will continue to accumulate interest while you are abroad. Britain's second largest bank, Royal Bank of Scotland, and HSBC are looking at American bank acquisitions while Barclays has been linked with Providian Financial, a US credit card company.

Cheque guarantee cards are not issued in the USA. Cheque fraud is rife, and many places, such as restaurants and service stations will not accept them as a matter of course. If you do pay by cheque, you will be asked for two pieces of identification such as student ID or passport, and driving licence or credit card. It is worthwhile getting a state ID if you do not have a driving licence: both of these are available from the Department of Motor Vehicles Licensing Office (www.dmv.org) in your state.

It is essential not to go overdrawn on a current account. Fees for bounced cheques can be punitive: between $10 and $25 per cheque. As well as this, the cheque is sent back to the payee, which if it is a shop or organisation is likely to charge another $10 to $25 fee. Individuals who knowingly write bad cheques may be charged with fraud.

Most banks offer overdraft protection, which can be a helpful feature, especially for students.

Chequebooks are not free, and have to be ordered in bulk from the bank, usually in sets of 20. This will cost around $25. It is common to have your full name, address and telephone number on your chequebook. Cheques are always returned to the account holder after cashing.

Finally, before opening an account check to see that the institution is federally insured so that your deposits are guaranteed up to $100,000 in case of corporate bankruptcy, fraud or theft. Banks which are included in this scheme advertise with special federal deposit insurance stickers in the window.

International and Internal Money Transfers

The most common form of international transfer is electronic, via the SWIFT system. This is instantaneous, and because of the five to eight-hour time difference, UK banks are able to transfer funds at same day value. This means that when you order funds from your UK branch the money will be changed into dollars at the exchange rate that is in effect at that moment, and not at the next day's rate. Lloyd's Bank advises that almost every bank has the SWIFT system, but that it is worthwhile banking with a large bank, which will be more likely to be a correspondent of a UK bank. UK banks can only transfer funds to correspondent banks, which will then, if necessary, move the funds on to another bank.

The SWIFT system allows notification to be sent to the bank from which funds are to be withdrawn, and for the authenticated payment instruction to be returned instantaneously. Unlimited amounts can be transferred in this way.

An express transfer costs around £20, and a standard transfer, which takes about five days, £10. Other forms of international transfers are banker's drafts and international money orders. These are sent by post and are relatively uncommon.

Internal money transfers. These can be arranged by electronic transfer (the SWIFT system or the CHIPS system) between banks across the country. The cost would be between $10 and $25, depending on the distance.

Other Banking Services

US banks offer all the services that are available from banks in Europe, with some exceptions such as foreign exchange facilities (see above). US banks also have a function similar to UK building societies, arranging mortgages and other low-interest loans. If a bank provides this service it will be called a savings bank. High-interest accounts are available at most US banks. These are of between two- and five-year deposit terms, and at the time of writing are offering interest rates of between 3.5% and 4%.

Savings Banks in the USA do not generally deal with any but the very smallest business customers: they are almost exclusively for private bank accounts. Businesses are catered for by the commercial banks.

Currency

The US monetary unit is the dollar ($), which is divided into 100 cents. Dollar notes (referred to as 'bills') come in the following denominations: $1, $2, $5, $10, $20, $50, $100. Naturally, the dollar and pound exchange rate fluctuates and is determined by the money markets. In the past few years despite Sterling's strength against the old European currencies, it declined against the dollar as the American currency became increasingly adopted as an international standard of security. Recently, the dollar has drifted downwards against the pound and the Euro and fell 21% against a basket of six currencies from January 2002 to the end of 2004. The current exchange rate on the dollar is $1 = £0.53 and $1 = €0.77. Exchange rates can be checked before departure at www.xe.com.

Useful Contacts

The big five international accountants and smaller specialist companies offer expatriate financial services such as taxation planning.

PricewaterhouseCoopers, 1 Embankment Place, London WC2N 6RH; ☎020-7583 5000; www.pwcglobal.com.

KPMG, 8 Salisbury Square, London EC4Y 8BB; ☎020-7311 1000; fax 020-7311 3311; www.kpmg.com/ or www.kpmg.co.uk.

Arthur Andersen, 180 Strand, London WC2R 1BL; ☎020-7438 3000; www.andersen.com.

Ernst and Young, 1 More London Place, London SE1 2AF; ☎020-7951 2000; www.ey.com.

Deloitte, Touche Tohmatsu, 180 Strand, London WC2R 1BL; ☎020-7936 3000; fax 020-7583 1198; www.deloitte.com or www.deloitte.co.uk.

Merril Lynch & Co, 4 World Financial Center, 250 Vesey Street, New York, NY

10080; ☎212-449 1000. Financial management and advisory company.
Wilkins Kennedy, Bridge House, London Bridge, London SE1 9QR; ☎020-7403
1877; fax 020-7403 1605; www.w-k.co.uk). Specialists in ex-pat taxation.

TAXATION

As a general rule, all non-US citizens (foreign nationals) living, working or
investing in the United States are subject to federal, state or local taxes.
How much you are taxed as a foreign national depends on your status as a
resident alien or non-resident alien: this is discussed further below.

The basic federal revenue law is the Internal Revenue Code, which deals with
the collection of income taxes, estate and gift taxes, employment taxes and
excise taxes. There is no VAT in the United States but states levy their own sales
taxes at varying rates.

Federal taxes are administered by the Internal Revenue Service (the IRS),
which is a government agency of the Department of Treasury. In addition to
federal taxes, states and municipalities can also levy taxes, which can sometimes
be fairly severe, although they are seldom above the level of federal taxes.
Seven of the states do not require anyone to pay income tax: Alaska, Florida,
Nevada, South Dakota, Texas, Washington and Wyoming. New Hampshire and
Tennessee only levy a tax on dividends and interest income. Most charge up to
10% on income. State taxes are covered in more detail below.

Income Tax

If you are earning you must file an income tax return on Form 1040, on or
before 15 April: the tax year is 1 January to 31 December. Paying income
tax, whether you are a permanent resident or not, is of crucial importance.
US residents are taxed on their worldwide earnings, while non-residents are
taxed on what they earn in the USA only. The income tax threshold (personal
exemption) is $3,100, and taxes deducted from those earning less than that sum
will be refunded. On top of that couples or single people can claim a standard
deduction. In 2004, the standard deduction for a single person was $4,850.
A portion of earnings is subject to withholding taxes (that is, the employer is
responsible for deducting the tax from earnings) and you will be required to fill
in a form W2 for federal withholding and a similar form for state and municipal
withholding. State income tax is filed on a different form in each state: forms
are available from the state tax office or the post office.

Student scholarships are liable for 14% Federal taxation on living expenses,
not on tuition expenses, and are also subject to State tax. Non-resident aliens
are taxed on all income derived from US sources. The statutory rate is 30% but
this can be reduced by tax treaty.

There are various tax treaties which have been set up with other countries (including the UK) which are designed to safeguard an individual or company against paying some taxes twice. A dual citizen of the UK and the US might be liable to tax on earnings in both countries. A Totalization Agreement serves the same purpose in the case of Social Security payments.

Green card holders, and those who have what is called a 'substantial presence' in the USA are taxed as US residents. 'Substantial presence' means (with various exceptions) spending more than 183 days in the country at any one time. Be very careful of the 183 day rule: it is extremely complicated. Days spent in the country from the previous two years can actually be counted as more than one day – you may have been in the USA for only 150 days in the past two years and still be liable to resident taxation. It is impossible here to go into the minutiae of federal tax law: if you are not sure where you stand, get professional advice.

Generally speaking, if you are in the USA with no intention of abandoning your 'tax home' in another country, and you have no application pending for permanent status, you are classed as a non-resident alien. Some individuals are exempt from resident's taxation: diplomats, employees of international organisations such as the United Nations, their families, teachers and trainees, students, and professional athletes. Tax exemptions are extremely complicated and cannot be covered in detail here. Some types of employee with certain functions are exempt from specific taxes. Aliens on temporary assignments in the USA – those working for multinationals for a set period, for instance – can deduct temporary living expenses (meals, lodging, transport, telephone and laundry expenses) from their gross earnings.

Earnings for personal services of holders of J-1 visas who are employees of foreign employers are specifically exempt from US taxes. The individual must not be in the country for more than 90 days, and must not be paid more than $3000. Some tax treaties allow for a more liberal reading of this ruling: again, it is important to get professional advice on this area.

As a rule non-residents are taxed at a flat rate of 30% on earnings. Residents and Citizens are taxed at the rates listed in Table 9.

Other taxes

VAT. There is no VAT in the USA. Most states (except Alaska, Delaware, Montana, New Hampshire and Oregon) impose sales tax, of between 4.5% and 9% on goods sold.

Social Security Tax. Social Security tax consists of the Old Age Survivors and Disability Insurance (OASDI) which was introduced in 1935, and a programme of Health Insurance (HI), called Medicare, for people over 65. The program insures for lost income due to retirement, disability or death and is administered by the Social Security Administration.

TABLE 9 — INCOME TAX

Married filing jointly

Income	Tax
Up to $14,600	10%
$14,600 – $59,400	$1,460 plus 15%
$59,400 – $119,950	$8,180 plus 25%
$119,950 – $182,800	$23,317.50 plus 28%
$182,800 – $326,450	$40,915.50 plus 33%
$326,450 or more	$88,320 plus 35%

Married filing separately

Income	Tax
Up to $7,300	10%
$7,300 – $29,700	$730 plus 15%
$29,700 – $59,975	$44,090 plus 25%
$59,975 – $91,400	$11,658.75 plus 28%
$91,400 – $163,225	$20,457.75 plus 33%
$163,225 or more	$44,160 plus 35%

Single

Income	Tax
Up to $7,300	10%
$7,300 – $29,700	$730 plus 15%
$29,700 – $71,950	$4,090 plus 25%
$71,950 – $150,150	$14,652.50 plus 28%
$150,150 – $326,450	$38,548.50 plus 33%
$326,450 or more	$94,727.50 plus 35%

Head of Household

Income	Tax
Up to £10,450	10%
$10,450 – $39,800	$1,045 plus 15%
$39,800 – $102,800	$5,447.50 plus 25%
$102,800 – $166,450	$21,197.50 plus 28%
$166.450 – $326,450	$39,019.50 plus 33%
$326,450 or more	$91,819.50 plus 35%

Almost all types of employment and self-employment are covered. Some non-resident aliens are exempt, depending on the type of visa they hold. Temporary workers on H visas are exempt, as are employees of foreign governments. Social Security payments are withheld by the employer.

For 2004, the social security tax rate was 6.2%, which applies to the first $87,900 of an employee's wages paid by the employer. The Medicare tax rate is 1.45%. The self-employed are also taxed at a rate of 15.3% on profits.

State and Local Contributions. State and local income taxes vary widely from state to state. In some areas, such as New York, they are fairly severe; elsewhere there are no state taxes, as in Nevada. Taxes paid to the state and locally can be counted as deductions from the gross wage for federal income tax purposes. Some states have different residency status and exemption rules: the local tax office or post office will have more information.

Gift Tax. Applies to US residents and (with exemptions) to non-resident aliens, on gifts of over $11,000 annually.

Estate Tax. There is no federal inheritance tax (although it is levied in some states). Estate Tax applies to all deceased persons' estates.

Pension Plan Coverage. You may be eligible to participate in a US tax-qualified pension plan during your stay or assignment. For example, you may be able to join your company's 401(k) plan, which would permit you to contribute up to $13,000 in 2004 (this figure will increase each year by $1,000 until the limit is $15,000 in 2006) of your salary on tax-deductible basis and to benefit from matching employer contributions. If you are aged 50 and over, an additional catch up contribution is allowed. The additional contribution amount is 2004: $3,000; 2005: $4,000; and 2006: $5,000. You need to check with a professional adviser what the tax implications are in the USA and your home country. If you decide to withdraw the money from a fund on leaving the US, that sum will be subject to US taxes.

Further Information

Further information can be obtained from:

Internal Revenue Services, Department of the Treasury; ☎1-800-829 1040; www.irs.gov. Local offices throughout the country.

Social Security Administration, 6401 Security Boulevard, Baltimore, MD 21235 ☎410-965 1234; and 200 Independence Avenue W, Washington, DC 20201; www.ssa.gov.

The publication *Foreign Nationals Working in the United States* is available from PricewaterhouseCoopers, 1 Embankment Place, London WC2N 6RH; ☎020-7583 5000; www.pwcglobal.com.

HEALTH

The US Healthcare System

The United States has some of the most expensive healthcare in the world and is the only developed nation that does not have a full government-supported healthcare system.

Much of this disparity though is attributable to the structure of American medicine, which is an extremely profitable industry: Pharmaceutical companies turn over millions of dollars in the search for new and lucrative drugs, doctors are highly motivated and even more highly paid, and hospitals are the best equipped in the world. But litigation is common and as a consequence all medical practitioners and institutions must take out punitive insurance policies and these costs are then passed on to the patients.

Unfortunately it is not the case that with this highly sophisticated health industry, every citizen is guaranteed similar standards of care. There are two state health care schemes, Medicare (for those over 65 and the disabled), and Medicaid (for those below a certain income level). Anyone falling outside the categories of the elderly or the very poor, must pay. Personal medical insurance ensuring the best treatment is confined to those who can afford to buy it from personal income or those lucky enough to be employed by companies willing to offer corporate membership of a medical insurance scheme. Loss of employment can often mean an entire family will lose its coverage overnight.

Although you will never be refused admission to hospital or left on the street by an ambulance because you cannot produce a credit card, it is crucial that you are insured for medical expenses. If there's only one piece of sound advice about visiting or living in the US, it's that medical insurance is mandatory before you set foot on American soil unless you happen to be very wealthy. An unforeseen medical emergency could literally bankrupt you within days. Admission for hospital treatment may require a deposit of between $5,000 and $15,000. The daily costs of a bed alone will seem extortionate: a private room alone can be around $1000 a day and medical treatment will be added on top. Hospitals sometimes pass debts on to debt collectors who may follow you back to your own country and demand payment on behalf of their client. A half hour visit to a doctor may cost $300 alone without any tests.

If you have any illness that requires regular drugs make sure that you take sufficient supplies with you. American pharmacists will not honour foreign prescriptions.

If you are sent out to the USA with a company it is more than likely that medical insurance will be part of the package: check this with your personnel department. Students will be able to benefit from cheaper premiums for the under 25s. Most colleges have a clinic or health centre, which will offer free advice and basic treatment. They do not run emergency units or out-of-hours service so it is a good idea to check which hospitals and emergency units they recommend.

Restrictions on Entry

No vaccinations are required to enter the USA from any country. But green cards (residency) will not be granted to applicants already in the USA as refugees or aliens on immigrant visas if they are found to have HIV antibodies or AIDS (or any other communicable disease) at the required medical examination. Irrationally and unjustly, temporary visitors with HIV are also denied entry unless they have received a waiver despite the fact that hundreds of thousands of Americans already carry the virus. Possession on entry of the drugs for treating

HIV and AIDS may be sufficient to prevent entry. If you are HIV positive you must apply for a waiver to accompany your visa and indicate that you are not suffering from symptoms of infection, that you have sufficient insurance to cover any medical expenses and also that the visit will not exceed 30 days.

Treatment

The treatment that you are offered in the USA will be very different to what you are used to in the UK. Family medicine is not common: instead of a GP dispensing prescriptions to everybody who comes to the surgery, there are specialists in each particular field. However, 'primary care physicians' are often consulted as the first point of reference particularly by patients in HMO plans (see below). Sometimes a specialist in internal medicine, an 'internist', functions as the equivalent of a European GP or general doctor who may then refer a patient to a particular specialist. It's quite common, particularly within cities, to use several separate specialists like a gynaecologist, dermatologist, or an osteopath. A mother will often use a women's clinic, her children will go to children's clinics and so on. Most doctors never make home visits although in the larger cities there will be special 'House-Call' units that will send a doctor to your house for a fee of $100 to $200.

For those who can pay, the quality of medical care in the US is extremely high. The country has some of the best hospitals and medical research facilities in the world. It's not uncommon for doctors to have their own testing laboratories within their offices so the process of testing is much quicker. In the highly litigious atmosphere of the USA, a doctor's greatest fear is a malpractice suit and, as a result, is unlikely to advise a couple of days in bed when you complain of headaches and dizziness. They will take samples and carry out a series of tests for the simplest ailment, to determine exactly what is wrong. You will be encouraged to have blood and cholesterol tests on a routine basis. Preventative medicine is therefore a major feature of American healthcare.

In the USA, the patient is the consumer, and you can take your custom elsewhere if you are not satisfied with the treatment. Hospitals are advertised on hoardings, on the radio, the TV, in magazines and on supermarket trolleys. 'We will help you realise your dream birthing experience', runs a radio advertisement for a New York hospital. As the consumer, you have the choice, and as with all free market systems, this can overwhelm you to the point where you simply feel confused. Nevertheless the best hospitals in American cities as in Europe tend to be teaching institutions attached to local universities. The magazine US News and World Report publishes an annual survey of hospitals ranked according to specialties, which is available at www.usnews.com.

A great advantage of being the customer in the health market is that doctors will always tell you exactly what they are doing and what they propose to do. You will never be left in the dark, or patronised by a doctor who does not feel it is necessary to let you in on the complexities of the treatment. Appointments are comparatively easy to schedule and the doctor can give each patient ample time.

At the end of a course of treatment or a stay in hospital you will be presented with an itemised bill. Fees are quite steep: around $200 for a consultation, $100 for a lab test, $50 for antibiotics. Refer all bills to your insurance company before you pay them, and if you are paying for your own treatment, double check the bill: it is common for hospitals to make mistakes and you may find yourself paying for treatment that you have not had.

Emergencies

The emergency number is usually 911, which will alert the police as well as an ambulance. Most cities have private ambulance services which will cost from $100-$200, but will probably come quicker than the public ambulance. They might be covered on your insurance. Hospitals have emergency rooms, the equivalent of casualty in the UK. Ambulances are obliged by law to pick you up for treatment; scare stories about car accident victims being left in the road to bleed because they can't produce a credit card are almost certainly untrue.

Minor Complaints

For minor complaints, tests and diagnoses there are 'walk-in centers' or 'urgent care centers', often located in town centres or shopping malls. Payment is on the spot, though some will defer payment until insurance comes through.

Dental Treatment

Dentistry is a sophisticated science in the USA. It is unlikely that you will suffer any pain at all, more than likely that your dentist will exclaim over the gaps in your teeth (American teeth, as well as American dentists, are the best in the world) and refer you on for cosmetic treatment with an orthodontist.

If you plan to stay in the USA for more than a year, have your teeth checked before you go, and take a copy of your dental records with you, which will save time and money if you have to go for treatment.

Group Healthcare Organisations

Health Maintenance Organisations (HMO's) are group benefit plans sponsored by a variety of different organisations from the government to employers, hospitals and insurance companies. They can be independent or attached to a hospital, but usually function quite separately, running their own clinics with independent doctors and nursing staff. They have grown over the last 15 years and now treat some 30 million patients a year. All medical costs are taken care of by a monthly subscription, generally much cheaper than conventional insurance premiums. While offering better value than individual insurance plans, HMOs generally offer more limited medical coverage. For example you will have to choose a doctor from a limited list of approved medical practitioners.

Preferred Provider Organisations (PPO's) are run on more or less the same lines, but are funded with greater collaboration between insurance companies and the medical profession to produce services at a better price. For more information see *Useful Addresses*, below

Insurance

Because of the costs of medical treatment in the United States, many European insurance companies will not insure expatriates going out for a long period. Instead they advise you to get your insurance from a US company such as BlueCross or UK-based companies such as Expatriate Insurance Services Ltd or BUPA (addresses below) which specialise in expatriate insurance

It is not uncommon to find expatriates who decide to take the risk of having no insurance at all, weighing up the cost of treatment against the lifetime costs of an insurance policy. But to reiterate, this is not at all sensible. American medical costs can be financially devastating. It is highly recommended to take out medical insurance during any stay in the US. Planning for an medical emergency may seem unduly neurotic, but it only takes an accident say while travelling or a case of severe food poisoning to send a 'healthy' person to hospital with all of the attendant costs.

Philip Jones stresses the importance of having healthcare insurance
The one thing to be aware of is healthcare. We are fortunate enough to have health insurance and as a result our health care is excellent. However, many, many people don't have insurance. There is no universal coverage and should you not have insurance then you can be refused access to healthcare or be left with enormous bills. For anyone moving here, it is something to be aware of.

Costs

It's hard to outline a 'typical' policy because medical insurance is a complicated business. Costs vary according to a large range of factors such as where will you be living, age, pre-existing conditions, number of children, or whether you are a smoker.

On a typical policy from a US insurance company, a couple aged between 25 and 34, with two children under 18, might pay $180 per month, with $34 extra for each child. The policy would have a $100 reserve, and costs of between $100 and $50,000 would be paid up to 80%. Costs of between $50,000 and $100,000 would be paid in full, and may in some circumstances stretch to a million dollars. Optional extras like maternity, dental or optical cover can be added too. There would be a $10,000 maximum evacuation payout (to get you back to your own country), after five days in hospital.

If you are going to be staying in the USA for six months or less it would be best to get a standard travel policy from an insurance company in your own country. They have the advantage of being cheaper, and have upper limits of around £2.5 million. However short your stay you should get a policy covering you for at least £15,000.

There are companies who will insure students under the age of 26 for up to two years for between £537 and £706, fully comprehensive with an upper limit of £2 million. Adults travelling on non-student classification (not business) can also be insured.

When choosing an insurance policy you need to look out for certain conditions that apply to different policies. In particular you should look out for the following:

Pre-existing conditions: make sure that the policy defines this term. It can either mean the existence of a medical condition that has been treated, or simply a condition that has existed prior to taking out a policy. It becomes crucially important if you are unaware of such conditions as heart murmur or ulcers. It is expensive to include pre-existing conditions in a policy, so look for policies with loose interpretations of the term.

Co-payment: this is the reserve on a policy. Some policies pay out 70%-80% up to a certain amount and 100% thereafter. There may also be different co-payments for different medical conditions.

Specific limits: some policies may specify dollar limits for certain conditions and ailments, and will only pay up to a certain amount.

Deductible: Each year the policy holder might, for example, have to pay the initial $2,000 of costs before any reimbursement from the insurance company begins.

Exclusions: Some policies exclude certain injuries, for example for dangerous sports.

Medical Evacuation: J-1 exchange visas are required to have medical evacuation coverage. This will pay to have the insured transported home for treatment. It is rarely used, and so is not an expensive addition to the policy.

Repatriation: The policy pays to have the insured's remains transported home if they should die while in the USA. This is also a required benefit for J-1 visa holders.

Useful Addresses

American Diabetes Association, 1701 North Beauregard Street, Alexandria, VA 22311; ☎1-800-342 2383; www.diabetes.org. Supply ID cards with information on holder's condition and needs.

Centers for Medicare and Medicaid Services, 7500 Security Boulevard, Baltimore,

MD 21244; ☎ *410-786 3000.*

International Association for Medical Assistance to Travelers (IAMAT), 1623 Military Road, Niagara Falls, NY 14304; ☎716-754 4883; e-mail info@iamat. org; www.iamat.org. Supply free pamphlets, and a world directory of fixed rate physicians. Membership is free, but donations are appreciated.

MedicAlert Foundation International, 2323 Colorado Avenue, Turlock, CA 95382; ☎209-668 3333; fax 209-669 2450; www.medicalert.org. For travellers with conditions such as weak hearts or diabetes, the MedicAlert Tag and membership costs $35 with $20 annual renewal fee, and gives information on the holder's condition in case of accidents.

Insurance Companies

USA

BlueCross BlueShield Association is a countrywide network of health insurance organisations which are administered locally. Check www.bcbs.com for your local plan.

CNA, 333 S Wabash, Chicago, IL 60604; ☎312-822 5000; www.can.com/. Specialises in tailored insurance plans for students visiting the USA for study or cultural exchange.

International Medical Group (IMG), 2960 North Meridian Street, Indianapolis, IN 46208; ☎317-655 4500 or 1-800-628 4664; fax 317-655 4505; e-mail insurance@imglobal.com; www.imglobal.com.

UK

Atlas Insurance, 37 King's Exchange, Tileyard Road, London N7 9AH; ☎020-7609 5000; www.atlasdirect.net. An expert in travel insurance and works in partnership with American insurer CNA (see above).

Axa Healthcare PPP, Phillips House, Crescent Road, Tunbridge Wells, Kent TN1 2PL; ☎01892-612080; www.axappphealthcare.com.

BUPA International, Russell Mews, Brighton BC1 2NR; ☎01273-208181; fax 01273-866583; www.bupa-intl.com.

Columbus Travel Insurance, Southgate Place, 41 Southgate, Chichester, West Sussex PO19 1ET; ☎0845-330 8518; e-mail admin@columbusdirect.com; www.columbusdirect.com.

Endsleigh Insurance Services, Shurdington Road, Cheltenham, Gloucestershire GL51 4UE; ☎0800-028 3571; www.endsleigh.co.uk.

Expacare, Columbia Centre, Market Street, Bracknell, Berkshire RG12 1JG; ☎01344-381650; fax 01344-381690; e-mail info@expacare.com; www. expacare.net. Specialists in expatriate medical insurance.

Expatriate Insurance Services Ltd, from the UK ☎0870-330 0016, International ☎+44-1273-703469, from within the USA ☎1-800-436 6267; e-mail info@expatriate-insurance.com; www.expatriate-insurance.com. Specialise in arranging international health, travel and life insurance.

HMO's and PPO's

America's Health Insurance Plans, 601 Pennsylvania Avenue NW, South Building, Suite 500, Washington, DC 20004; ☎202-778 3200; fax 202-331 7487; e-mail ahip@ahip.org; www.ahip.org. Represents companies providing health insurance coverage.

American Association of Preferred Provider Organizations, PO Box 429, Jeffersonville, IN 47131; ☎812-246 4376; fax 812-246 4630; www.aappo.org.

CRIME AND THE POLICE

The bald statistics on crime in the United States are uncompromising. Twenty per cent of US citizens rate crime as the most serious problem in the country; the homicide rate is now seven times that of Canada and more than 20 times that of Germany; homicide is the third most common cause of death amongst elementary and middle school children – schools in many cities have airport-style X-ray screening to prevent pupils bringing weapons into class. A child is 15 times more likely to die of gunfire in the USA than in Northern Ireland at the height of the Troubles. Thirty-two people per 1,000 households are likely to be the victims of violent crime in an average year.

The Clinton administration tried to pass a number of laws to deal with the problem, but had to steer a complicated path between the right, calling for more punishment and more executions, and the left, which wants rehabilitation and prevention. At the centre of the debate is the gun lobby, which in the form of the National Rifle Association (NRA) is a powerful political force with a large membership. The right to bear arms is a freedom enshrined in the constitution as a legacy of the Revolutionary militias created by local communities to resist British rule. It is a right cherished by many Americans but seen as baffling by many other nations where regulation of firearms is perceived as a logical attempt to protect the public. The debate over controlling weapons is frequently conducted in congress and during presidential elections.

It is indisputable that President George W. Bush is far less inclined to propose or support further gun control. Instead, he favours stronger penalties against criminals. When he was governor of Texas he supported the state's highly controversial law that allows residents to carry concealed guns, ostensibly for protection. In other states, guns are licensed to be kept in the home for self-defence.

Certainly the NRA favoured President Bush in the 2000 presidential campaign, spending $10 million in advertising and political donations to defeat his opponent Al Gore. To complicate matters, states each pass their own firearm laws in addition to Federal regulation.

The crime bill passed in 1994 banned the manufacture and sale of guns classed as assault weapons, that is, semi-automatic rifles like AK47's. But observers say that as 83% of violent crime involves handguns, which are not touched by the law, it had limited effect. For all the power of the gun lobby, there are signs that Americans are getting sick of the ubiquity of firearms in their society. The terrible spate of playground and mass public shootings in recent years when schoolchildren brought weapons of war to the classroom (not by any means an exclusively American phenomenon), has woken many people to the fact that guns mean less rather than more freedom.

More recently, municipalities and crime victim groups have begun lawsuits to place responsibility for gun crime on the manufacturers. On their part, the gun makers have frequently counter-sued, arguing that their opponents are trying to interfere with free enterprise.

Other new government measures include millions of dollars for more police, but as the most violent cities (Detroit and Washington) already have huge police forces, that does not seem to be the answer either.

For a great number of its citizens America is a deadly place to live, more so than many other countries in the world. Many cities are still plagued by high rates of violent crime, often caused by turf wars among drug dealers or gangs. Having said that, it's important to keep this in perspective. Not all cities share the same crime rates and urban neighborhoods vary as they do in the rest of the world.

The most violent and crime-ridden cities are often not the ones that foreigners would go to: Odessa, Texas, is more dangerous than Miami or New York City, for example, which often feels far safer than London owing to the fact that almost unlike anywhere else in the world the city is open for business around the clock. In Manhattan, you will frequently see people walking on the streets at four in the morning past shops and restaurants that have been open all night. But in other newer cities, largely planned for the age of the car, middle class professionals have frequently left 'downtown' for the suburbs. A new trend too is for developers to build and maintain 'gated communities' which all visitors have to enter through a permanent security post.

Some cities have gained from urban renewal and improved policing. Most notably, New York has famously experienced a dramatic decline in violent crime over the past decade. Some commentators have attributed this to higher police numbers and former Mayor Guiliani's policy of 'zero tolerance'. But this approach to urban policing remains controversial. New York police during this time have often been accused of brutality particularly against minorities and there have been several instances of individuals being inexplicably gunned down or seriously injured in custody.

Most murders happen within the family or within groups that know each other. They also happen in areas that it is not easy to stray into by mistake. There are parts of every city in which it is dangerous to walk, and it is a relatively simple matter to find out what those parts are. This does not mean that you have to be paranoid: the New York subway is marginally less populated at night but precisely because it operates a 24-hour service, you need never be alone on a station platform or in a carriage.

> Unfortunately, many big American cities suffer from high levels of drug related crime which make certain districts dangerous to travel through let alone visit. But the best advice is to use your common sense. If you stray into an area that looks seriously run down and abandoned then it may well not be a safe place. Likewise it's sensible not to walk in dark areas at night.

Listen to what people tell you about an area. A park might look charming and tranquil, but if the guidebook or a local tells you that it is unsafe, take their advice. It will take a long time to get to know an area well enough to make your own decisions. When driving, do not allow anyone except a policeman to flag you down. In cities, keep all car doors locked.

The most likely thing that will happen to you, if you do not take proper precautions, is that you will fall victim to a pick-pocket or bag-snatcher. The way to avoid this is to use your common sense: don't let your handbag swing ostentatiously on your shoulder, don't count your money in public, don't look too much like a tourist, ambling around appearing lost and wearing a camera around your neck! Those most likely to be robbed or mugged are those who appear vulnerable: don't stop on the street to peer at a map, or hurry along in a panic. Walk with purpose.

An increasingly popular movement across America is BAMM – Bay Area Model Mugging (www.bamm.org). Started in California, it teaches women full-contact self defence against attacks, and goes against the prevalent myth that women are generally too weak to withstand a male attacker. You are taught not only how to fight back, but also how to observe your environment, prevent negative encounters, use your voice to attract attention, and gauge the weaknesses of your attacker. In short, it teaches you how not to be – or seem to be – a victim.

In the *Traveller's Survival Kit USA and Canada*, published by Vacation Work, you will find advice on how to limit the dangers of mugging. In short: always carry $50-$100 'mugger money'; if threatened, don't try to resist or make sudden movements – your attacker will be extremely wound up and will not hesitate to use his weapon if panicked; direct his hand to your wallet or purse; stay absolutely still until you are sure he has gone; flag down a cab and go straight to a police station; collect the number of the police report to facilitate your insurance claim, and ask for a lift home.

The Police

There are four main law enforcement agencies in the USA: city police, state police, the National Guard and the Federal Bureau of Investigation (the FBI, the 'Feds'). The state police (also known as state troopers) operate the highway patrol, the National Guard are civilian reservists who are called up to deal with civil disturbances (one-time Vice President Dan Quayle was, notoriously, a member of the National Guard during the Vietnam war, which some say was a form of draft dodging). The FBI deals with major crime and offences across state borders.

You are most likely to come into contact with the city police if you are mugged, or if you are caught jaywalking (crossing the road on a 'Don't Walk' signal). The state police are responsible if you break down, or are caught speeding. Needless to say the police will not accept ignorance of the law in mitigation of a traffic violation, or other misdemeanour. The law varies from state to state and from city to city, and it is important to be familiar with any peculiarities of the area you are living in. In some very popular tourist towns, special laws are reactivated every summer in order to cope with the artificially high population: you might find yourself up against summer drinking laws, or laws covering large gatherings, without realising it.

SOCIAL LIFE

'America is more like a world than a country'. Martin Amis

There is nothing typical about America or Americans. The sheer size and diversity of the continent's fifty states makes it difficult to draw any conclusions, and generalisations are always misleading.

Everything about America is unexpected, the more so to European eyes even though they have been brought up on a diet of Americana – films, TV, Marvel comics, fast food. They expect to understand, to recognise, and are all the more surprised when nothing is as they thought.

People from Britain in particular do not expect America to seem foreign, yet it is. Everybody speaks English, and the assumption is made that with the common tongue comes all the rest: people must think the same because they speak the same. One of the great delights of travelling in America is that you are always surprised when you expect not to be. San Francisco? Roller-coaster streets, clapboard houses and trams ... Dallas? No problem – oil wells and bootlace ties, steer horns on the fender and a gun rack in the cab... New York? Easy – subways and cops, foul-mouthed cabbies and Huggy Bear on every corner...

The fact that all this actually exists delights the traveller, but what is really interesting is the fact that America is truly foreign. If we think we know America we do not know the reality of it: the size of the country, the smells, the variety of the people. You realise you are in another country as soon as you step off the plane, but it is brought home to you with a jolt when you order a glass of water in a Pizza Hut in LA, and the waitress says 'What?' 'Er, water please' you repeat, at which she looks at you with scorn and incomprehension. Only after several repetitions do you understand that you must pronounce it 'wahder'. Without the hint of a smile she turns her back as you run a nervous finger under your collar. The barriers of a common language.

In a country of 286 million inhabitants spread over a land mass into which Britain would fit like a small piece of jigsaw, we should expect to find some variation in the way people lead their lives. The differences between Los Angeles and New York can be greater than those between London and Paris – after all, they are many times further away from each other, and are separated by several time zones.

Los Angeles, a vast conurbation of 13.5 million people, is spread out in a series of satellite communities, connected by 750 miles (1,207 km) of freeway, in a 70-mile (112-km) wide basin between the Pacific and the mountains. The city basks in an almost constant temperature of 68° F (20° C). New York, by contrast, is more familiar. The climate is harsh in winter and steamy in summer, but at least it changes. The city has a subway, and its people move around on foot. The country around New York, with its wooded hills and gorgeous autumn colours, is similar to a lot of Britain.

Between these two ends of the country lies a world. If you drive from the west coast to the east you pass through four time zones, and cover nearly 3,000 miles (4,828 km). You may drive for hundreds of miles without seeing another car, and come across towns that are separated from their neighbours by a three-hour drive. Within this continent live people as diverse as the Texans, who still fly the confederate flag and call themselves the Lone Star State, liking to think that they are not quite a part of the union, and the Amish of Pennsylvania, who shun the 20th century in all its forms.

To attempt to describe the social life or customs of such a continent is difficult. Besides, there are several books on the subject already. What follows are at best generalisations, but should give a flavour of the country.

Manners, Customs and Social Attitudes

America is a nation of immigrants. Vast numbers of Americans arrived, and are still arriving, as refugees, 'huddled masses yearning to be free'. Many, even those who of the second, third and fourth generation, feel rootless. When they set foot in a new environment they make themselves at home as quickly as possible. In every town there is a civil society or social club of some sort:

the Rotary, the Kiwis, the Elks, the Lions, the Jaycees, the Parent-Teachers Association, The Junior League, the Garden Club, the Shriners. These (especially the last) are often an excuse for men to get together and throw bread at each other in restaurants, and play silly practical jokes, but they are also ready-made societies that are instantly recognisable. In a new town you are unlikely to be lonely, with so many formal and informal organisations ready to welcome you.

There are two conflicting sides to the American character: on the one hand they are fiercely individualistic, but on the other they place great value on being a team player. To Americans the British are stuffy, tweedy, polite, but they themselves have rigid sets of rules. One of the great myths about Americans is that they do not stand on ceremony, unlike the British, who are obsessed with protocol. Americans, however, can be very formal. You may go to a dinner party and find that your neighbour quietly stops you in mid-flow because the host is saying something and it is rude to talk at the same time. You may go to a party in California and find that although everybody is getting gently and gaseously drunk on watery beer, when you light a cigarette it is regarded as the height of bad manners. Always expect the unexpected, and take your cue from what others are doing.

Americans have a reputation for spontaneity and openness. An English couple at a party in New York said that they were going into New England to see the fall, and were amazed when another couple who they did not know offered them their house to stay in. They did stay there, and it transformed their holiday. To meet people as friendly as that is common, but it is equally common to meet the reverse side of that particular coin, and to assume that because everybody addresses you as an old friend they can be called upon to behave that way. When dealing with American manners, remember that the shared language might lead you to take things for granted, that you would not do if you were in France or Germany.

Making Friends

This shifting population is romanticised in literature and films – see Kerouac's *On The Road*, and hundreds of road movies. So there's an enduring appeal in the idea that moving on holds the promise of a better life. The average American moves once every four or five years, and companies often relocate their employees every two years. Professionals accept the fact that to progress in a country the size of a continent that they may need to relocate frequently and across great distances. Many employers, especially the large ones with offices across the nation, make every effort to make relocation attractive. There will be company social clubs and special events within firms so that new arrivals can meet their co-workers. Local communities are also active in helping new arrivals meet 'the neighbors' and will invite them into local homes. Culturally,

Americans invite participation. This might involve joining the Parent Teacher Associations (PTAs) or attending events organised by local churches, women's groups or joining a local golf/tennis/ country club.

Students, for example, will move far from their home towns and states to study at good colleges. Having made a circle of college friends they might on graduation need to move again thousands of miles from their friends. So Americans expect to relocate and are used to making new friends. Frankly, this social fluidity is often a welcome relief from the formalities and strictures of European social interaction. If you attend a party in the US, particularly if you're new to your area, people will show a genuine interest. They will ask all about you and your family with a genuine interest. At times it may seem pushy to the more reserved European, but it does usually demonstrate a spontaneous hospitality.

In general, it is much more common to be invited into someone's home, and on a much shorter acquaintance than it is in Britain.

> **Anthony Goodman found Americans to be incredibly welcoming to new neighbours**
> *When we arrived we were showered with homemade cookies and invitations to visit. Having previously lived in London in apartments where you didn't really even know the people living below you, this was very supportive.*

To outsiders Americans have a reputation for forming superficial friendships, but this reflects an eagerness to expand their social circle and contacts with greater ease than many British people. As an expat you should expect though to spend a year or more finding compatible people with whom you can form close friendships.

> **Philip Jones also made friends easily**
> *Americans are amazingly friendly and generous. They have traditionally loved the Brits and are very welcoming. There are also an enormous number of English people in the States. That has always been the case but it is even more true now. It is hard to go anywhere in New York now and not hear English accents.*

For British people in the US, to communicate with and find other expats, you might want to take out a subscription to *Union Jack* (PO Box 1823, La Mesa, CA 91944; ☎619-466 3129; e-mail ujnews@ujnews.com; www.ujnews.com), a national newspaper published for Brits in the US (subscriptions $30 for 12 issues). The paper lists adverts for clubs, immigration lawyers, and shippers, and publishes news about the UK.

FOOD AND DRINK

'Pigs in a blanket, sixty-nine cents. Eggs roll'em over and a package of Kents.'
Tom Waits

Apple pie, clam chowder, Louisiana gumbo, jambalaya, enchiladas, barbecued oysters, corn fritters, strawberry shortcake, pastrami, rye bread. Beefburgers, Coca Cola, thick shakes. Every regional delicacy has its alter ego: for all the delicious dishes that 200 years of immigration have contributed to the country, there is a bland, mass-produced, cholesterol-rich quickie.

The American palate is not very brave, and everyday food tends to be tasteless and\or sweet. It is actually possible to be served M&Ms as an appetiser, and huge and sickly desserts are common. For all this there is a grand tradition of American food. In a country which is populated by Irish, Poles, Jews, Germans, Ukrainians, Chinese, French, Japanese, Thais, Vietnamese, Mexicans, English, Indians, Russians (and so on until you have named just about every nation on earth), diversity in dishes could be expected. Wherever you go in the States you will find regional dishes.

In much of Europe, and especially in Britain, this tradition has been lost. But sampling regional delicacies is one of the joys of a trip through America. The gumbo (okra soup) that you get in Louisiana really is the best, and the New England clam chowder is a reflection of the region's outstanding seafood. Cal-Mex and Tex-Mex are hybrids of American produce and traditional Mexican cooking which is much spicier than the usual American diet. But it is possible to eat well in the restaurants of large cities as increasing affluence has prompted an interest in cookery from around the world. Other areas of the country specialise in local produce.

Many scientists believe there is more obesity in America than in any other nation because of a genetic imbalance. But it could also be because of the amount they eat. In a restaurant, it is impossible to order a small portion. If, wishing to take the edge off your hunger, you order the small salad, you can be sure that it will come garnished with whole quarters of watermelon and an entire lettuce. French bread rolls are aptly called 'submarines'.

Typically, American meals are straightforward. Breakfast consists of cereal and coffee, lunch of a sandwich, and supper of meat and two veg. Eateries and diners line every strip of highway from New York to San Francisco. There are 'family restaurants' which cater for whole families, and in every state the restaurants serve the local cuisine. In the midwest and Texas beef features prominently, and fish and seafood can be found in towns along the coast lines of Florida, Louisiana, New England and California. In the South, soul food – grits, cornbread, beans – can be delicious. Mexican restaurants are ubiquitous, as are Chinese and Italian. In contrast to much of Europe, Indian food (that is, from the subcontinent) is quite hard to come by.

There is one culinary tradition that is done so well that to miss it is to miss one of the greatest pleasures that the country can offer. Ask an American expatriate what they miss most about living abroad, and they will talk about waffles, and maple syrup, and eggs roll'em over, and grits, and sourdough bread. Brunch is a great American tradition, a breakfast usually taken late in the morning on a weekend and so vast that lunch is unnecessary. Many restaurants and hotels will serve brunch, encompassing elaborate buffets of cereals, fruit, eggs, meats, and pancakes. Americans will try to make you understand, with the peculiar pride that people have in the seemingly trivial old traditions, that their breakfast cannot be beaten. It is true.

Tipping. Rightly or wrongly, waiting staff depend on tips for much of their earnings. You should always tip at least 15% in an American restaurant, and if the service is particularly good, 20%. If you undertip, it is more than likely that the waiter will ask, quite politely, if there was any problem with the meal. On the whole, service in restaurants far exceeds that of Europe. The US has cultivated a culture of service and 'the customer is king'. It's rare to meet a surly waiter or waitress who exudes resentment. In most diners, for example, you'll meet an effusively sunny Cheryl or Diane (names are often worn on badges) who greets you like a long lost friend. They really work for their tip and they depend upon them. It's important to reward their efforts particularly if you are going to be living in that community and plan to be a regular customer. In New York State, local sales tax (includes state and municipality levies) is 8½% and diners simply double the tax which is usually the last figure on a bill before the final sum.

Alcohol

Roadside bars are exciting: dark and forbidding, with one or two truckers sitting morosely at the end of a long bar, a pool table, and a person serving who is at best suspicious, at worst hostile. If you go into one on a bright day you walk into darkness, and peer about for a while before you locate the bar. They are everything we expect from America. But the beer (and don't share these feelings with the barman) is typically weak: Coors, Miller or Budweiser. A new development is the microbrewery, or brewpub, where the beer is brewed on the premises and is often excellent.

If you are under 21, you cannot drink in bars in America. Bar staff work by the rule of thumb that you must *look* at least 25 if they are going to serve you without an ID. Whenever you go out, take identification with you. A photocopy of your passport is often not sufficient, as bars are used to underage drinkers trying to pass off photocopies of their brothers' ID cards as their own.

Liquor laws vary from state to state, and affect such things as when and where you can drink or buy alcohol. In some states, mostly in the south and southwest, different counties have different policies: you may find that one county is dry or alcohol-free while the bars in the neighbouring county are raucous. Alcohol is completely banned on many Native American reservations.

As a general rule, bars may open some time between 9am and noon, and close between midnight and 3am. In many states you will find alcohol is forbidden on Sundays.

The neighbourhood pub hardly exists in America, except in places like California and Florida where British expats live, and pubs with names like 'The Cock and Bull' cater for their nostalgic yearnings. Instead there is a multitude of bars, seedy or romantic, according to your state of mind. There will almost always be a pinball machine, and a pool table. They can be very lively places, with a good mix of different types of people (although the men usually outnumber the women by a large margin). There are also cocktail lounges, much more genteel affairs, where your drink will be put on a little paper doily and the conversation, and music, is muted. You will be served by a waiter, and pay when you leave. A tip will be expected. Singles bars are a variation on the same theme: Americans tend to be more open about their relationships than Europeans, and consequently frequent such places in a much more phlegmatic frame of mind.

In bars and restaurants beer is sold by the glass, can or bottle in 12 fl oz measures, costing around $2.50, but this depends naturally on whether you're stopping in a roadside saloon or in a swanky Manhattan cocktail lounge. In most bars you can also buy a pitcher of draught beer, considerably cheaper than buying by the glass. Spirits are sold in measures which are approximately double the English optic measure, for around $2. The most popular whisky is Bourbon (Jack Daniels, Jim Beam or Wild Turkey), but scotch can be found in most places. The best scotch and malt whiskies (like Johnnie Walker Black Label, or Glenfiddich), can be twice as expensive than they are in Europe. Vodka and gin are also popular. Bear in mind that American spirits are generally much stronger than they are in the UK (80% or 90% proof rather than 70%).

ENTERTAINMENT AND CULTURE

Theatre

New York is the heart of American theatre and its centre is known across the world as 'Broadway,' which invented the modern musical as we know it today. Broadway roughly corresponds with London's West End and where you will find all the most successful shows, many of which are the highly successful musicals which have originated in London over the past 20 years.

The smaller and often more experimental theatres are known as 'Off-Broadway' where you will find more company based and ensemble theatres. The smallest theatres on the fringe, often fifty-seat studios are known collectively as 'Off-off Broadway.'

Take a credit card for booking: the most comprehensive listings are in the Sunday *New York Times* (www.nytimes.com), *New York magazine* (www.newyorkmetro.com), the *Village Voice* (www.villagevoice.com), the *New Yorker* (www.newyorker.com), and *Time Out New York* (www.timeoutny.com). There is also a telephone listings service, New York City on Stage (☎212-768 1818).

There are free summer shows at Shakespeare in the Park in the Delacorte Theater in Central Park. In the big cities you will find the best Broadway shows in the larger theatres, and smaller theatres putting on a selection of fringe shows. Some cities like Chicago, Boston and San Francisco have particularly active and critically successful theatres. Contact the local tourist office or chamber of commerce for details.

Prices on Broadway can be high, often as much as $100 for the best seats. Elsewhere, tickets are more affordable, and you can buy unsold (standby) tickets half-price on the day of performance. This is usually cash only. The best place to buy cut price tickets for both Broadway and Off-Broadway shows is the TKTS booth on Times Square or Bowling Green Park near Wall Street. Each day at 11am unsold theatre tickets go on sale for 25% to 50% less than the normal price. You may need to queue but it's the best way of seeing a show for far less. Bear in mind too that the booths only take cash or traveller's checks. For updated daily information ☎212-221 0013.

Classical Music, Opera and Ballet

Some of the most famous companies in the world are based in the United States, where corporate sponsorship of classical music, opera and ballet is as common as it is in Europe. In New York, the Lincoln Center is home to some of the world's leading performing arts organisations: the New York Philharmonic, the Metropolitan Opera, The New York City Opera, the New York City Ballet and the American Ballet. The Center has several auditoria: the Metropolitan Opera House (the Met), Avery Fisher Hall and the Alice Tully Hall. The great American orchestras are in Boston (the Boston Symphony's classical season, The Boston Pops, takes place from mid-May to mid-July), Chicago, Cleveland, New York and Philadelphia. The leading opera companies include Boston, Chicago, New York, San Francisco, Santa Fe and Seattle. The San Francisco Opera is the oldest major company in the west; the San Francisco Ballet (which is more than 60 years old) and the San Francisco Symphony are equally distinguished companies. The country's famous ballet companies are the New York City Ballet, the American Ballet, the Joffrey Ballet (New York and San Francisco), the National Ballet in Washington and the Pittsburgh and Philadelphia Ballet Companies.

Prices are as high as you would expect for major establishment performing arts: a ticket to the opera or ballet in the big cities costs between $50 and $200. However, although standard prices are high, tickets are often subsidised, and some performances can be seen for as little as $30. Standing tickets at around $10 are sold at some of the big venues like the Met in New York. Concerts and performances are of course not limited to the major halls: in every large city there are hundreds of smaller and more intimate venues with correspondingly cheaper seats.

In the summer the New York Philharmonic gives free performances in Central Park, and outdoor classical concerts are held in many venues across the country, including the Hollywood Bowl in Los Angeles.

> **John Philip Jones found a healthy cultural life away from the big cities**
> Syracuse offers an extremely rich cultural life, with opera, a symphony orchestra, and world-class chamber music. It also has a good theatre. New York City is not too far away (five-hour drive!).

Cinema

Hollywood dominates in America just as it does in the rest of the world. Tickets cost from $8 to $12, usually bookable by credit card. In New York there is a special cinema hotline (777-FILM), with details of screenings around the state.

Cinemas are usually classed as 'First-Run', or 'Revival and Art House': the former are everywhere and the latter can be found in most big cities. One of the great symbols of America – the drive-in movie – has sadly lost out to the video. But some people are nostalgic for their youth and are renovating drive-ins. They are still few and far between, although if you ask around you may find one not too far away. Enthusiasts should check out some of the devotees' websites. A particularly good one (at the time of writing) is the Drive-In Theater Guide at www.driveintheatre.com

Small towns have multi-screen complexes which show all the latest releases: it is difficult to find anything remotely art-house or avant-garde outside the big cities.

Films are classified G (general audience), PG (parental guidance), PG-13 (parents strongly cautioned, some scenes may be unsuitable for children under 13), R (no children under 17 unaccompanied by an adult), and NC-17 (no children under 17).

Gambling

Americans have a strangely ambivalent attitude towards gambling. It is illegal in most of the country, yet they spend $650 billion a year on legal gambling with a further $380 billion wagered illegally on sporting contests, more than on cinemas and sport combined. Although gambling is banned in most states, gambling cities such as Las Vegas, Nevada and Atlantic City, New Jersey, and some Native American reservations, which are exempt from state laws, make up for the lack of opportunity elsewhere. Nevada's state revenue depends on gambling, as did the revenue of the Mafia, although recently the Mob – or what remains of it – is turning elsewhere for funds, and legitimate companies are buying up and building casinos.

In a place like Las Vegas ('Armageddon in neon', as it's been dubbed) it is difficult to resist at least a flutter, and often as difficult to stop. The main clientele of the big casinos is as far from sophisticated as it is possible to be: housewives, with shopping baskets full of quarters, feeding the slot machines, their husbands at the roulette tables. Casino owners recognise that it is essential that gambling is not perceived as seedy or in any way disreputable, or the ordinary punters – those who would otherwise be sunning themselves in Florida, and on whose endless supply of small change the business relies – would stay away. Although in many casinos the drinks are free, and the layout is designed for maximum disorientation to make it as difficult as possible to leave, children are allowed and a family atmosphere is encouraged.

As well as casino gambling, there are state lotteries and, of course, the horses. Horse racing is mostly limited to flat racing, and off-track betting is illegal in all but three states: Connecticut, New York and Nevada. All betting is based on the totalisator (tote) system, where the total amount placed is divided among the winners. Bets are placed to win, place (come second), or show (third). An each way bet is the same as in the UK: first, second or third. For listings and a guide to form, buy *Daily Racing Form* which can also be viewed at www.drf.com.

Museums

America has some of the best museums in the world, usually very well-presented, informative and very interesting. Museums like the Metropolitan in New York, the National Gallery in Washington, and the Getty in Los Angeles have outstanding collections on a level with the great collections of Europe. But in the US these collections were built up and then donated by families which grew enormously wealthy on commodities and services like oil, steel, or banking in the 19th century. Most large cities like Boston, Chicago, Philadelpia, Houston, and San Francisco also have superb collections of art and antiquities that can take days to view in their entirety, reflecting the wealth of the country and its diverse immigrant heritage. The Smithsonian Institution in Washington DC houses a range of separate museums dedicated to Space, Natural History, ancient civilizations and American history. Prices for normal museums range from $10 to $15. In the cities get hold of a local newspaper for listings.

Living museums are one of the things that Americans do particularly well. Every state has its particular piece of history which it wants to preserve, and often it is done in typically grandiose style, in the form of a living museum. All over the country historical towns, battlefields, houses of the famous, and landmarks are preserved and in some cases rebuilt. Some of the best known are Colonial Williamsburg in Virginia, an entire 17th century town preserved (and recreated), Dearborn in Michigan, Sturbridge Massachusetts, Mystic Connecticut, and the seaports of New York and Baltimore. Presidential libraries like the Kennedy Library in Boston and the Reagan Library outside Los Angeles are popular tourist sites as they commemorate both the achievements of individual presidents and also particular eras of American history.

These are always well worth a visit, but are unfortunately very expensive as tickets can be as much as $20 for one person: to take a family, and pay for all the souvenirs that your children will demand, can be a chastening experience.

Sport

Baseball. Baseball is the great American unifier. More than football, baseball is the sport that most regard as quintessentially American. Every major city has a nationally competing team, and every county has a league. Fathers tutor their sons early in the mysteries of the game: they like to see it as more than a game, as preparation for life, learning to be a team player. Just as the British have any number of cricketing metaphors, Americans talk about 'ballpark figures' (a very rough estimate) and have expressions like 'three strikes and you're out', referring to the number of criminal convictions that you are allowed before you are locked up for good. An outing to a baseball game is a highly recommended way to immerse yourself in authentic American culture. You'll eat popcorn and hot dogs while watching a game among an enthusiastic crowd of families with little of the aggression sometimes found in European soccer stadiums. There's even an organ to build up the excitement. One advantage to baseball is that it is much quicker than cricket and does not last longer than a few hours.

The rules of baseball are very similar to rounders: teams win by scoring a number of runs around a circular pitch. 'Hitters' are given three attempts ('strikes') at balls thrown by a pitcher, (who pitches from the 'mound') and run as far as they can round the pitch – but at least to first base – without being struck out. A home run is when the hitter runs all the way round without stopping.

There are two main leagues, the National and the American. Each team plays 162 games a year – five times a week – in the spring and summer, leading up to the World Series in the Fall, which is played between the winner of each league. Although it is called the World Series, Canadian teams are the only ones from outside the US to participate.

There are more than 6,000 baseball themed books in print. As a starting point try *The Official Encyclopaedia of Major League Baseball* (Ed. John Thorn). Try also *The Great American Novel* by Philip Roth.

Football. In fall and winter, football is played. Americans call European football 'soccer', and the football that they play more closely resembles rugby.

To most Europeans, American football is as incomprehensible as cricket is to Americans. It has the same amazingly well-informed following and draws the same eccentric fans (Richard Nixon said that if he hadn't gone into politics he would have been a pro-football commentator, and was by all accounts an expert in the game). There are stupendous amounts of money to be made, and one of the major breeding grounds is the college football league played in the summer. Many colleges will recruit promising players in the hope that they will nurture a future star.

In football, an egg-shaped ball has to be thrown and caught over a line to score a goal. That is the point, but like all games it becomes more complicated the more the game is studied. What baffles foreigners is the endless parlaying on the pitch, and the set moves that seem to take away all spontaneity. One of the most important (and highest paid) players is the quarterback, on whom most of the set moves depend. It is his job to throw the ball an immensely long distance, after it has been passed to him in a series of preordained moves. The other members of the team take out their opposite number, again in a predetermined fashion. Teams spend days watching and rewatching their own and their opponents' moves on video to try to spot weak points.

Teams play 16 games throughout the fall and winter, on Sunday and Monday evenings, culminating in the Superbowl in January. This is watched by men at home, eating snacks, drinking beer, and throwing popcorn at the screen. One drawback for a sport is the fact that the player's faces are hidden by visored helmets which obscures the human drama of their emotions from the spectators.

Other Sports. Other important American sports are basketball and ice hockey, played in indoor arenas throughout the United States. Like some football and baseball players, basketball stars can achieve fabulous wealth and superstar status.

Soccer is becoming increasingly popular, especially among schoolchildren. The resounding success of America's hosting of the 1994 World Cup and their team's passionate performance in France in 1998, has boosted the game's ratings. Although it is unlikely ever to gain recognition as a national sport, more than 11 million Americans now play soccer regularly, and there are plans to begin a new national league.

Cricket, sadly, has less chance of finding a place in America's heart. For those Brits who cannot bear to miss the thwack of leather on willow, and who get dewy-eyed at the thought of the shadows lengthening on the village green, the West Indian community in New York plays 12 games every weekend in summer in Van Cortland Park, and on Staten Island there are frequent games between the British and the West Indians.

Amateur Sports. Americans take their sport very seriously, never more so than when it is amateur. Hunting, shooting and fishing, tennis and golf, are all extremely popular. By 'hunting' the Americans mean taking a rifle and shooting birds and\or other animals. They do not mean foxhunting, which is regarded as an English aberration, and is practised only in Virginia, Maryland and other parts of New England. In America, riding to hounds is certainly an elitist occupation, but other forms of hunting are followed by all income groups.

Tennis and golf, in a country where land is plentiful and relatively cheap, can also be played by those without huge incomes. There are public courses and clubs, which will allow anyone to play cheaply, and will not reject you if you are a woman or went to the wrong sort of school.

Camping and Hiking. These are also very popular pastimes. Contact the National Parks Service in Washington DC for details of parks and the best times of year to go. You can also look for campsites in each state and make reservations at www.reserveamerica.com.

Festivals

There are events and festivals happening all the time in the United States, from the Mardi Gras in the two weeks before Shrove Tuesday in New Orleans to state fairs in the summer and 4th July Independence Day celebrations in every town, large and small, in the land.

The following is a brief list of some of the main festivals around the US. Nothing is more galling than to arrive in a place only to discover that the most exciting festival of the year has just ended: it is well worth checking with State Tourist offices before you go travelling so that you can plan your route accordingly.

February

Daytona 500, Daytona Beach, FL; www.daytona500.com. The most famous stock car race in the world. Book accommodation at least six months in advance.

May

Indianapolis 500, Indianapolis, IN. A month-long festival of events leading up to the famous car race.

June

A Taste of Chicago, Chicago, IL. A gigantic food festival that takes place in June and July, serving food from the city's restaurants to some four million people; ☎ 312-744 3315.

July

Boston Pops Fourth of July Concert, Boston, MA. One of the thousands of Independence Day events: can be particularly moving.

Kutztown Folk Festival, Kutztown, PA. A celebration of the culture of the Pennsylvania Dutch; ☎610-638 8707.

Cheyenne Frontier Days, Cheyenne, WY. The biggest rodeo event in the world: the last full week in July.

August

State agricultural fairs take place in almost every state, usually in August. The biggest are in Wisconsin, Milwaukee (early August), Illinois (Springfield, early August), Minnesota (St Paul, last week in August, first week in September).

Burning Man, Black Rock Desert, NV; www.burningman.com. A festival dedicated to alternative performance and art which transforms the desert into a temporary city of 25, 000.

September

Pioneer Days, Fort Worth, TX. Good ole boys in western-style celebrations in the stockyards. Three days in late September.

Misissippi Delta Blues Festival, Greenville, MS. One of the biggest blues events in the country.

October

The State Fair of Dallas. The Dallas State Fair Park is a national monument, and this three-week extravaganza is held around and in it. Prize cattle, livestock and more good ole boys in the Lone Star State.

November

Macy's Thanksgiving Day Parade, New York City. Held annually on Thanksgiving Day, a parade of carnival animals, balloons and floats takes all day to pass through the 'canyons of Manhattan' from 86th Street and Central Park West to Macy's department store at 34th Street and 7th Avenue.

December

The National Christmas Tree Lighting/Pageant of Peace, Washington, DC. Annual festival that begins with the lighting of the presidential tree on the White House lawn, on the second Thursday in November, and is followed by nightly choral performances at the Ellipse

These are only a handful of festivals and events that take place across the United States every year from local village fairs to large events drawing hundreds of thousands of people from across the country. Visit www.festivalfinder.com for information about 2,500 music festivals across North America. Festivals.com is a guide to global festivals but provides extensive detail on events in each state of the US. There is also a list of every state tourism website.

SHOPS AND SHOPPING

America, the land of shopping malls and supermarkets, can still surprise visitors with its small, independent shops. True, these are mostly in the big cities, and the cosy street of shops in the small town has long gone, but shopping need not be the air-conditioned nightmare that we are led to believe. Wherever you shop, you will find that prices compare very well with Europe. Food, clothes, books, compact discs and electrical goods are all cheaper in the States.

One of the great charms of some cities, particularly New York and San Francisco, is how old-fashioned they are. Visitors are surprised by how small and interesting the streets are at ground level. It is worth walking around New York's Greenwich Village, or SoHo, or Haight-Ashbury in San Francisco, to see that America is not a land of soulless malls, but that it is easy to find excellent little shops, selling everything from T-shirts to walking sticks, if you only look for them.

As out-of-town shopping centres and high street arcades spring up all over the UK, the awesome power of the American shopping culture becomes less of a novelty. It is, still, an experience. It is no exaggeration to say that America is a shopper's paradise, (although paradise can mean many things to different tastes). Since the first 'Shopping and Entertainment Complex' opened in Bloomington, Minnesota in the 1950's, the shopping mall has become the American shopping experience personified. We are now used to malls in the UK, and so to describe one would be pointless. What you must be ready for, however, is that the biggest American malls are bigger, shinier, more air-conditioned, with more pervasive muzak and longer and quieter escalators, than anywhere in the world.

The best shopping is to be found on a handful of famous streets: Rodeo Drive in Beverly Hills, Lake Shore Drive in Chicago, Worth Avenue in Palm Beach, and 5th and Madison Avenues in Manhattan. It is an experience to walk down one of these streets and to feel, for once in your life, that you are sharing the same space with the truly rich. Of course, the dream is rudely shattered when you step into one of the shops and are treated with a certain coolness by the assistants, who can place you in an income bracket before the door has sighed shut behind you.

Shopping in small-town America has nearly disappeared, as huge out-of-town shopping centres have sucked all the custom away from downtown (the town centre), which has become a grey expanse of vacant lots and boarded-up shops.

The well-heeled residents have fled to the suburbs, leaving the poorest families to make what they can of it. This is a bleak picture, but it is happening all over the country.

Dedicated shoppers should not despair, however. The mall has its peculiar attractions, if only that you can buy anything you could possibly want under one (very big) roof. Shopaholics should head for the great department stores like Macy's or Bloomingdales in Manhattan, or Saks Fifth Avenue for big-name men's tailoring. In San Francisco Ghirardelli Square or the San Francisco Shopping Center combine shops, restaurants and 'entertainment'. For the biggest of them all, in the unlikely setting of South Dakota and attracting 20,000 tourists a day, Wall Drug combines drugstore, mall and museum of American eccentricity in one.

Factory shops ('outlets') are also popular, selling goods direct from the manufacturer at discounts of up to 70%. They are usually located outside city centres and may contain hundreds of different outlets under one roof. There is a comprehensive list of outlets at www.outletbound.com, which also publishes a paper guide listing 11,000 factory outlet stores in the USA and Canada (toll-free outlet info line 1-888-OULET-2).

For information on the big department stores have a look at their generally very good websites: www.sears.com, www.bloomingdales.com and www.walmart.com are just three.

Sales Tax

Nearly all states have a sales tax on goods sold, the equivalent of VAT on shopping in the UK. Both the state and the local municipality levy charges and in total the charge ranges from 4.5 to 9% depending on which state you are shopping in. Only Delaware, Montana, New Hampshire and Oregon do not impose a sales tax. Level of tax and exemptions vary on different items, and often cause strange anomalies between states: you might find that there is a lower tax on cigarettes in one state, in which case everyone from the neighbouring state will buy their cigarettes across the state line. Tax is often exempted on larger items that are going to be shipped out of the country: in tourist shops this will be standard.

TIME

Continental United States covers four main time zones: *Eastern Time* (the east coast as far as Michigan, Indiana, Georgia and Florida; *Central Time* (as far west as North Dakota and Texas), *Mountain Time* (south from Montana), and *Pacific Time* (the Pacific coast: Washington, Oregon, California and Nevada). Eastern time is five hours behind GMT, Central six hours behind, Mountain seven hours and Pacific eight hours. You will have to take account of time differences when calling within the States: remember that 9am in New York is 6am in California. The 24-hour clock is hardly ever used in timetables.

METRICATION

Petrol is measured in gallons, distances in miles, weights in pounds and ounces. The US gallon is smaller than the UK imperial gallon, pints can be dry or liquid, and the pound is the largest measure of weight: the average man weighs 168 pounds, never 12 stone. Clothing sizes also need clarification: they are all measured slightly larger than in Europe.

Metrication is slowly being adopted. Metric units – the International System (SI) – is being used to an increasing extent by industry, coordinated by the Office of Metric Programs. Complete conversion of industry is expected by the end of the century. US scientific language is almost entirely metric, and all public schools teach the metric system.

TABLE 10	CONVERSION TABLES	
US	**Imperial**	**metric**
1 dry pint	33.6 ounces	
1 liquid pint	0.8327 imp pint	
1 US gallon	0.8327 imp gallon	4.5 litres
1 short cwt	100 lbs	45 kg
1 short ton	2,000 lbs	
14 lbs	1 stone	6.4 kg
1 lb	1 lb	.45 kg
1 mile	1 mile	1.6 km

TABLE 11	TEMPERATURE

Farenheit	0	10	20	30	40	50	60	70	80	90	100
Celsius	−18	−12	−7	−1	4	10	16	21	27	32	38

Women's clothing sizes (men's sizes are identical in the USA and the UK)

UK	8	10	12	14	16	18
US		8	10	12	14	16
Europe	36	38	40	42	44	46

Shoe sizes

UK	3	4	5	6	7	8	9	10	11	12
US	5	6	7	8	9	10	11	12	13	14
Europe	36	37	38	39	40	41\42	43	44	45	46

PUBLIC HOLIDAYS

Holidays falling on a Sunday are usually taken on the following Monday; those falling on a Saturday are taken on the preceding Friday:

New Year's Day	1 January
Martin Luther King Day	3rd Monday in January
President's Day (Washington's Birthday)	3rd Monday in February
Memorial Day	Last Monday in May
Flag Day	14 June
Independence Day	4 July
Labor Day	1st Monday in September
Columbus Day	2nd Monday in October
Veteran's Day	11 November
Thanksgiving	4th Thursday in November (Friday usually taken as holiday as well)
Christmas	25 December

RETIREMENT

CHAPTER SUMMARY

- America can offer the retired person a gentle climate, low cost of living and a culture that is comparatively easy to adapt to.
- Florida and California are the most popular destinations for both Americans and non-Americans, but Arizona and Colorado are growing in importance.
- **Red tape.** US immigration laws are no easier on retired people than they are on anyone else: there are no special 'retirement visas'.
- Non US citizens without green cards will only be able to stay on temporary visas for periods of up to six months at a time.
- **Settling in.** Although there are few expatriate clubs in the US there are large numbers of other clubs and societies that can help you establish a social circle.

BACKGROUND INFORMATION

The United States has the most diverse landscape in the world, and the most varied climate. Several states have the perfect weather for those who like their sunshine gentle. Many retired people love the year-round blue skies of Florida or California with their constant temperatures and warm seas.

As well as the climate and the landscape, America offers a great variety of leisure activities. From the natural and dramatic beauty of the Grand Canyon, Monument Valley, or the redwood forests of northern California to the grand *kitsch* of Disneyland, everything for the tourist is done in style and (usually) with taste. Above all, Americans know how to build museums. They are expensive, but informative and interesting, and often very big. It is very difficult to be bored in the States.

Prices are generally lower than in Europe. A gallon of petrol is famously cheap, but all the consumer durables, cars, washing machines, electrical goods, clothes, property and many other goods are also very reasonably priced.

For the British retiree, another inestimable advantage to America is the common language. This is important for anybody moving to a new country, but doubly so if you are retiring, as you will probably be at an age when learning a new language would be an effort you can do without. For other Europeans, the fact that at some stage in her history America has taken in representatives of almost every race on earth, means that it is always possible to find a community from your own country.

There is one major disadvantage to America as a place to retire to: immigration laws. The zeal of the Immigration and Naturalization Service is discussed elsewhere, but it is important to mention here that America, unusually, has no special retirement category in its immigration laws. If you want to retire, you have to do so on one of the visas available to everyone: there are no special dispensations for the over 65s. This is all covered in detail in the body of the chapter. What it means is that unless you have a green card or are a US citizen, you will probably be able to stay in the country for only six months at a time.

This of course may be no great disadvantage. A lot of people will regard it as the perfect way to spend their retirement: six months in the sun, six months at home seeing the grandchildren. This need not be too expensive: because most people are in the same boat, the rental sector in popular retirement areas like Florida is geared towards six-month lets.

Visa categories change constantly, and there may well be a new retirement visa introduced in the future, or one which allows an eight-month stay, for example. Meanwhile, think of the advantages and enjoy your retirement.

The Decision to leave the UK

Unless you are marrying a US citizen, or already have citizenship or a green card, the decision to leave permanently need not be taken. For the reasons given above and in the following sections, the vast majority of retired foreigners in the United States spend only part of the year there. This makes life much easier. You need make no irreversible decisions about selling the house and moving wholesale to the other side of the Atlantic. It also gives you the opportunity to get to know the country and decide which state suits you best. When you are certain that you want to settle in the USA, you can take the necessary steps towards getting more permanent status. This is not easy, but it is a good deal easier if you know the country. The following sections give details of the various immigration options open to retirees.

RESIDENCE AND ENTRY REGULATIONS

There is no provision in federal immigration law for retired people. Unlike many other countries, anybody wishing to retire to the USA, with enough funds to support themselves, cannot do so on a special retirement visa. The regulations, as outlined in *Residence and Entry*, stand for anybody of any age who wishes to spend time in the United States.

However, retirees with $500,000 to invest can now take advantage of legislation, signed off in December 2003, which has created a retirement visa in all but name. The USCIS has redefined the EB-5 visa, called the Pilot Program, whereby EB-5 applicants may invest in a USCIS designated Regional Center and apply for a green card, issued to the applicant, spouse, and all children under the age of 21. Regional Centers offer 'immigrant investor programs' which are virtually passive investments, enabling you to genuinely retire, or for that matter, do anything you choose. Visa processing takes about a year and 21 months after entering the US you have three months to apply for removal of conditions after which the investment may be sold.

Without a green card or the funds for an EB-5 visa, it is impossible to legally spend more than six months of the year in the USA. One way to get round the problem is to use a B1 or B2 visa, for temporary visitors on business or pleasure, valid for six months at a time. These visas used to be valid indefinitely, but are now valid for ten-year periods. They allow multiple entry, so the holder can spend six months in the country, leave and return for another six months subject to the discretion of immigration at the port of entry. Opinion is divided as to whether it is a good idea simply to cross the border into Canada, Mexico or the Bahamas, and return immediately: the immigration authorities are increasingly denying entry if they suspect that you are using your visa to reside permanently in the USA. As a B visa holder you must retain a home outside the USA.

Some retirees decide that six months of the year is enough for them: they can spend the winter in America, and return home for the spring and summer. Those who are semi-retired may set up a company or buy an existing business (on an E-1 visa), or try for an intra-company transfer visa (an L-1). Both have advantages. The E visa is, potentially, renewable every five years as long as the business is maintained and you fulfil your obligation to employ a few US citizens. To qualify for an E-visa you need to have made an investment in your company in the States (usually of around $100,000 but you may have an application approved for less than that), to employ people (usually one or two but there is now lower limit), and to show that the business is profitable.

However, it should be noted that E-1 and E-2 visas have non-immigrant status, with no right to a green card. There will come a time when age or illness forces retirement and the visa will not be renewed. Any children emigrating under their parents E visa will not be eligible for free schooling and will lose their entitlement to remain in the US at age 21.

The L visa allows you to apply for a green card after two or three years and exempts you from a major step in the application process: that of labour certification (proving that your job cannot be done by an American). The disadvantage for those on the way to retirement is the work involved with starting a new business and the additional risk of doing so in an unfamiliar business environment. This applies to both E and L visa applicants.

There are two ways to qualify for an L visa. The first is to be transferred by your company to a branch, affiliate, subsidiary or joint venture in the USA. You must have been employed outside the USA for at least one of the past three years as a manager, executive or person with specialised knowledge. Another way of qualifying is to set up a branch, or sister company to a company that you already run in your own country: you will then have L visa status as an employee of the American side of the company. The two operations can be run in tandem until you are eligible to apply for a green card, and then the home country branch can be wound down, and you can retire on your resident's status. This sounds simple, but there are major pitfalls. It is essential to get professional advice to ensure that you are applying for the right visa for your status (see *Residence and Entry Regulations* for addresses of immigration lawyers).

POSSIBLE RETIREMENT AREAS

It is unlikely that you will be thinking of spending most of your retirement in America without some knowledge of the country and the advantages and disadvantages of the various states. The most important criteria are affordability (the cost of living in that state and the cost of property purchase or rental), climate, and the ease of getting there from your home country. Another consideration should be the numbers of fellow expatriates that you are likely to meet: most people would prefer to be somewhere with a sizable community from their own country.

There are few statistics available on the number of foreigners actually retiring to the United States. According to a survey from the American Association of Retired Persons, 52% of the country's older population – 16.2 million people – live in nine states. California, New York, Florida, Pennsylvania, Texas, Illinois, Ohio, Michigan and New Jersey all have more than one million people aged over 65.

The most popular states for expatriates of all nationalities, and for American retirees, are Florida and California. They have agreeable climates, affordable property, and Florida has the added advantage for foreigners of being readily accessible from Europe. Another advantage is that owing to its popularity as a holiday destination, flights are frequent and comparatively cheap. California's popularity is waning slightly, mainly because it is 3,000 miles further away from Europe. New York State and Massachusetts have always been popular, but the soaring price of property in these states has dissuaded a lot of people from buying there. Arizona and Colorado are attracting more foreigners: they are both in the early stages of rapid development, which means that property prices are low but the economy and facilities are getting better. A recent US survey found that they are the two most popular states for Americans to own a home, and observers say that many UK buyers are following suit.

One of the problems of retirement in the United States is that, without a specific 'retirement visa' there is no real community or club for retired foreigners. There are a few associations such as the Florida Brits Club (see below), which have been set up to bring expatriates together, but there is little specifically for retired expatriates. The last section in this chapter has some addresses of clubs and organisations for expatriates. This section outlines selected states that are popular with foreigners. Many of these people will be retired, and spending up to six months of the year in their second home. The descriptions cannot begin to be exhaustive: for more information see the *Regional Guide* in Chapter Six, *Employment*, or contact state chambers of commerce for real estate guides.

Florida

There are vast areas of Florida in the process of development, and as a result the state is being heavily advertised as the most desirable place to buy a home. Retirement developments are being sold at the moment, some with several golf courses attached. Florida is the main expatriate and retirement state, popular with Europeans as well as Canadians and Americans. It has the biggest concentration of over-65s (18%) in the country, and the smallest population of under-18s. Between 3,500 and 6,000 British people own second homes in Florida. This does not count the large number of people who rent their holiday home year after year. Being on the east coast, Florida is easily accessible from Europe, but it has a far warmer climate than the rest of the east coast states. One of the reasons for Florida's popularity is the number and variety of diversions: Disney World, the Everglades National Park, Universal Studios, the Kennedy Space Center, and hundreds of beaches. The area south of Orlando, Palm Coast and Amelia Island in the northeast of the state are the areas that attract the most British property buyers. Other popular areas are Naples (southwest), Newport and Sarasota on the central west coast. At the bottom of the range it is possible to find a three-bedroom freehold house with two bathrooms for $150,000 but prices can then go sky high depending on what you are looking for.

If you're looking for advice and information about becoming expatriates in the USA, The Florida Brits Group (18 Grange Close, Skelton, York YO30 1YR; ☎01904-471800; email FlaBritsCl@aol.com; www.FloridaBritsGroup.com) is a good place to start. Established in 1990, with a membership of more than 1,200 couples all of whom own holiday homes in the sunshine state of Florida. The group gives advice on buying and running holiday property in Florida and organises regular events in the UK for British homeowners. Membership is a one-time joining fee of £20 per couple. The group sells a Florida Homeowners Information Pack providing advice on wills, taxes, legal issues and rentals (price

£16.50, includes P&P). It also has good associations with business brokers in Florida and visa consultants in the UK to assist would-be emigrants source visa qualifying businesses for E2 visas. There are two publications which could be helpful: *The Complete Guide to Life in Florida* (International Property Magazine; ☎01708-450784); and *The Practical Guide to Florida Retirement*, Betty McGarry (Pineapple Press, Price $9.75).

Property Contacts

Florida Home Realty, 10200 State Road 84, Suite 107, Davie, FL 33324; ☎954-475 4860; e-mail info@floridahomerealty.com; www.arvidarealty.com.

Florida Property & Business Services LLC, PO Box 41, Chichester, West Sussex, PO20 1ND; ☎01243-536026; e-mail FloridaPBS@aol.com; www.FloridaPBSLLC.com. Accountants providing a service to property owners in Florida.

The World of Florida, St Ethelbert House, Ryelands Street, Hereford HR4 OLA; ☎01432-845645; fax 01432-845640; e-mail homes@worldofflorida.co.uk; www.worldofflorida.co.uk. Specialise in villas to buy and rent in Florida.

Colorado

This is one of the most beautiful states: 35% of it is given over to national parkland in some form. Colorado is in the process of development, and its economy is considered healthy. Along with Florida and Arizona it is one of the most popular states for expatriates. Fort Collins, in the north of the state, is an attractive part of the state, and is reported to be one of the fastest-growing communities in the USA. It has over 300 days sunshine a year, and is close to the Rocky Mountain National Park, Estes Park and the Poudre Valley, all of which have wonderful views. There are a number of developments springing up, and houses are reasonably priced: in Fort Collins a single mid-range family three-bedroom home will cost around $250,000. Of course, it's possible to find a cheaper home or one that costs far more. One of the great advantages of Colorado is the varied landscape and climate: although it has the highest average altitude of any of the states, and more famous-name ski resorts (among them Aspen and Vail) than any other state, it also attracts walkers and hikers in the summer. Developments around Fort Collins have facilities for golf, horse-riding and boating.

Arizona

Arizona has recently been at the top of the tables for activity in the homes market, with almost 30% more new sales, and for increases in employment. It is one of the boom states, with land being reclaimed from the desert and turned into new business parks at an unprecedented rate. Real estate prices are still reasonable: the price of an average new home in Scottsdale costs around $236,000. The cost of living is one of the lowest in the country: Phoenix, the largest city in the state, is an affordable place to live. Winter temperatures in the high 60s make Arizona a favourite with retirees, as does the famous scenery. But during summer, the desert setting is merciless as temperatures climb above 100° F (37° C) and make it unwise to spend any length of time outside an air-conditioned environment.

Arizona is the Grand Canyon State, and also has Monument Valley and some wonderful desert scenery. It is a prime tourist state: the Grand Canyon is one of the seven natural wonders of the world. Many property developers are concentrating on the Scottsdale/Phoenix area, where 'gated' communities are being built with secure entry, pools and sports facilities. They also have golf clubs, restaurants and shopping nearby.

California

The state that for many people sums up America has long been a mecca for sun-worshippers and those in search of a better quality of life. The climate hardly changes in California; apart from a few days of light rain in the spring, the sun smiles down on the reclaimed desert that makes up most of the south of the state – the most populated part. It is a popular retirement state, though less so with Europeans than with Americans. One of the best things about California is the variety of the landscape, which has everything from the high Sierra mountains to the desert: Death Valley is the lowest point in the country, 656 ft (200 m) below sea level. There are also the Redwood forests in the north, the vineyards of the Napa Valley, and the Pacific coastline which stretches the length of the state. The weather changes gear the further north you go: the climate of San Francisco is markedly cooler and wetter than Los Angeles. California's economy improved considerably in 2004 and residential construction increased again. A popular area is Santa Monica, 15 miles (25 km) west of downtown LA. It is near the sea, with all amenities, but with practically no public transport. The Santa Clarita Valley is a community development, appreciated by families. Another planned community is Westlake Village – Agoura Hills: the official real estate brochure for the area says the 'quality of life is enhanced by the relative serenity of ocean breezes'. In the San Francisco area Palo Alto is an old-fashioned community with trains to the centre; Los Altos is a dormitory town popular with foreigners because of its European appearance.

Texas

Another popular retirement state with Americans, Texas has a high standard of living, a healthy economy, and an excellent climate in the south. It is the second biggest state after Alaska, with relatively cheap real estate, although it is extremely difficult to find rental property. Because of many advantages, the state is attracting international companies, and the main expatriate population is a shifting one of workers and executives on temporary contracts and secondment. Galleria, west of Houston, is a mixed residential and business area with good access to shopping and recreational facilities. There are international schools in Houston and Memorial (a quiet, wealthy, tree-lined neighbourhood). Another popular area is Plano, separate and to the north of Dallas. It has lakes and reservoirs nearby for boating and fishing, and public transport is excellent.

PENSIONS

If you are living in the USA or visiting regularly, and you are entitled to a UK (or EU) state retirement pension, you will get the same rate as if you were in the UK, including all state pension increases. You should let your local Social Security office know your date of departure and your overseas address. When you return to your own country it is essential that you tell the relevant office that you are back. You can receive a retirement pension from both the USA and the UK (and EU) if you have enough insurance under each country's scheme to qualify you for a pension. The social security reciprocal agreement between the USA and most European countries will help you to receive a US pension if you do not have enough UK (or European) insurance. The normal system that operates is that if you have at least six quarters of insurance coverage (the equivalent of one and a half years full employment) in the USA, but you do not have enough to qualify for a US pension, the insurance that you have paid in the UK or Europe can be combined with your US insurance to help you qualify for a US pension. The amount of pension that you are entitled to will be calculated in your country of origin, based on the amount you would have earned if you had been paying insurance there all along.

This applies only to a basic retirement pension, not to state earnings related pensions and any occupational pensions. If you have a personal pension scheme in your own country this can be transferred to a US personal pension scheme by the insurance company that provides the scheme. The company has to make an application to the Inland Revenue Pension Schemes Office (or the appropriate office in your country) in order for the transfer to be approved, and then arrange for the scheme to be transferred across to a US insurance company. If you have been sent abroad by your company you should have been continuously covered by the company's occupational pension arrangements, which will enable you to build up rights towards your pension. Your employer will have made one of three arrangements for you: you may have remained in the home company pension scheme, transferred to your host company's scheme, or you have been transferred to an international offshore pension scheme. Depending on length of service, you should be entitled to draw your pension in the USA (see also *Taxation* in Chapter Four, *Daily Life*).

Widow's benefits can be paid in the same way as retirement pensions. If your husband was insured under both UK and US schemes, the same rules apply as for retirement pensions, above. If you are entitled to US Retirement or Disability Benefit, it may be reduced if you are drawing a UK retirement pension, under rules called the Windfall Elimination Provisions. However, these rules do not apply if you are drawing UK widow's benefits, so it may be worthwhile to continue drawing UK widow's benefits until you are 65, rather than claiming UK retirement pension at 60.

Regulations governing pensions are complicated, and you should get professional advice before deciding on any course of action. See *Useful Addresses* below.

Useful Addresses

When you contact the organisations below you should include your full name, date of birth, your UK national insurance number or pension number, and your US Social Security number.

HM Revenue & Customs (previously *Inland Revenue*), Pension Schemes Office; ☎0115-974 1777; www.inlandrevenue.gov.uk/pensionschemes.

Overseas Pension Service, Department for Works and Pensions, Tyneview Park, Whitley Road, Benton, Newcastle upon Tyne NE98 1BA; ☎0191-218 7777; www.thepensionservice.gov.uk. For information on the UK social security scheme.

United States Embassy, Federal Benefits Unit, 24 Grosvenor Square, London W1A 7AE; ☎020-7499 9000; fax 020-7495 7200; www.usembassy.org.uk. For information on the US social security scheme.

US Social Security Administration, Office of International Operations, 6401 Security Boulevard, Baltimore, MD 21235; ☎800-772 1213 (within the US); www.ssa.gov/international. For other enquiries regarding contributions in the US.

Taxation

Taxation is covered in detail in *Daily Life*. If your pension is being paid from the UK into a US bank account, if you are non-resident in the USA and are resident in the UK (for taxation purposes), your pension will be taxed at source by the local UK tax office, and paid to your US bank account net of tax (i.e. with the tax already deducted). If you are claiming exemption from UK taxes on the basis of non-residence in the UK, then your pension will be paid gross to your US bank account, and taxes will be deducted in the USA. Under present laws, 85% of your UK government social security income may be taxed, if it reaches levels of $30,000 to $40,000. It is important to understand also the tax treaties and totalisation agreements in force between the United States and the UK. Generally, if you are a non-resident of the USA and a resident of the

UK, even if you are spending six months of the year in the USA, these two agreements ensure that you do not have to pay income tax or social security in both countries. You should get the advice of a tax practitioner in order to make sure that you are paying the right amount of tax, and are not being penalised in both countries.

Useful Addresses

Chastang, Ferrell, Sims and Eiserman, Certified Public Accountants and Consultants, Fifth Third Center, 999 Vanderbilt Beach Road, Suite 601, FL 34108; ☎239-514 3782; fax 239-514 3783; e-mail info@cfseonline.com.

Expatriate Advisory Services, 14 Gordon Road, West Bridgeford, Nottingham NG2 5LN; ☎0115-981 6572; fax 0115-945 5076.

US Pensions

US retirement benefits are paid on a system of work credits, measured in three-month (quarter-year) units called quarters of coverage. In order to draw benefits you need to have a certain number of years' work to your credit. Retirement benefit is paid to workers at the age of 65. A reduced amount can be claimed as early as age 62. Your eligibility for state retirement benefits from your country of origin and from the USA is described above. Under reciprocal arrangements you may combine national insurance payments to make you eligible for a pension in either country. Generally, you will not be eligible for full US retirement benefits until you have worked in the country for 10 years.

Occupational (company) and personal pensions plans are similar to those available in much of Europe. Company tax deferred retirement plans are usually called 401(k) plans: you are allowed to invest a certain percentage (adjusted annually) of your income. Personal retirement plans, either an Individual Retirement Account (IRA), or a Keogh Retirement Plan for the self-employed, are also available, although they are not as widespread in the United States as they are in Europe. They are sold by most financial institutions, including banks, insurance companies and savings associations.

Occupational pension schemes are extremely complex. They generally fall into two broad categories, those that are financed entirely by the employer, and those to which both employer and employee contribute. Within these categories are defined contribution plans and defined benefit plans (fixed contributions and fixed benefits respectively). There are many other types of pension scheme, including profit share schemes, employee stock ownership plans (ESOPs), money purchase schemes and simplified employee pension plans. Employers will supply all their employees with information on the pension scheme that they operate. For further information, contact The Pension Rights Center (1350 Connecticut Avenue NW, Suite 206, Washington, DC 20036, ☎202-296 3776; e-mail pensionhelp@pensionrights.org; www.pensionrights.org).

HEALTH INSURANCE

You are not eligible for Medicare until you have been resident in the USA for at least five years. Medicare is the federal programme of health insurance (HI) included in the social security provisions. It is available to all US citizens who are over 65, and who have paid social security taxes. Those over 65 are automatically covered, unless they have not been in the USA for five years. It is essential that you are covered by an insurance policy from your own country if you are thinking of going to the United States for any length of time. Even if you have secured a green card and you are going to live in the USA, if you are over 65 and have not been in the country for five years, you will not be eligible for Medicare. It will also be almost impossible to buy insurance at this age. Any American over the age of 65 who is buying insurance is doing so only to top up Medicare (which typically pays hospital bills less deductibles – drugs, dental costs – for the first 60 days of treatment), and no insurance company would cover you for the sort of sums necessary for full insurance. It is not unknown for people to be bankrupted by major surgery when they have not been properly insured. There is a list of insurance companies in the *Daily Life* chapter.

WILLS, TAXATION, AND LEGAL CONSIDERATIONS

The making of wills is also covered in *Setting Up Home*. This section will deal with the various legal and taxation considerations that have to be taken into account should you die while living in the USA.

You should get the advice of an attorney when making your will. There are two types of inheritance law for those who die intestate. Most states have common law: the estate is divided among all surviving relatives, including the spouse and children. Nine states (Alaska, Arizona, California, Idaho, Louisiana, Nevada, New Mexico, Texas, Washington and Wisconsin) have community property law, in which property acquired by a husband and wife after their marriage is regarded as owned by them in community, and is divided up as such after death.

You should make a will regardless of the size of your assets. If you get married, the marriage automatically revokes previous wills, and if you separate or divorce, you should change your will. Remember that it will be to your advantage to establish your domicile outside the United States in order to avoid US death taxes. If you have a green card or have become domiciled (see below), this option is not open to you. If you are domiciled, you can make a will that establishes a 'credit shelter trust', which ensures that both you and your spouse can use the $1.5 million (rising to $2 million in 2006 to 2008) estate tax exemption amounts separately.

The US equivalents of inheritance tax or death duties are Estate and Gift

Taxes. A federal estate tax is imposed on the market value of assets that an individual owns at death. In addition, all the states impose death taxes at much lower rates than the federal rates. There is a also a gift tax which is designed to prevent people giving away all their assets before death.

The important criterion with estate taxes is not whether you are resident or non-resident, but whether you are domiciled or non-domiciled in the USA. This is very subjective, but as a basic rule of thumb, if you have a green card, or have been permanently in the country more than five years (normally this will beholders of L, E and G visas) you will be considered domiciled. If you have been in the country for less than five years, or if you stay for a few months at a time, and have a home in another country, you will be considered non-domiciled.

Tax rates have been cut following the budget bill introduced by President Bush in 2001. Estates of domiciled people are taxed at 48%, declining year by year until 45% in 2007. An exemption is allowed on the first $1.5 million, which will rise to $2 million in 2006 (by 2009 the exemption will rise to $3.5 million). Non-domiciled people are taxed at the same rate but only on US assets, with an exemption limited to the first $60,000.

It is important to remember that if you buy a US home, no matter what your nationality or visa status, it will be subject to estate tax when you die. In addition to the Federal Estate Tax, there may be levies imposed by state governments so this needs to be considered in estate planning too.

Gift tax is only imposed for non-domiciled people if the gift is tangible (real estate). A gift of property therefore is liable to gift tax, but US stocks or bonds, which are considered intangible, are not liable. However, stocks and bonds will be subject to estate tax at your death. You should also make your spouse the owner of any life insurance policies.

One method of distributing assets after death is to set up a revocable living trust, which effectively puts all your property into a trust. The advantage is that you remain in control of decisions affecting the property but on death all assets are not put into probate. In many states, if land or homes exceed a valuation of $20,000, the estate is automatically entered into probate, the process whereby each will is ratified by the courts and involves unnecessary expenses which may cost up to 10% of the entire assets. Consult EstatePlanCenter (531 Reddington Drive, Redding, CA 96003; ☎530-221 7911; fax 530-221 7917; e-mail questions@estateplancenter.com; www.EstatePlanCenter.com) or the American Association of Retired People (601 E Street NW, Washington, DC 20049; ☎1-800-687 2277; www.aarp.org) for further detailed advice.

DEATH

All deaths must be reported to the local town hall: the death of a foreigner should also be reported to the relevant embassy or consulate in order that it can be registered in the deceased's country of birth. There are various things to be taken into account when arranging a funeral in the United States. The most important decision is whether you would like the body to be shipped home or not. The cost will vary depending on the state: in New York it costs around $1,500, plus the standard airfare. Pricing is fixed by weight. In the Yellow Pages under 'Funerals' you will find several funeral directors which specialise in shipping. Cremation costs start at $500, but will normally cost much more. The American Association of Retired People says that the average total cost of a traditional funeral is $4,600 but flowers and other costs can add another $1,000. Burial can cost a further $2,600. In certain states this will be higher or lower, depending on the density of the population and the availability of space.

HOBBIES AND INTERESTS

The over 65s are a powerful and vocal lobby. They are also numerous and wherever you go you will find an array of societies and a wide range of recreational activities designed expressly for the retired.

There are sports and social clubs with expatriate members in all areas of the United States, and especially in metropolitan areas and places like Florida and the east and west coasts where expats congregate. Membership of a sports club can be expensive, but fees vary so widely depending on the state, the city, and the type of club that it is difficult to give an average. In general, the YMCA (101 North Wacker Drive, Chicago, IL 60606; ☎312-977 0031; www.ymca.net) is one of the most reasonably priced organisations, with annual subscriptions of between $400 to $1,000 (seniors enjoy better rates). For more information, contact the local chamber of commerce or look in the local Yellow Pages under 'Clubs'.

The United States has a tradition of religious tolerance: freedom of religion is enshrined in the First Amendment of the Constitution. The Roman Catholic Church has around fifty million members, and the nearest equivalent to the Church of England is the Episcopal Church, with some three million members. You will find that church attendance is higher than it is in Britain and many parts of Europe. Because of the history of immigration to America, you will also find that no matter what your nationality or denomination, there will be a church to cater for your needs. In many communities the church is the social as well as religious centre, organising discussion groups, outings, sports events, dinners and musical evenings. If you are not a churchgoer but are at a loss as to how to start meeting people and making a social life in a new area, you will find that the local church will make you feel extremely welcome. Americans are very friendly towards new arrivals, and never more so than in a church group. If you need more information about churches and religious centres, look in the Yellow Pages under 'Religious organisations' or 'Churches'.

Whatever your hobby or interest, it is unlikely that you will not be able to find a soulmate. As an example of the variety of clubs, meetings and events, here is a selection from the *What's On* column of a local paper in New York state. In a packed week, there was a meeting of CHANGES (Citizens Helping A New Generation to Evolve Sustainably), an archaeology lecture on 'New Perspectives on Prehistoric Cultural Change', the twice-monthly meeting of the New Horizon Senior Citizens Club of Yorktown ('New Members Welcome!'), a meeting of Suburban Singles ('tonight's discussion topic, How do you feel about the risks/joys of 'Falling in Love'?'), several harvest suppers, a keep-fit evening run by the American Heart Association, a traditional clam chowder lunch, a slide lecture on 'The History of England thru Embroideries', craft fairs, Roast Beef Dinners, Turkey Dinners, a Polynesian Chicken Stir-Fry Dinner ('Sponsored by the Calvary Bible Church, with Entertainment by the Bleach Boys (sic) Hawaiian Dress Optional')... the list goes on. This sort of thing is replicated in tens of thousands of small towns throughout America, and the hospitality of the average American will ensure that you are made welcome.

CLUBS, ASSOCIATIONS, AND USEFUL ADDRESSES

The Florida Brits Group, Peter and Jean Stanhope,18 Grange Close, Skelton, York YO30 1YR; ☎01904-471800; email FlaBritsCl@aol.com; www. FloridaBritsGroup.com. Membership of 1,200 Florida-property-owning couples.

Union Jack, PO Box 1823, La Mesa, CA 91944; ☎619-466 3129; advertising only, toll free ☎1-800-262 7305; e-mail ujnews@ujnews.com; www.ujnews. com, is a very useful source of contact information for British expats; it is a newspaper published monthly that can be obtained on subscription for $30 per year. It lists expat clubs and organisations, and classified advertisements for immigration attorneys and shippers.

American Association of Retired Persons, 601 E Street NW, Washington, DC 20049; ☎1-800-687 2277; www.aarp.org. Advice on relocation, retirement housing, taxation and financial planning. Bibliography of retirement directories.

Administration on Aging, 1 Massachusetts Avenue, Washington, DC 20201; ☎202-619 0724; www.aoa.dhhs.gov. Local services for seniors in their locality. Of limited help to individuals but may be able to provide some useful contacts.

America's Guide Senior Infoserver, www.americasguide.com. Information on retirement communities, homes, and sheltered accommodation nationwide.

SeniorNet, 121 Second Street, 7th Floor, San Francisco, CA 94105; ☎415-495 4990; fax 415-495 3999; www.seniornet.org. An online community and resource for retirees with chat rooms, news, and advice.

Firstgov for Seniors, www.seniors.gov. The federal government's online information hub for retirees.

Section 2

WORKING IN THE UNITED STATES

EMPLOYMENT

PERMANENT AND TEMPORARY WORK

STARTING A BUSINESS

EMPLOYMENT

CHAPTER SUMMARY

○ **Looking for work.** Information on both specific vacancies and possible employers to contact on spec can be obtained from advertisements in the media, websites, consultants, chambers of commerce and professional associations.

○ **Working practices.** Europeans may be surprised by the combination of a strong work ethic and a casual approach.

  ○ Salaries in the US are higher than in Europe and there tend to be more additional benefits provided, but working hours are longer and there are fewer days off.

○ **Permanent work.** Prospects for finding work are particularly good in areas to do with high technology and medicine.

○ **Short-term employment.** A number of very well established possibilities exist for young people to get summer jobs on children's camps or year-long placements as au pairs in private households. Voluntary positions are also available. Legal schemes that enable foreign students to take their choice of paid casual work are described in detail below.

○ **Economic overview.** After low unemployment in the last decade the new century began with a down turn but this can be seen as an inevitable part of the economic cycle.

  ○ Like other highly industrialised nations, the US has shifted from being a producer of goods to a provider of services; three-quarters of the workforce is now employed in service industries.

THE EMPLOYMENT SCENE

The latest figures show that the employment market in the USA is improving and during 2004 more than two million jobs were created. In February 2005, the economy added 262,000 new jobs bringing the new job total to 2.4 million in the preceding 12 months. Currently, the unemployment rate stands at 5.4% albeit just slightly lower than the December 2001 rate of 5.8% which was the highest figure in six years. Manufacturing was the worst affected with greater job losses during President Bush's first term than in any other four-year period since World War II. The non-manufacturing economy, on the other hand, did quite well. Sectors like electronics, aviation, industrial machinery, and cars were badly hit by the economic downturn at the beginning of the new millennium and US exports remain troubled. During 2000 and 2001 many workers in IT, the Internet and New Media suffered a wave of redundancies as the stock markets drastically cut the valuations of over-inflated companies who were trading at prices far in excess of traditional revenue and stock price ratios.

The US economy and confidence have been undeniably influenced by the worst attacks on the country in sixty years since Pearl Harbor. Following the terrorist assaults of 2001, 100,000 people in the airline industry and a further 60,000 in the travel industry lost their jobs. However, the economy had officially already entered a recession, which was only the second US recession in 20 years, indicating how buoyant the US economy had been since the close of the 1970s and that decade's energy crises. In time, passengers recovered their nerve, especially when new security measures in airports and on planes were seen to be working. Forecasts predict growth in manufacturing output and a revival in consumer demand.

The Department of Commerce secretary, Carlos M Gutierrez, said early in 2005 that: 'President Bush's tax relief has helped America create three million jobs since May 2003. To sustain our economic recovery, the Bush administration is pursuing pro-growth policies including making tax relief permanent, eliminating trade barriers, and reforming and strengthening entitlement programs. Under President Bush's leadership, more Americans are working than have ever worked before.'

According to the US Bureau of Economic Analysts, three sectors made notable contributions to faster US personal income growth in 2004 – professional services, finance, and construction. The top three states, North Dakota, Iowa, and South Dakota, benefited from record or near-record production of corn, soybeans, and other crops. The area of the US with lowest unemployment rate is the Great Plains region, which includes the Dakotas, Nebraska, Kansas, and Oklahoma. These states offer the greatest protection against the 'knock-on' effect whereby individual companies take down others in the same community in a chain reaction of bankruptcies. States most vulnerable to this effect are Hawaii,

Alaska and Washington. Contrary to popular belief, high-growth companies exist in all sectors of the economy. Technology companies from computing to bio-technology are not necessarily going to be the most successful companies. A survey by the National Council on Entrepreneurship found that high growth companies exist in all areas of the US and span the spectrum of economic activity. Finding the right job also entails picking a well-managed company with good prospects for success and a contented workforce.

OPPORTUNITIES FOR IMMIGRANTS

The USA continues to be a favoured overseas posting for company employees. The London-based consultants Employment Conditions Abroad found in a survey that increasing numbers of foreign workers are now being posted to the USA. It is the largest area for expat movements both in terms of numbers, and the size of the country, and they anticipate that the trend will continue. This however applies only to those already employed by large companies with HQs, subsidiaries, branches or agencies in the USA. But this is hardly surprising.

> Prospects for foreigners are best in high technology fields and niche markets. Highly-qualified engineers and managers in the computer industry, and in some areas of medicine such as physiotherapy and occupational therapy, are still in demand. Software designers and systems engineers with five to ten years experience will find a ready market for their skills in the USA.

This view of the country sitting at the foot of the rainbow is nurtured by Hollywood, but its romantic appeal has such resonance that some people will literally risk their lives on fragile boats to get there. This continues a tradition first started by the *Mayflower* in 1620. The concept of the American Dream is irresistible for many people even if it is a schmaltzy simplification of the life lived by a majority of the population who must balance their salaried incomes against the stream of financial obligations, from running a car to paying taxes. Anyone who has spent time in some of America's downtown urban areas or passed through slums on a train can testify that entrenched poverty still exists within the US and that misfortune can literally take anyone off to Skid Row.

Nevertheless it is important to acknowledge that the United States has historically seen immigration as representing a blood transfusion, a one-way flow of nutritious talent and drive. Certainly, emigrating to the US for professional reasons continues to bear fruit for many individuals seeking the good life and a chance to improve their standard of living. These immigrants also make valuable contributions to their adoptive country.

Working in the US is often a boon to one's professional credentials, especially if you return to your native country. But a sense of proportion is important. You will still encounter all of the problems of working life you experienced back home and you may well be working longer hours for that larger house.

Although the outlook in some areas is not optimistic, foreign workers will always be popular. It is often cheaper to employ expatriates: recruitment costs may be higher, but there is less risk of the employee on a working visa being poached by rivals because of the bureaucracy and expense involved in giving sponsorship. Training costs may be minimal, and there is a better chance of loyalty from a foreign employee if she or he migrates from abroad expressly to work for a specific company. (See also *Executive Employment Prospects* below). Foreign workers tend to be highly motivated to succeed because they have invested their skills, education and resources in making the move.

RISKS

While employers may appreciate the value of hiring foreign employees, there are certain risks for immigrant workers. The disadvantage of the working visa system is that someone can relocate him or herself to the USA to find that the job is unsuitable or even face redundancy without the opportunity to find new work. After navigating the legal and financial hurdles to obtain one job, are you likely to want to endure the application process for a second time within one year? During the late 1990s, system engineers and software designers were recruited from India's booming computer sector to find that they were laid off shortly after arriving when the economy ran into trouble.

Another factor to consider is that some employers are reported to use the working visa system to pay lower wages. By law H1-B workers must be paid the median wage in their job category, but some foreign workers admit they ask for raises less frequently and are less likely to make complaints at work for fear of jeopardising the company's sponsorship. It might be easy in some cases to find work in the States but you are also fairly expendable, particularly if you are a relatively new employee and cheap to fire. This is not to say individuals shouldn't try to find jobs in the USA but must understand the limitations of a working visa, which explains why a residency with its freedom to move jobs is worth its weight in gold.

RESIDENCE AND WORK REGULATIONS

The US visa system is covered in detail in *Residence and Entry Regulations*. There is no work permit as such, instead the US Citizensip and Immigration Services (USCIS) issues a range of 'non-immigrant' visas (more than 70 in all), to cover every possible reason to enter and stay in the country. Some visas allow you to work: the most common of these is the L visa, which allows the holder to work for the company which sent him or her to the USA, and for no other company. The B visa allows the holder to conduct temporary business in the US such as holding meetings, attending conferences and so on. A common application is for an H visa whereby an American company sponsors an individual for possessing specialised knowledge linked to a degree. Other visas are for different categories of work; for example J visas are for participants of an approved Exchange Visitor Programme (see section on Short-Term Employment below) and O visas are issued to artists of 'extraordinary ability or achievement'. Another fairly common visa is the E (Treaty Trader) visa, issued to nationals of countries with a treaty of trade and navigation with the USA, who are going to carry on trade with the USA and that country. There are about 50 treaty countries, including the UK and most of the EU. Because the USCIS rules are extremely complex, it is advisable to get professional advice from an immigration lawyer unless your company is taking care of the visa application for you.

SKILLS AND QUALIFICATIONS

Details on individual professions are given at the end of this section, under the heading *Permanent Work*. The US State Department has given advance certification for work permits for people with advanced degrees in dietetics, nursing, pharmacy, physical therapy, medicine and surgery. The advanced degree requirement will sometimes be waived (with the exception of medicine and surgery) if you have a regular degree and specialised experience. This means that working visas in certain categories will be issued more readily.

The necessity for degrees and certificates varies from profession to profession. In some fields, such as computing, experience is everything and qualifications almost worthless. The same applies in journalism, and many secretarial posts. To practice professional nursing it is necessary to pass a state licensing exam, for which you need a qualification in your home country. Several professions require a qualification recognised by an American body. Librarians need a master's degree from a school accredited by the American Library Association, and entry to law, accountancy, banking and financial services is dependent upon a series of qualifications. If you are employed by a law or accountancy firm with operations in the USA, you will be able to get a posting without specific US qualifications. Although the US system is based on common law, as it is in England, as an individual it would be very difficult to find work in a US law firm without passing US law exams. Accountancy is regulated by state accountancy boards, 35 of which will consider applications from people with overseas qualifications. *The Encyclopaedia of Associations* (see below) lists trade and professional associations in the United States, which will be able to advise on the qualifications necessary to work in particular professions in the USA. See also *Permanent Work* at the end of this section, and *Professional Associations*, below.

SOURCES OF JOBS

THE MEDIA

UK Newspapers and Magazines

Several newspapers published in the UK carry advertisements for jobs in the USA. Many papers can give excellent leads and useful information, even if they do not have formal 'Situations Vacant' advertisements. The *Guardian* carries international job adverts within its supplements from Monday to Thursday and Saturday. The *Financial Times* carries adverts for mainly senior business and executive positions, and has regular supplements and special reports on countries and sectors. These will often cover individual states in the USA, contact the paper direct for details. The *Times* on a Thursday is particularly good for executive positions as is its 'Crème de la Crème' executive secretary section on Wednesdays; both it and the *Independent* have overseas jobs, though not in dedicated sections. For academic positions, the *Times Higher Education Supplement* (published Fridays) is a fruitful source.

A UK paper dedicated to the job search is *Jobsearch UK* (weekly), which has one page of overseas jobs.

One of the best magazines to read is the *Economist*, which has an extensive section advertising senior positions in business, finance and industry, many of them overseas. There are also a handful of dedicated magazines such as *Nexus* (monthly) and *Job Finder*.

New Scientist has advertisements for science and technology jobs, while *New Statesman and Society* and *The Spectator* have advertisements for jobs in particular areas, notably charities and politics. There will be (albeit infrequently) US-based positions advertised.

If you are looking within a particular sector, trade associations and their respective journals will be useful sources. The journals will be available in public libraries, and the associations themselves will often help you even if you are not a member. The *Directory of UK Associations* has comprehensive listings.

Other trade-orientated magazines can provide useful leads: *Campaign* and *Marketing Week* for advertising, the *Bookseller* (publishing), and the *Administrator* (company administration, company secretarial) are all available in newsagents and libraries. Accountants and lawyers should contact their associations for advice on job-hunting.

International and European Newspapers and Magazines.

By their nature the international journals are too broad in their outlook to carry many adverts for specific jobs. The exceptions: the *Economist* (see above) and the *Financial Times* (which has a US edition, see *Daily Life*) are useful sources for senior managers. Otherwise, the *International Herald Tribune* and the *Wall Street Journal Europe* are useful for general business information.

US Newspapers and Magazines

The best way to job hunt through the US papers is to send off for the domestic editions of the city or area that you want to work in: get a copy of the *Chicago Tribune*, the *New York Times*, the *Tennessean*, the *Cleveland Plain Dealer*, or the paper from whichever city in which you intend to work (see *Daily Life* for addresses). Otherwise, the only truly national newspapers are *USA Today* and the *Washington Post*. The former's London office, USA Today International Corporation (10 Wardour Street, London W1V 3HG; ☎020-7559 5859, fax 020-7559 5880; e-mail europe@usatoday.com; www.usatoday.com) places adverts in the domestic edition. They advise that it is worth buying the domestic editions for jobs vacant ('Help Wanted') advertisements, and the international edition (available from most big London newsagents) for nationwide financial and industry news. For listings of US specialist journals see *Benn's International Media Directory*.

Directories

Vacation Work (www.vacationwork.co.uk) publishes and distributes a number of annual directories covering short-term work. *Summer Jobs Abroad* and *Summer Jobs for Students in the USA* give advice and comprehensive lists. Other directories such as *Internships USA* deal mainly with unpaid, part-time executive work placements (see *Short-Term Employment*, below). The *International Directory of Voluntary Work* lists a certain number of placements in the USA. The University of London Careers Advisory Service (49-51 Gordon Square, London WC1H 0PN; ☎020-7554 4500; e-mail careers@careers.lon.ac.uk; www.careers.lon.ac.uk) has a *Guide for UK and Overseas Students* with exhaustive information on companies offering employment in the EU or worldwide. This is aimed primarily at graduates. *Getting Computer Jobs Abroad*, published by the magazine *Computer Weekly*, has a detailed section on the United States. For directories it is best to go to main reference libraries (in London, the Central Westminster Reference Library, 35 St Martin's Street, London WC2H 7HP; ☎020-7641 4636; www.westminster.gov.uk/libraries; or Senate House Library at the University of London; ☎020-7862 8500; e-mail enquiries@shl.lon.ac.uk; www.shl.lon.ac.uk).

Useful Websites

There are literally dozens of job hunt websites with lists of vacancies classified by professional categories or regions. Local newspaper websites are a quick way of finding vacancies whether abroad or within the US. Many allow you to post a CV (resumé), search for companies, view internship possibilities, and find advice about relocation to the US. Here is just a sample of some reliable job search sites:

America's Job Bank: www.ajb.dni.us. Run by employment commissions of state agencies containing jobs in both public and private sectors.

CareerMart: www.careermart.com. Fast and up-to-date career site.

CareerMosaic: www.recruitmentresources.com/careermosaic.html. A large job search Internet engine.

CareerBuilder.com: www.careerbuilder.com. Leading recruitment resource. Searches the classified ads of more than 130 local American newspapers.

JobBank USA: www.jobbankusa.com/jobs.html. Specialises in providing employment services to job seekers. Includes a database of vacancies, news about job fairs, employer information and posting resumés online.

Monster: www.monster.com. A huge searchable database of jobs in the US and around the world, plus information on large employers.

Net-Temps: www.net-temps.com. Leading job board for temporary, temporary-to-permanent, and full-time employment.

PLACING EMPLOYMENT WANTED ADVERTISEMENTS

There are some advantages to placing an *employment wanted* advertisement in the local newspapers of the state or city in which you want to work: you can write your own job description and you can be selective about where you work. As well as this, a foreign advertisement in a local newspaper will always get noticed (there is still some cachet in having an English secretary in certain types of firm, for example). Be cautious about respondents. Ask how long they have been in business, if and where they are registered, how many other people they employ, and what the remuneration for the job is. If you are at all suspicious, get something in writing and contact the local city hall or chamber of commerce for advice on how to find out more about the company. Women especially should not agree to meet anybody without being absolutely sure where they are going, and whom they are going to see. If in any doubt, make sure you let at least one person know your movements and how long you will be.

There is a list of major newspapers in the *Daily Life* chapter above. If the area in which you want to work is not listed, contact the local chamber of commerce for names of newspapers. Although each state has at least one daily that goes statewide, US papers are very local, so try to be fairly exact about the area you choose.

The following is a sample advertisement. It is important to put it in the *weekend* edition, as well as the daily. Make sure you include your country code in the phone number.

> **SITUATION WANTED** English Secretary, 28, computer literate (Word, DTP), legal experience, some Spanish spoken. Seeks permanent position in Los Angeles or surrounding area. Resumé available. Contact Janet Ellis.

AGENCIES & ORGANISATIONS

UK Agencies

Engineering and Construction

AndersElite, Capitol House, Houndwell Place, Southampton, SO1 4HU; ☎02380-223511; e-mail CDI-AndersElite@cdicorp.com; www.cdicorp.com.

Medical and Nursing

O'Grady Peyton International, 1/3 Norton Folgate, London EC1 6DB; ☎0870-700 0140; fax 0870-700 0141; e-mail routeeurope@ogradypeyton.com; www.ogpinc.com.

PHP Health Professional, Central House, 1 Ballards Lane, Finchley, London N3 1QX; ☎0800-581917. Sponsors nurses through exams needed to practice in the USA.

Computers and IT

Abraxas, 180 Oxford Street, London W1D 1NN; ☎020-7255 5555; fax 020-7636 0333; e-mail corporate@abraxas.com; www.abraxas.co.uk.

Sales and Marketing

NHA International Ltd, Badgemore Park Golf Club, Gravel Hill, Badgemore, Henley-on-Thames, Oxfordshire RG9 4NR; ☎01491-842700; fax 01491-842703; e-mail trqcon@nhaint.com; www.nhaint.com.

Other

VIP International, VIP House, 17 Charing Cross Road, London WC2H 0QW; ☎020-7930 0541; fax 020-7930 2860; e-mail vip@vipinternational.co.uk; www.vipinternational.co.uk. International hotel and hospitality recruitment company: visa restrictions mean that there are very few opportunities in this area for executives, but the company also recruits for temporary positions on board luxury cruise lines.

US Agencies

Agencies specialise in particular disciplines, and the most prolific, as in the UK, are those offering temporary jobs in secretarial work. Fees are usually paid by the employer, but you should check whether you will be required to pay in advance. Look under Employment Agencies in the Yellow pages.

Guidance can also be sought from relocation and support agencies such as *International Consultants of Delaware*, 625 Barksdale Road, Suite 109, Newark, DE 19711; ☎302-737 8715; fax 302-737 8756; e-mail icd@icdel.com; www. icdel.com. A provider of educational evaluation services.

Chambers of Commerce

There is a Chamber of Commerce in all major cities and in every state. They exist to promote business, and provide information on all aspects of living and working in the local area. State Chambers of Commerce supply information packs with business contacts, rates and taxes, commercial and residential property contacts and prices, business start-up materials and other relevant information. Addresses listed in the Yellow Pages.

BritishAmerican Business Inc (BABi) at 75 Brook Street, London W1K 4AD; ☎020-7467 7400; fax 020-7493 2394; www.babinc.org, has more than 400 UK and US corporate members. Membership is by company only, with yearly fees of between £700 to £3,855. Membership gives access to various EU/UK/US committees, business information sources and databases, and an extensive events programme.

International Chambers of Commerce

BritishAmerican Business Inc, 52 Vanderbilt Avenue, 20th Floor, New York, NY 10017; ☎212-661 4060.

US Chamber of Commerce, 1615 H Street NW, Washington, DC 20062; ☎202-659 6000; www.uschamber.org.

See *Useful Business Information State by State* for addresses of city Chambers of Commerce.

PROFESSIONAL ASSOCIATIONS

Accountancy

National Society of Accountants, 1010 N Fairfax Street, Alexandria, VA 22314; ☎703-549 6400; fax 703-549 2984; e-mail members@nsacct.org; www.nsacct.org.

American Institute of Certified Public Accountants, 1211 Avenue of the Americas, New York, NY 10036; ☎212-596 6213; fax 212-596 6200; www.aicpa.org.

American Accounting Association, 5717 Bessie Drive, Sarasota, FL 34233; ☎941-921 7747; fax 941-923 4093; e-mail Office@aaahq.org; www.aaahq.org.

Agriculture

Agriculture Council of America, 11020 King Street, Suite 205, Overland Park, KS 66210; ☎913-491 1895.

American Dairy Association, 10255 West Higgins Road, Suite 900, Rosemont, IL 60018; ☎1-800-853 2479; www.dairyinfo.com.

American Forest and Paper Association, 1111 19th Street NW, Suite 900, Washington, DC 20036; ☎1-800-878 8878; e-mail info@afandpa.org; www.afandpa.org.

Banking/Insurance/Financial Services

American Bankers Association, 1120 Connecticut Avenue NW, Washington, DC 20036; ☎1-800-BANKERS; www.aba.com.

Financial Women International, 1027 West Roselawn Avenue, Roseville, MN 65113; ☎651-487 7632; fax 651-489 1322; info@fwi.org; www.fwi.org.

American Association of Insurance Services, 1745 S Naperville Road, Wheaton, IL 60187; ☎630-681 8347; fax 630-681 8356; e-mail info@AAISonline.com; www.aaisonline.com.

Insurance Information Institute, 110 William Street, New York, NY 10038; ☎212-346 5500; www.iii.org.

Chemical/Pharmaceutical

American Institute of Chemists, 315 Chestnut Street, Philadelphia, PA 19106; ☎215-873 8224; fax 215-925 1954; e-mail info@theaic.org; www.theaic.org.

American Pharmacists Association, 2215 Constitution Avenue NW, Washington, DC 20037; ☎202-628 4410; fax 202-783 2351; e-mail infocenter@aphanet.org; www.aphanet.org.

Construction

American Institute of Constructors, PO Box 26334, Alexandria, VA 22314; ☎703-683 4999; fax 703-683 5480; e-mail admin@aicnet.org; www.aicnet.org.

Electrical

American Electronics Association, 5201 Great America Parkway, Suite 520, Santa Clara, CA 95054; ☎408-987 4200; www.aeanet.org.

Engineering

American Institute of Chemical Engineers, 3 Park Avenue, New York, NY 10016; ☎212-591 8100; fax 212-591 8888; e-mail xpress@aiche.org; www.aiche.org.

American Society for Agricultural Engineers, 2950 Niles Road, St Joseph, MI 49085; ☎269-429 0300; fax 269-429 3852; e-mail hq@asae.org; www.asae.org.

American Society of Mechanical Engineers, Three Park Avenue, New York, NY 10016; ☎1-800-843 2763; e-mail infocentral@asme.org; www.asme.org.

Institute of Electrical and Electronics Engineers, 3 Park Avenue, 17th Floor, New York, NY 10016; ☎212-419 7900, fax 212-752 4929; www.ieee.org.

Institute of Industrial Engineers, 3577

Parkway Lane, Suite 200, Norcross, GA 30092; ☎800-494 0460 or ☎770-449 0460; fax 770-441 3295; www.iienet.org.

Legal

American Bar Association, 321 North Clark Street, Chicago, IL 60610; ☎312-988 5522; www.abanet.org.

Media/Performing Arts

Actors' Equity Association, 165 W 46th Street, New York, NY 10036; ☎212-869 8530; fax 212-719 9815; www.actorsequity.org.

American Federation of Television and Radio Artists, 260 Madison Avenue, New York, NY 10016; ☎212-532 0800; fax 212-532 2242; e-mail info@aftra.org; www.aftra.org.

American Federation of Musicians, Paramount Building, 1501 Broadway, Suite 600, New York, NY 10036; ☎212-869 1330; fax 212-764 6134; www.afm.org.

National Writers Union, 113 University Pl., 6th Floor, New York, NY 10003; ☎212-254 0279; fax 212-254 0673; e-mail nwu@nwu.org; www.nwu.org.

Newspaper Association of America, 1921 Gallows Road, Suite 600, Vienna, VA 22182; ☎703-902 1600; fax 703-917 0636; www.naa.org.

Medical

American Medical Association, American Medical Association, 515 N State Street, Chicago, IL 60610; ☎1-800-621 8335; www.ama-assn.org.

American Nurses Association, 8515

Georgia Avenue, Suite 400, Silver Spring, MD 20910; ☎301-628 5000; fax 301-628 5001; www. nursingworld.org.

Secretarial

International Association of Administrative Professionals, 10502 NW Ambassador Drive, PO Box 20404, Kansas City, MO 64195; ☎816-891 6600; fax 816-891 9118; e-mail service@iaap-hq.org; www.iaap-hq.org.

Miscellaneous

American Advertising Federation, 1101 Vermont Avenue NW, Suite 500, Washington, DC 20005; ☎202-898 0089; fax 202-898 0159; e-mail aaf@aaf.org; www.aaf.org.

National Retail Federation, 325 7th Street NW, Suite 1100, Washington, DC 20004; ☎202-783 7971; fax 202-737 2849; www.nrf.com.

American Association of Exporters and Importers, 1050 17th Street NW, Washington, DC 20036; ☎202-857 8009; fax 202-857 7843; www. aaei.org.

Travel Industry Association of America, 1100 New York Avenue, NW, Suite 450, Washington, DC 20005; ☎202-408 8422; fax 202-408 1255; www.tia.org.

American Institute of Mining, Metallurgical and Petroleum Engineers, 8307 Shaffer Parkway, Littleton, CO 80127; ☎303-948 4255, fax 303-948 4260; e-mail aime@aimehq.org; www.aimeny.org.

STATE EMPLOYMENT AGENCIES

Job Services, the state operated employment service, operates a network of some 2,000 local offices in major cities around the country. These 'Employment Service Centers' provide free counselling, testing and job placements, and allow access to computerised listings of possible openings across the country. They are listed in the Yellow Pages under Employment Service or Job Service.

COMPANY TRANSFERS

The 'special relationship' between the UK and the USA is now stronger than ever in industry and commerce. The American Chamber of Commerce in the UK lists 10,000 US companies that have subsidiaries, parents, distributors or agents in the UK, and 8,000 UK companies which have business links in the USA. Many of these companies will send staff overseas on secondment. If you are starting your career it would be a good idea to consider the possibility of securing a position in a US company, or a UK company with links with the USA.

For more information see the *American Chamber of Commerce Directory* (available in libraries – you do not have to be a member of the Chamber), or identify the major companies operating in both countries in the following directories. For US companies and their subsidiaries see *Moody's Register*, *Ward's Business Directory* and *Thomas Register*, all of which list companies by industry sector; for UK companies and their subsidiaries consult *Kompass* (www.kompass. com), *Kelly's*, *Sell's Directories*, or *Who Owns Whom* (Dun & Bradstreet), a directory of companies and their subsidiaries throughout the world. In London, the Business Collections at the British Library have extensive resources which give details of UK companies and their subsidiaries worldwide. You can contact the Library at Business Collections at British Library (Science, Technology and Business), St Pancras, 96 Euston Road, London NW1 2DB. General enquiries can be made on ☎020-7412 7676 or you can use the Lloyds-TSB information line which is free to use for 10 minutes, ☎020-7412 7454/7977. Alternatively, the City Business Library, 1 Brewers' Hall Gardens (footpath between London Wall & Aldermanbury Square), London EC2V 5BX; ☎020-7332 1812; www. library.uncg.edu/news, run by City of London.

The UK Trade and Investment's excellent website at www.uktradeinvest.gov.uk gives detailed information on all aspects of exporting and building trade links.

APPLYING FOR A JOB

The best way to get a job, according to the US Bureau of Labor Statistics in the Department of Labor, is to apply to a company direct. Thirty-four percent of applicants are successful this way. The next best method is to network (including asking friends and relatives for help), which works for 26% of applicants. Only 14% get the job they want by answering newspaper advertisements. Other means, such as using private and state employment services and agencies, trying to get a school placement or taking civil service tests, are used by less than 6% of those who find jobs. Contrary to popular opinion therefore, buying the newspaper every day for the 'help wanted' columns is not as likely to end in success as sending your resumé on spec. This is not to say that you should not apply to newspaper advertisements, but do not be put off by rejections: an advert in a major daily will have been seen by thousands, and answered by hundreds of people, all in a situation similar to yours.

If there are many ways of finding a job, there are as many methods used by recruiters to find the perfect applicant. It is important to remember when applying for any job, whether in the USA or in Europe, that the recruiter may be almost as apprehensive as you. Recruiting is a time-consuming and very expensive business, and it is essential to get it right first time. The consequences of bad recruiting – the person appointed turning out to be a plausible layabout who leaves after six months, for example – are serious. Selecting five or six people for interview from 600 resumés is difficult enough. Using the 40 minutes of an interview to find out if the person sitting nervously opposite you is worth $100,000 a year, as well as being the sort of character you can work with every day, is indeed a challenge.

Companies use different systems to make recruitment less of a lottery. Professional agencies will be used when a series of employees are required at once (for the opening of a new department, or a new plant), and head-hunters will be brought in if a very senior post is vacant. It can be worthwhile to contact agencies that deal with recruitment in your field. They will always talk up your chances of getting a job, and the reality is that they are often a lot less useful than they appear to be, but it does no harm to cast your net as wide as possible.

Some companies use psychological tests to get to the 'real' character of the candidate. Opinion is divided as to the usefulness of the different tests that are in vogue at any one time. Psychometric testing is in favour at the moment (your personality is categorised according to a series of psychological tests), but handwriting analysis is still used by a surprising number of large and well-known companies. The theory behind all these tests is that you cannot get to the true nature of an individual through the formal setting of an interview, and that it is important to find out if the person will fit in with the group he or she will be joining. You will find that psychometric testing is used more at the senior end of the job market, and in certain professions – banking and financial services, for example. In the media and the creative, arts-based jobs, recruitment is often by the back door, but when a job is formally advertised the selection process will be conventional. This is true for the majority of companies and the majority of jobs: the right candidate will be found in the old-fashioned way, via resumé or application form, covering letter and interview.

LETTERS OF APPLICATION

As in the UK, make sure that you are concise, to the point, and legible. If you are replying to an advertisement, start your letter, 'I would like to apply for the position of ... as advertised in Dry Cleaning News'. The second paragraph should describe your educational background and experience. The covering letter is an introduction to the resumé, so it should concentrate on the areas that best qualify you for the job, highlighting certain points that are not detailed in the resumé. For example, if you are applying for the job of Assistant Editor at Dry Cleaning News, and you have worked in a laundrette, draw attention to it by saying 'You will see from my resumé that I have some experience of such and such ...' Close the paragraph by talking yourself up a bit, saying that you think you are well-qualified and could make an important contribution to the team.

In the third paragraph, mention that you are enclosing all relevant material, are available for interview at any time, and look forward to hearing from them. Finish with 'Yours sincerely' (if you have addressed the person by name), 'Yours faithfully' (if the letter starts 'Dear Sir', or 'Dear Madam'). It is always a good idea to find out the name of the person you are applying to, as it makes the letter more personal. If you are applying on spec, this is essential. Your letter should be on one side of an A4 sheet. Anything longer will be read without concentration. Do not waffle: an application letter should always be to the point, but never more so than when dealing with Americans, who pride themselves on their ability to get down to business quickly. Make sure that you read advertisements carefully. If it asks for a handwritten letter, don't type it: recruiters are not impressed by an inability to follow the simplest instruction.

In the USA it is common for the sender to put their address in the top left-hand corner of the envelope.

It is sometimes the custom to write a letter after an interview, thanking your interviewer for taking the time to see you, and reiterating your interest in the job. If you have gone to see someone for advice as a result of an on-spec letter, you must thank them, but after a formal interview for an advertised job it is not necessary and is unlikely to make a difference to their decision.

THE RESUMÉ (CURRICULUM VITAE)

There are many different opinions about the writing and structuring of a resumé. Should it be short, or long? Should you include a biographical paragraph in the third person (as in, 'Janie Jones is dedicated, careful, and likes to see a project through...')? Should you detail all your academic achievements, or none at all? Should you include referees, or say that they will be supplied on request? There are certain facts about a resumé that are unalterable. It is a brief summary of your career: the 'hard' information about your qualifications and experience. It (and the covering letter) are going to get you an interview, or not. It will sit in a pile of up to 500 other resumés, and will be allowed perhaps three minutes of somebody's time. Given these facts, certain decisions can be taken. The resumé should not be more than two sides of A4, and should be clear and well-laid out. Presentation is vital. The resumé is there to put across facts as efficiently as possible, and to show its subject in the best possible light. If you do not have access to a word-processor, consider getting it done professionally (see the Yellow Pages for addresses). In the UK employers are usually good at spotting this, and tend not to like it, but it is more acceptable in the USA. Try not to make it too shiny and overproduced. Avoid large blocks of text: it should be easy on the eye, with the important sections, such as work experience easy to find and read.

Start with your name, address, telephone number, age and marital status. List your work experience, starting with the most recent job. Say what the job was, the dates you were there, and give brief details of your responsibilities. The more relevant it is to the job you are applying for, the more details you should supply.

The parts of the resumé that are going to sell you should be on the first page. On the second page list your formal education (schools, dates attended, degrees and certificates – with US equivalents if possible – and major subject areas of specialisation). If you are a recent graduate, add extracurricular activities that relate to the job that you are applying for.

List languages spoken, volunteer activities (if these are particularly relevant, put them on the first page, and draw attention to them in the covering letter), special skills (typing, shorthand), and membership of professional organisations.

Add a couple of lines of personal interests, what sports you play, what you do for recreation. If the recruiter has reached this stage of the resumé, he or she will already be interested in finding out more about you, and a shared interest in an unusual sport or hobby could get you an interview. Never lie about or exaggerate your interests. If you say you have travelled extensively in Australia, be prepared for an interviewer who may have done the same. Admitting that you only spent a week in Sydney will not impress.

If you list referees, make absolutely certain they know they might be contacted, and why. It is usually sufficient to say 'Referees supplied on request' at the end of the resumé.

THE INTERVIEW

Interviews affect people in different ways. Remember that your interviewer may be as nervous as you are. Bad interviewers are a hazard: they will not know how to put you at your ease, and they will not allow you to show yourself at your best. There is nothing you can do about it, except to be fully prepared for every eventuality.

You should find out everything you can about the company. Look up its website, or look in *Moody's Register of Companies, Hoover's Handbook, Forbes 500*, and other directories that list companies and their important characteristics. If you are able to show that you have taken the time to learn about the company, it will demonstrate that you are serious about the job.

Dress smartly. In the USA dress codes are more casual, but men should never go to an interview without a jacket and tie, and women should never wear trousers unless they are part of a suit, or very tailored. Use your common sense: an interview in a bank will call for a smarter turnout than one in a newspaper office. If you find your interviewer in a T-shirt, that is no problem: if you get the job you can moderate your dress accordingly. If you had turned up in jeans it would have looked as if you didn't care enough to make an effort.

Don't show that you are nervous. Any interviewer will expect you to be slightly apprehensive, and will make allowances. Remember, however, that the purpose of the interview is really to find out if you are the kind of person that will fit in: sweating and stammering too much will not bode well for future meetings. It is unnecessary to advise against smoking: lighting up in most American companies would get you thrown out before you got past the security guard.

The interview should start with simple questions, designed to put you at your ease. The answer to the question 'How was your journey?' is 'Fine', not a diatribe on the frightfulness of the subway system.

During the interview concentrate on what you are being asked. If the interviewer launches into a long piece about the company, beware of the unexpected question thrown in to see if you are listening or not.

Try to set your own agenda. To be invited to 'say something about yourself' is a gift: you can put your strengths to the fore. It is impossible here to go into all the sorts of questions you may be asked. Some seem easy: 'Tell me five of your weaknesses'. But trying to tell an interviewer one weakness that does not make you sound like a bad bet is difficult enough. Mention things that can be easily corrected: 'I need to improve my typing', for example. Don't say one of your faults is that you're a bit of a perfectionist – it's been heard before. If you are asked about your strengths, be honest, but be modest as well. Be prepared for the unexpected. You may be asked to complete aptitude tests, or other written tests.

An interview does not have to be an ordeal. One of the most important things to remember is that it is a tedious business for your interviewer, taking up time that could be better spent. If you can make the hour pass quickly and enjoyably, you will be remembered as good company. Try to turn the interview into a conversation, rather than a question and answer session. Most Americans like to deal straightforwardly with people, and are uncomfortable with ambiguity. Don't try to be clever, answer questions as honestly as you can, maintain eye contact, give a firm handshake, and look as if you are the sort of person it would be a treat to work with.

Useful publications for job applicants include *What Colour is Your Parachute? A Practical Manual for Job-Hunters and Career Changers* (Richard Nelson Bolles, Ten Speed Press, www.tenspeed.com, £14.99) and *Resumés That Get Jobs* (Macmillan General Reference). As always www.amazon.com has the best database of business books.

ASPECTS OF EMPLOYMENT

OVERVIEW

The central piece of legislation applying to all areas of employment (hiring, promotion, performance appraisal, compensation and benefits, dismissal, redundancy and so on) is Title VII of the Civil Rights Act 1964. This enshrines in law the right of the individual not to be discriminated against on grounds of sex, age, race or religion. State and municipal governments often have their own regulations, causing some overlap with federal laws; some states have passed laws which restrict discrimination for other reasons. Claims against employers initially go to the Employment Equal Opportunities Commission (the EEOC), and if no settlement is reached they can then be taken to a federal court.

Wrongful dismissal is an area of law that is still developing. Some courts, for example, have interpreted possession of an employer's letter offering a job, or a company's personnel handbook, as an actual contract, making it much more difficult to dismiss the employee. Similarly, employees who have been sacked for refusing to carry out instructions that are dangerous or illegal have successfully sued their employers. It is also possible to sue an employer for making statements, while firing someone, that cause emotional distress.

For companies sending employees to the USA, *ECA International* (Anchor House, 15 Britten Street, London SW3 3TY; ☎020-7351 5000; fax 020-7351 9396; e-mail eca@eca-international.com; www.ecaltd.com) is an employment consultancy providing information on all aspects of employment, including remuneration and benefits comparisons, taxation, cost of living indices, and so on. Membership is open to companies only.

WORK PRACTICES

It would be impossible to attempt to describe here how American business functions. It is a huge subject, and one that has been covered by many experts. As always, there are a few generalisations that can be made, but they should be treated with caution: what is relevant in the east may be completely different in the west.

Americans have a strongly defined work ethic, and work is generally taken very seriously in the States. They take fewer and shorter holidays than in Europe, and it is common for weekends and family life to be sacrificed if a job needs to be done. Good time-keeping is important. Arriving five minutes late for a meeting calls for an apology; if you are going to be 15 minutes late you should telephone beforehand with a good excuse. American businesses are often geared for quick results and present success: 'long-term' means looking ahead three years. This is thought to be one of the reasons why some industries are falling behind the Japanese and the Germans, who tend to look longer-term. You will be expected to work hard, with fewer breaks. You will find that smoking is forbidden in the office, and 'fag breaks' are very uncommon. You may find Americans are more aggressive and articulate in meetings than you are used to. You will also find that they are impressed by well-presented arguments backed up by hard-hitting data.

Confusingly, Americans are as renowned for their casual approach as they are for their punishing work ethic. First names are the norm (as indeed they are in most companies in the UK these days), and networking on the golf course or squash court is common practice. The appearance of informality can be deceptive: business meetings are held at breakfast, lunch or dinner; business entertaining takes place at a ball game or other sporting event; cocktail and dinner parties at colleagues' houses may well have a serious business purpose.

Another ritual that is gaining ground is dress-down Friday. Some major corporations have decided that if employees are allowed to wear casual clothes on a Friday it increases productivity. This of course comes with its own set of rules: if you are working for Chase Manhattan, dressing down is likely to require as much (or more) thought than putting on a suit and tie. Sports shirts, chinos and loafers is the accepted casual uniform.

Observers of the American business ethic have identified three key ways in which companies work. The first is to have clear lines of management, and detailed instructions. 'Who do I report to?' is often the first question a new employee asks. Secondly, employees expect constant feedback on their work (continual assessment is also the basis of the schools grading system), and thirdly, close supervision is expected. If you are managing American employees, don't take it for granted that they will react in the same way as their British counterparts: if you have to correct someone for any reason, get the advice of an American colleague first.

Achievement programmes in American companies are common, often with prize ceremonies. Financial success is highly valued, and rewarded.

A survey of *Fortune 500* company executives brought to light what they considered were the main elements to their success. The important thing was that they were all fully aware of the need to pursue their own careers, and the success of the company was seen as a means of achieving individual success, not as a means to an end. They also all embodied the great American values: they were pragmatic, assertive and, up to a point, egalitarian.

TELEWORKING

More than one sixth of America's working-age population – around 30 million people – do not owe allegiance to a single employer, and don't work in an office; teleworkers – or 'techno-peasants' as they've been dubbed – are the growing army of workers who have taken advantage of the opportunities given by affordable home computers and set up home offices. There are two types of teleworker: the person who works from home for many different people – a freelance journalist or a plumber, for example – and the person who works for a single company but does it from home instead of going into the office every day. Many companies are happy to have employees working from home – it means less overheads, and a happier employee is a more productive one. In the UK, teleworking is taking off at a slower rate. British Telecom (BT) has around 1,500 staff who work from home full time. It can seem very attractive. You don't need to put on a suit and subject yourself to the miseries of public transport. You can start and stop work when you like, and you can say goodbye to the backbiting and politics that colour office life. But be warned – many people find working at home lonely and depressing. While it can seem a luxury not to have to subject yourself to the nine-to-five routine, when your computer is next door to the spare bedroom it can be impossible to stop thinking about work. One of the great advantages of going into the office is that you can keep it separate from the rest of your life; teleworkers sometimes find that far from casting off their shackles, they have simply brought them home.

For more information on teleworking and the 'soho' concept (small office/ home office or companies with 20 or fewer employees) in the USA, WorkingSolo Inc (PO Box 952, New Platz, NY 12561; ☎ 845-255 7171; fax 845-255 2116;

e-mail wsoffice@workingsolo.com; www.workingsolo.com) provides news, information, and encouragement to the self-employed and microbusinesses.

WOMEN IN WORK & SEXUAL HARASSMENT

Women in american companies have all the same problems and preoccupations as they do in other countries. The issues of sexual harassment, and the glass ceiling preventing women from rising above a certain level in the hierarchy, are endlessly debated. Political correctness ('PC') is an area, which should be given the same respect as an uncharted minefield. The most important thing to remember is that America is a very litigious society, and issues are likely to go to law much sooner than in Europe. Women should be aware of any male-female tensions that exist in a company, and take their cue from female colleagues. Men should be very careful of what they say and do. What might be lighthearted fun in London could be construed as the grossest politico-sexual incorrectness in Los Angeles.

It is in the universities that the issue is most complex. Many male academics are genuinely worried about the PC lobby and its implications: a 59-year old male professor in New Hampshire has recently been suspended without pay for (apparently harmless) remarks made in the classroom, in a sinister parallel to a notorious play, David Mamet's *Oleanna*, in which an academic is destroyed by an over-zealous female student.

It is wise to be aware, however, that the debate is not confined to the rarefied atmosphere of the universities. Most company guidelines warn against behaviour that is likely to create 'a hostile and intimidating atmosphere', even though this may not be fully defined. Commentators have warned that to be accused of this sort of behaviour can carry the same sort of stigma as an accusation of indecent assault.

SALARIES

Salaries in the USA are higher than in Europe, and include more benefits and perks although Americans have to spend considerably more time at work. As in Europe there are wide discrepancies between different occupations and between the public and private sectors. The notion of a national average is fairly meaningless without looking at different fields. The average salary for catering managers is $32,000 while the average salary for high school principals, for example, is $80,000 and a university dean can earn up to $200,000. An average salary for a data processing manager is $88,000, but for an accountant $46,000. Starting salaries for graduates depend on a number of factors including the profession they are joining and their qualifications. A recent graduate with a bachelor's degree in social work from California State University is earning on average $17,350 but if they are graduating from the computer science programme they are earning $55,000.

The Federal minimum wage is set by the Fair Labor Standards Act of 1938. The act was last amended in 1997 to bring the minimum wage up to $5.15 an hour. Additionally, the act stipulates that overtime be paid after a statutory 40 hours a week, restricts child labour and guarantees equal pay for equal work regardless of sex, age, religion. Some state laws will require a higher minimum wage, and companies working on government contracts come under the Public Contracts Act, which may also require a higher minimum wage.

BENEFITS AND PERKS

Benefits packages tend to be more generous than in the UK, with medical coverage, profit sharing, and pension plans generally offered as standard. The situation as regards healthcare is undergoing major changes at the time of writing (see *Health* in *Daily Life*): as health insurance premiums increase many employers are cutting back. At the same time, government health reforms may require employers to pay up to 80% of their workers' health insurance. Any contract should be studied carefully for healthcare provisions. Many employers offer life insurance as part of a benefits package. Pension plans are organised similarly to UK pensions: there are government schemes to which the employer contributes and other schemes funded by employer and employee. Those on temporary and fixed-term contracts may not be eligible for company pension schemes.

Company cars are only provided to employees if it is absolutely necessary to the job. This is true even for senior executives.

WORKING HOURS, OVERTIME & HOLIDAYS

Americans are the most overworked people in the developed world and up to half of the workforce is estimated to be suffering from symptoms of work-related stress. On average Americans work 50 hours per week which is in stark contrast to the 35 hour working week in France.

Holiday entitlement tends to be much less than in Europe. The standard annual leave is two weeks, plus national and state holidays (see *Daily Life*). This compares very unfavourably with the situation in Europe and Australia where five weeks holiday per year is typical. Holiday allowance in the US is generally increased according to the number of years' service you have with the company.

Escape magazine calculated that Americans take only 9.6 days holiday per year and that a typical American couple are working 500 hours more per year than they were in 1980. As a consequence there is growing pressure to readjust this balance so that Americans can have more time for their family life and relationships. The impact of overwork on health is also being hotly discussed in the media. In the next five years this debate is likely to continue as a reaction takes place to a culture of excessive demands made by the workplace and career in favour of a better quality of life that is not simply measured in terms of income and promotion.

In factories working hours are normally from 8am to 4.30pm, and in offices 8.30am to 5pm. Overtime generally starts after a 40-hour week, although some unions have negotiated overtime after 35 or even 30 hours. Blue collar workers are generally entitled to overtime pay or compensation; this depends on the individual industry.

You will find that working hours can vary because of the varying time zones across the country. In banking and financial services and the stock market, the necessity to keep pace with the opening of the New York stock exchange means that on the west coast the working day starts at least an hour earlier.

TRADE UNIONS

Union membership in manufacturing has fallen dramatically in the last 10-15 years, while there has been a corresponding rise in membership of federal and state government unions. In 1995, 14.9% of the workforce was unionised, as against 13.2% today. But government workers are more unionised at 37.5% compared to the private sector's rate of 8.5% or the finance, real estate, and insurer sector at 1.9%.

American trade unions are organised locally. Members of 'locals' all tend to work in the same industry, or to work in the same firm (which results in several different trades represented in one local). The locals are in turn members of a national union (such as United Auto Workers), and most of the national unions are in some way affiliated to the American Federation of Labour and Congress of Industrial Organisations (AFL-CIO). The balance of power is shifting away from the locals towards the big national unions.

Collective bargaining between the local union and the employer normally decides any dispute, rather than a strike. Collective bargaining agreements between employers and unions often have no-strike clauses, and clear and well-established guidelines for employees to air their grievances. With these sorts of safeguards, strikes are fairly rare.

In unionised industries the union is recognised as the spokesman for any member with a complaint, and has a right to be present if the member wants to put the complaint to the management.

Employees have statutory rights to organise and join unions, and to strike. The law varies from state to state: in some states the closed shop is illegal, for example.

EMPLOYMENT CONTRACTS

Companies are not required by law to give their employees contracts, but in most cases there will be some sort of letter of agreement or contract offered. If you are being sent to the US with your existing job, you should check your contract or agreement with the host company. In particular, you should be aware that the following areas are treated differently in the USA, and there should be a provision for them in any contract of employment:

Sick pay: employees are allowed to take a certain number of days each year (usually six days) sick leave on full pay. This is a statutory requirement, but the contract should detail any extra allowances the company gives.

Medical Insurance: check that the company provides this, and that it is sufficient to cover your needs (see *Daily Life*).

Housing Allowance & Cost-of-Living Allowance (COLA): US employees working outside their home states are usually entitled to an allowance to cover extra costs. Sometimes this will include a certain number of days in a hotel. If you are coming out to the States from the UK your company should make some sort of allowance for this, which will be detailed in the contract. A relocation package is often given to managerial employees, which should cover removal and transport costs.

Termination Period: under Federal law employers are required to give at least 60 days' advance written warning of any layoffs, plant closures. There are no other specific obligations covering termination periods, but your contract should specify a period of notice (usually from one to three months) that both employer and employee must work to.

Check also for school fee allowances, overseas premiums, home leave allowances for family members, company car, moving expense reimbursement and 'settling-in' allowance, home maintenance expenses incurred in renting out your house in your home country, tax equalisation reimbursements, and other fringe benefits.